DEFENSIBLE SPACE

This book is based on a study which was financed in part by a grant from the National Institute of Law Enforcement and Criminal Justice of the United States Department of Justice. The opinions and findings are those of the author.

CRIME PREVENTION
THROUGH URBAN DESIGN

DEFENSIBLE SPACE

OSCAR NEWMAN

COLLIER BOOKS
A Division of Macmillan Publishing Co., Inc.
NEW YORK

Macmillan Publishing Co., Inc.
866 Third Avenue, New York, N.Y. 10022
Collier-Macmillan Canada Ltd., Toronto, Ontario

Defensible Space is also published in a hardcover edition by Macmillan Publishing Co., Inc.

Library of Congress Catalog Card Number: 73-187075

FIRST COLLIER BOOKS EDITION 1973

Printed in the United States of America

TO *Kopper*

CONTENTS

ACKNOWLEDGMENTS ix

PREFACE xiii

1 *Defensible Space* 1

2 *The Problem* 22

3 *Territoriality* 51

4 *Natural Surveillance* 78

5 *Image and Milieu* 102

6 *Current Practitioners of Defensible Space* 118

7 *Modifying Existing Environments* 163

8 *Summary and Recommendations* 187

APPENDIX A: *Methodology* 209

APPENDIX B: *Additional Statistics* 239

BIBLIOGRAPHY 252

INDEX 257

ACKNOWLEDGMENTS

The Project for the Security Design of Urban Residential Areas is an ongoing study of the effects of the physical layout of residential environments on the criminal vulnerability of inhabitants. The project involves both statistical analyses and extensive modifications to the existing plant and grounds of housing projects to test the efficacy of hypotheses. Funds for the research component of this work, and the preparation of this study, were made available by the National Institute of Law Enforcement and Criminal Justice of the U.S. Department of Justice. We are thankful to the Institute Administrators, Jerris Leonard, Clarence M. Coster, and Richard W. Velde, for making these funds available and to Martin Danziger, Assistant Administrator of the Institute, for his support and encouragement.

We are most indebted to John Conrad, Chief of the Center for Crime Prevention and Rehabilitation, the branch of the Institute through which this project was funded, for his professional guidance.

A significant test of the validity of our concepts involved altering buildings and grounds of existing housing projects for the purpose of performing "before and after" studies. We are thankful to the New York City Housing Authority for its active interest and cooperation in making sites and funds available for this purpose. We are particularly indebted to Simeon Golar, Chairman of the Authority, to the Members of the Board of the Housing Authority, Aramis Gomes and Walter Fried, and to the General Manager, Marcus Levy, for allowing portions of the Authority's current Modernization Budget to serve a double purpose by enabling us to undertake large-scale physical modifications.

We are thankful to Irving Wise, Director of Management, for his assistance during the past three years of our association with the Housing Authority—initially for his having arranged our first presentation; for his significant role in the November 1969 conference; and, on a continuing basis, for facilitating our work and coordination of our activities with the Authority's.

It is difficult to adequately thank Sam Granville, Deputy Director of Management for Tenant Relations, and formerly Director of the Authority's Modernization Program, for his truly tireless efforts on our behalf—first in helping to win support for our proposed work, and subsequently in teaching us the ropes on the inner workings of the Modernization Program and the Housing Authority.

We are indebted to Bernard Moses, present Director of the Modernization Program for his warm assistance and good humor and his capacity for turning obstacles into advantages, potential bureaucratic haggles into opportunities for experimenting with new ideas.

Professional praise and thanks are due to Max Schreiber, Chief Architect of the Authority, and Clair Fisher, Landscape Architectural Division Chief, for allowing us to share their knowledge and insights into housing design.

Special thanks are due to the New York Housing Authority Police and their Chief, Daniel J. Daly, for acquainting us with their work.

We wish also to express thanks to the following other staff members of the New York City Housing Authority:

—Harry Fialkin, Chief of the Statistics Division, for his having made available Housing Authority data on tenant profiles and on crime;

—Daniel Balk, Chief of the Engineering Division, and his staff for their technical assistance in the preparation of working drawings involving mechanical hardware;

—the individual housing project managers and their staff and to the many other members of the Authority who have been of assistance on a day-to-day basis.

As of November 1970, the Criminal Justice Coordinating Council of the Office of the Mayor of New York City has undertaken cosponsorship of a portion of our research related to the employment of electronic devices to improve the security of existing urban high-rise projects. These funds were provided by the Law Enforcement Assistance Administration, via the New York State Office of Planning Services, Division of Criminal Justice.

We are indebted to the members of the staff of the Criminal Justice Coordinating Council, in particular to Henry S. Ruth, Jr., Director of the Council, who encouraged us to become involved in the security of existing housing as well as in developing directives for new housing. If one considers that over four million people in our nation today live in public housing, even modest improvements can have great import. We are also grateful to Henry Ruth for his initial sponsorship of our work while Director of the National Institute in Washington.

We should also like to express our thanks to Peter Gray of the Criminal Justice Coordinating Council for his assistance in the preparation of our electronics proposal, and for the skill with which he guided it through the many city and state committees.

We are most appreciative of the efforts of those architects and planners who replied to our questionnaire, in particular to those who made their work available for use in our chapter on current practitioners. Here, I should like to address particular thanks to Bernard Guenther, Thomas R. Vreeland, Jr., and Roger Montgomery for also bringing the work of others to our attention.

In conclusion, I wish to acknowledge the work of the members of the staff of the Project for the Security Design of Urban Residential Areas at the Institute of Planning and Housing at New York University:

—Barry Hersh, City Planner, for his work in data gathering statistical analysis and his relentless efforts in coordinating the many facets of our activity;

—Stephen Johnston, Architect and Urban Designer, for his work in detailing our proposed modifications for construction, and his assistance in framing tests for our hypotheses;

—Jerry Rosenfeld, Architect and graduate student, for his coordination of the graphics and development of the visual component of this study;

—Betty Mackintosh, Bonnie Stone, and Barry Wood, graduate students in City Planning, for their tireless efforts at interviewing and observation in the development of supporting data;

—Dr. Lucille Nahemow, Social Psychologist and Environmentalist, for her assistance in structuring interviews and in the development of the "pre- and post-test" models;

—Stanley Fisher, Director of the Computer Facility of City University of New York Graduate Center, for his development of the computer programs employed in the various analyses performed on the data;

—Sally Felvey, who during the initial period of getting the project underway, occupied the grueling and, at times, thankless role of Administrative Assistant, and in the preparation of this study served in the additional roles of editor and typist.

Finally, I should like to express personal thanks to Dr. George Rand, Psychologist and Co-Principal Investigator in the first year of our study, for his encouragement, insights, and many significant contributions.

OSCAR NEWMAN

Director of the Institute of Planning and Housing
New York University
January 1972

PREFACE

This book is based on a study of the forms of our residential areas and how they contribute to our victimization by criminals. More broadly, it examines one aspect of how environment affects behavior. Housing officials in the late 1960s had already come to recognize that certain building types were having disastrous effects on their occupants. Enough damage had been done to human lives and property for the government, through the 1968 Federal Housing Act, to issue guidelines that families with children no longer be located in high-rise buildings, unless no other options were available. These directives were born of experiences repeated in city after city throughout the country. But no opportunity to study the phenomenon in detail and to isolate its working ingredients came until later.

In response to the alarming increase in urban crime rates, the President and Congress passed the Safe Streets Act of 1968 which resulted in the allocation of funds both for supplementing existing crime deterance efforts and for undertaking research into new techniques for crime prevention. The study which produced this manuscript was funded under these auspices.

In this book we outline the problems produced by many of our most familiar housing types; we isolate the factors affecting the behavior and attitudes of people living in them, and suggest remedies for both new and existing residential developments. The research methods used in our study are explained both within the main body of the text and at greater length within the appendixes.

We have chosen to direct this work at a rather wide readership. It was initially intended primarily for housing developers, architects, city planners, and police. But, as the scope of the work grew and the significance of our findings became more apparent, it was felt that the manuscript should be reworked so as to make it more universally available. Rather than reduce its professional and academic content, however, effort was made to keep technical terms to a minimum and explain those whose inclusion was felt to be mandatory.

Over the past three years, the Project for Security Design of Urban Residential Areas at New York University has been examining housing developments in every major city in the country. In each city, efforts were made to study housing of all income groups for the purpose of comparison. A variety of study techniques were employed, including interviews with inhabitants, project managers, and police who serve these developments. Where recorded data on crime, vandalism, and maintenance costs was available, it was incorporated into the analysis. In New York City the analysis was the most comprehensive and detailed.

There are 169 public housing projects in the City of New York, which contain 150,000 apartment units, housing a total of 528,000 people. The New York City Housing Authority which manages these projects keeps extensive data on its tenants, their ages, incomes, years of residence, previous backgrounds, and history of family pathology.[1] In addition, the New York City Housing Authority has its own sixteen-hundred-man police force which is required to file detailed reports of all criminal or vandal activity, as well as simple complaints.

These police reports are the most detailed of their kind kept anywhere.[2] They not only describe the nature of the crime and complainant, but pinpoint the exact place of occurrence within the project or its surrounding area. With this data it has been possible to determine exactly where the most dangerous areas of buildings are, as well as to compare crime rates in different building types and project layouts.

The New York City Housing Authority's facilities have proven a very rich data resource for still other reasons: almost every conceivable housing type and project site plan has been employed by the Authority in the building of one or more of its developments in the years since 1936 when it first began its program. Its projects range in physical characteristics from two-story row houses to thirty-story elevator apartment buildings.[3] Some of the Authority's larger projects house as many as 3,150 families, while others (recent in-fill housing developments) contain as few as 150 apartment units.[4] The number of units in a project does not necessarily correlate with its overall size or ground area. Some housing estates, built prior to 1954, composed of walk-up apartments (with elevator service in a few taller buildings) are spread over as many as sixty-five acres but house only sixteen hundred families.[5] By contrast, some recently completed projects housing over sixteen hundred families can be found located on as little as fifteen acres.[6] This range of physical characteristics, sizes, and densities, and the use of various architectural features to achieve similar ends, has provided an incomparable laboratory for measuring the effects of different housing environments on crime and vandalism.

Still one other peculiar and useful aspect of the New York City Housing Authority's pattern of project development is the nature of the spread of these different building prototypes over the greater New York City area; they do not entirely follow the pyramidical pattern typical of most American cities. Because of changing housing policies, economic factors, or peculiar land acquisition opportunities over the years, it is possible in New York to find high-rise high-density groupings at 190 units to the acre as far as twenty miles out from central Manhattan, located in the midst of predominantly single-family residential areas.[7] Similarly, relatively low-density projects at only seventy-eight units to the acre can be found in the central areas of New York, the result of early liberal housing policies; their continued survival in high-density Manhattan is the result of a well-functioning building maintenance program and a reluctance on the part of the Housing Authority to tear down anything it has built.[8]

These contrasting locations of different building prototypes have allowed us to examine the exclusive effect of the peculiar physical design of a project, independent of its urban location. In most other American cities, low-density housing is found at the periphery of urban areas, as are low crime rates. This correlation might lead one to deduce that low density is the critical factor affecting crime rates. But as higher incomes and other social variables influencing crime rates also correlate with suburban locations, this causal assignment of crime to density may be spurious. Thus the occasional location in New York City of low-density housing projects in core urban areas and high-density projects in suburban locations has provided an opportunity for a unique comparative analysis.

A further essential step in ascertaining the extent to which the physical design of housing is in itself a variable affecting crime rates requires a balanced accounting for the other factors which also influence crime. Traditionally, crime has been correlated with income, age, family pathology, and so on. A fair test of hypotheses concerning the impact of the physical environment on crime therefore requires comparison of communities in which the social characteristics of the population are as constant as possible: where the only variation is the physical form of the buildings.

The advantage in restricting the statistical portion of the study to New York City Housing Authority projects accrues from the fact that there is only a limited variation in the social characteristics of its resident population. Had we attempted an in-depth comparative analysis of the effects of physical design on crime rates in the range of housing in the private sector, the extreme variations in social characteristics of tenants in private versus public housing would have complicated comparison endlessly.

All these factors, coupled with the wealth of computerized data kept by the New York City Housing Authority on tenant characteristics, location, and the extent of crime and vandalism have enabled us to test most of our hypotheses regarding the effect of the design of residential environments on the victimization of inhabitants.

Because of our location in New York and work with the Housing Authority projects, it should come as no surprise that many of the examples used to illustrate defensible space mechanisms are from New York City. We beg the indulgence of the New York City Housing Authority, who may find it unfair to be so singled out and scrutinized. The New York Housing Authority is the largest operating authority in the country. Its record of enlightened policies and management is second to none. Contrasted to housing projects of like size in other large cities, crime in New York City projects is significantly lower. It is worth mentioning, too, that we have found the Authority's current design directives to the architects of its new projects much in advance of any employed elsewhere in the country. For every New York project used in this book to illustrate poor "defensible space" design, there are two which could have been presented to illustrate good design.

Our recognition of the significance of territoriality is by no means new to the architectural and sociological professions. Elizabeth Wood, Jane Jacobs, Marc Fried, Walter Firey, and Lee Rainwater are among the many who have intuitively recognized the potentials within this approach for development of a new rationalism for housing design.

To date, most of these students of the territorial needs and prerogatives of urban dwellers have been able to bring little more than extensive personal experience and naturalistic observations to their exposition of the problem. Their insights are nevertheless cogent, and we have assimilated many of them into the development of our own hypotheses.

For historical purposes, it is important to pay particular tribute to Elizabeth Wood and Jane Jacobs for their initial formulations of the problem and commitment to the principles embodied in this study. Both also share an abiding involvement in public policy. There are many others who could be cited as intellectual predecessors, espousing similar theoretical principles: Robert Sommer, Edward Hall, Christopher Alexander are some of the more obvious. It is important, however, to recognize the unique impact of Jacobs and Wood who entered directly into the foray while operating within the economic and social constraints of their times.

NOTES

1. See Appendix A, figure A4 and table A5, for a sample of the New York City Housing Authority transcript of tenant data form, and for the record format of the tenant data statistics tape.

2. See Appendix A, figures A1, A2, and A3, for a sample of the incident report form, transcript of incident report form, and a list of all coded crimes included in the NYCHA Police data.

3. Polo Grounds, Bronx, New York, a 1,614-unit project composed of four, thirty-story buildings.

4. Queensbridge Houses, Queens, New York, a 3,149-unit project composed of twenty-six, six-story buildings; Saratoga Avenue, Brooklyn, New York, a 125-unit project composed of one, sixteen-story building.

5. Breukelen Houses, Brooklyn, New York, a 1,595-unit project composed of thirty, three- and seven-story buildings.

6. St. Nicholas Houses, Manhattan, New York, a 1,526-unit project composed of thirteen, fourteen-story buildings.

7. E. R. Moore Houses, Bronx, New York, a 463-unit project composed of two, twenty-story buildings.

8. Harlem River Houses I, Manhattan, New York, a 577-unit project composed of seven, four- and five-story buildings.

DEFENSIBLE SPACE

1

DEFENSIBLE SPACE

The crime problems facing urban America will not be answered through increased police force or firepower. We are witnessing a breakdown of the social mechanisms that once kept crime in check and gave direction and support to police activity. The small-town environments, rural or urban, which once framed and enforced their own moral codes, have virtually disappeared. We have become strangers sharing the largest collective habitats in human history. Because of the size and density of our newly evolving urban megalopoli, we have become more dependent on each other and more vulnerable to aberrant behavior than we have ever been before.

In our society there are few instances of shared beliefs or values among physical neighbors. Although this heterogeneity may be intellectually desirable, it has crippled our ability to agree on the action required to maintain the social framework necessary to our continued survival. The very winds of liberation that have brought us this far may also have carried with them the seeds of our demise. It is clear to almost all researchers in crime prevention that the issue hinges on the inability of communities to come together in joint action. The physical environments we have been building in our cities for the past twenty-five years actually prevent such amity and discourage the natural pursuit of a collective action.

The anonymous cities we have built, for maximum freedom and multiple choice, may have inadvertently succeeded in severely curtailing many of our previous options. Collective community action, once easy, is now cumbersome. But even in the absence of a community of minds, joint action has become essential to the survival of urban life in America. Police forces operating without community consent, direction, and control are a wasted effort—more irritant than deterrent. Means must be found for bringing neighbors together, if only for the limited purpose of ensuring survival of their collective milieu. Where the physical design of the living environment can be used for this purpose, it must be so exploited.

Over the past fifteen years, the crime problem in our urban metropolitan areas has become severe enough to prompt a major exodus of middle-income families to the suburbs. However, the results of 1971 crime survey statistics indicate that the crime problem is shifting to the outer reaches of the city.[1] The horizons of escape promised by suburbia and the barricaded inner city towers seem to be narrowing. The only recourse now appears to be total lockup and self-restriction of movement: a self-imposed curfew and police state.

This book is about an alternative, about a means for restructuring the residential environments of our cities so they can again become livable and controlled, controlled not by police but by a community of people sharing a common terrain.

Over the past three years, the New York University Project for Security Design in Urban Residential Areas has been studying the nature, pattern, and location of crime in urban residential areas across the country. Our conclusion is that the new physical form of the urban environment is possibly the most cogent ally the criminal has in his victimization of society. The concentration of population in large metropolitan areas has produced an urban form that makes hapless victims of its occupants.

The time has come to go back to first principles, to reexamine human habitat as it has evolved, to become attuned again to all the subtle devices invented over time and forgotten in our need and haste to house the many. For even within the widespread chaos of our cities, it is still possible to find isolated examples of working living environments which are crime-free, although at times located in the highest crime precincts of cities. Architectural design can make evident by the physical layout that an area is the shared extension of the private realms of a group of individuals. For one group to be able to set the norms of behavior and the nature of activity possible within a particular place, it is necessary that it have clear, unquestionable control over what can occur there. Design can make it possible for both inhabitant and stranger to perceive that an area is under the undisputed influence of a particular group, that they dictate the activity taking place within it, and who its users are to be. This can be made so clearly evident that residents will not only feel confident, but that it is incumbent upon them to question the comings and goings of people to ensure the continued safety of the defined areas. Any intruder will be made to anticipate that his presence will be under question and open to challenge; so much so that a criminal can be deterred from even contemplating entry.

Defensible space is a model for residential environments which inhibits crime by creating the physical expression of a social fabric that defends itself. All the different elements which combine to make a defensible space have a common goal—an environment in which latent territoriality and sense of community in the inhabitants can be translated into responsibility for ensuring a safe, productive, and well-maintained living space. The potential criminal perceives such a space as controlled by its residents, leaving him an intruder easily recognized and dealt with. On the one hand this is target hardening—the traditional aim of security design as provided by locksmiths. But it must also be seen in another light. In middle-class neighborhoods, the responsibility for maintaining security has largely been relegated to the police. Upper-income neighborhoods—particularly those including high-rise apartment buildings—have supplemented police with doormen, a luxury not possible in other neighborhoods. There is serious self-deception in this posture. When people begin to protect themselves as individuals and not as a community, the battle against crime is effectively lost. The indifferent crowd witnessing a violent crime is by now an American cliché. The move of middle- and upper-class population into protective high-rises and other structures of isolation—as well guarded and as carefully differentiated from the surrounding human landscape as a military post—is just as clearly a retreat into indifference. The form of buildings and their arrangement can either discourage or encourage people to take an active part in policing while they go about their daily business. "Policing" is not intended to evoke a paranoid vision but refers to the oldest concept in the Western political tradition: the responsibility of each citizen to ensure the functioning of the *polis*.

"Defensible space" is a surrogate term for the range of mechanisms—real and symbolic barriers, strongly defined areas of influence, and improved opportunities for surveillance—that combine to bring an environment under the control of its residents. A *defensible space* is a living residential environment which can be employed by inhabitants for the enhancement of their lives, while providing security for their families, neighbors, and friends. The public areas of a multi-family residential environment devoid of defensible space can make the act of going from street to apartment equivalent to running the gauntlet. The fear and uncertainty generated by living in such an environment can slowly eat away and eventually destroy the security and sanctity of the apartment unit itself. On the other hand, by grouping dwelling units to reinforce associations of mutual benefit; by delineating paths of movement; by defining areas of activity for particular users through their juxtaposition with internal living areas; and by providing for natural opportunities for visual surveillance, architects can create a clear understanding of the function of a space, and who its users are and ought to be. This, in turn, can lead residents of all income levels to adopt extremely potent territorial attitudes and policing measures, which act as strong deterrents to potential criminals.

The spatial layout of the multi-family dwelling, from the arrangement of the building grounds to the interior grouping of apartments, achieves defensible space when residents can easily perceive and control all activity taking place within it. It is not of course intended that residents take matters into their own hands and personally restrict intrusion. Rather, it is suggested that they employ a full range of encounter mechanisms to indicate their concerned observation of questionable activity and their control of the situation: offers of assistance to strangers in finding their way, as a means for determining their intent and the legitimacy of their presence; continued in-person surveillance and the threat of possible interference; questioning glances from windows; and finally, to be able to set up a situation which will stimulate residents to call the police and insist on their intervention. As we have seen too often lately, the ability of even secure middle-class Americans to intervene, if only by calling the police, is not something that can be depended on any longer. Similarly, self-initiated police intervention in ghetto areas meets at times with community disapproval, even when the community feels intervention is required. The defensible space environment extends the area of the residential unit into the street and within the area of felt responsibility of the dweller—of both low- and middle-income. By contrast, the resident living within large, apartment tower developments feels his responsibilities begin and end within the boundaries of his own apartment. He has learned to be detached even from what he sees outside his own window.

In our newly-created dense and anonymous residential environments, we may be raising generations of young people who are totally lacking in any experience of collective space, and by extension, of community rights and the shared values of society. In many ways, therefore, defensible space design also attempts to attack the root causes of crime. In the area of crime prevention, physical design has been traditionally relegated the role of *mechanical prevention*, leaving intact the structure of motivation and attitudes which eventually lead to the criminal event. Defensible space design, while it uses mechanical prevention, aims at formulating an architectural model of *corrective prevention*. Our

FIG. 1. Mud House in the African Sudan. The stoop symbolically defines the entry to the dwelling. It declares simply, but emphatically that this is where the territorial prerogatives of the tribe, defined by the compound, are overridden by the dictates of the members of the family unit. (Reprinted, by permission, from Joop Hardy, "Door and Window," in *Forum*, No. 8, 1960. Photo by Aldo Van Eyck.)

FIG. 2. Neolithic Settlement, Hacilar, Turkey. Excavation and reconstruction of extended family compound and individual house. There are two entries to the enclave, both of which lead to a central communal area shared by all dwellings. The entry to each family unit is then further defined by a smaller transitional court off the communal area. (Courtesy of The Hamlyn Group)

Excavation of extended family compound

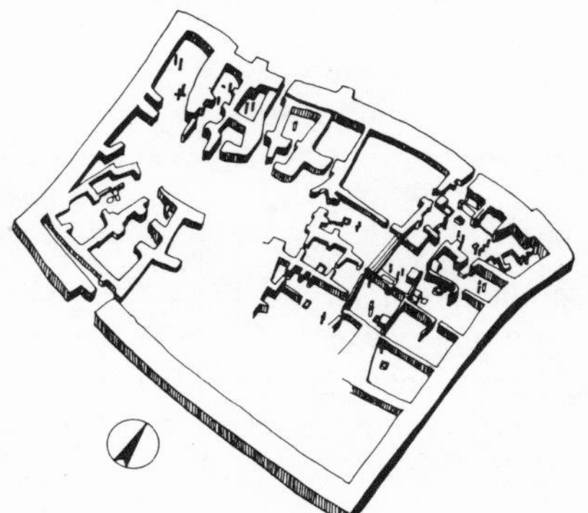

House within family compound

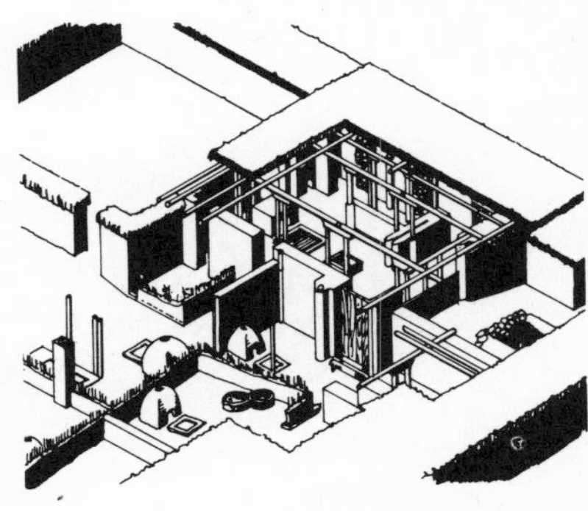

FIG. 3. Street in Herculaneum. Note stoop at entry to each house and positioning of windows to survey street entry. (Reprinted by permission from M. Grant, *Cities of Vesuvius*, p. 64. Photo by Werner Forman © 1971 by The Macmillan Company.)

present urban environments, created with such speed and determination, may be little more than the spawning grounds of criminal behavior.

In the evolution of human habitat over the past thousands of years, men in every culture have developed cogent devices to define the territorial realm of their dwellings. The nature and function of these mechanisms evolved slowly through change and adaptation during use. So long as human environment was built within a tradition, simply repeating previous forms ensured the preservation of past learned experience. With the breakdown of building tradition, through the rapid evolution of new techniques and the need to answer the pressing problem of accommodating higher densities, the simple repetition of past practice has become difficult, if not impossible. Unfortunately, the accumulated traditions inherent in the residential forms of the past were not held within the conscious verbal bank of human knowledge. In architectural history there is ample evidence of territorial definition and symbolization in the forms of previous residential environments. There is unfortunately no parallel evidence of their overt discussion. The tradition, grown over thousands of years in man's piecemeal search for a form of residence in an urban setting, has been lost.

In building the residential environments of twentieth-century cities, there was no reference to tradition, simply because the needs seemed so totally new and unlike any experience in the past. In our rush to provide housing for the urban immigrants and to accommodate our high population growth rates, we have been building *more* without really asking

FIG. 4. Street in Eighteenth-Century Dutch Town. Note how the realm of each dwelling unit is defined by the raised platform at the point where the entry meets the street. Windows further reinforce territorial claim by providing unmistakable surveillance from within the dwelling. (Photo by author)

FIG. 5. Row-House Street typical of Nineteenth-Century American Cities. It contains the identical ingredients which define the dwellings' relationship to the street found in the Dutch town (fig. 4). (Photo by author)

what? The high-rise prototype, with its myriad of resident janitorial and security staff, worked well for upper-middle-income families with few children but cannot be simplistically transplanted, minus the accompanying staff and accouterments, for the use of large, low-income families. It is clear that we built without much thought and without much concern and are now stuck with the results. As will be shown in later chapters, poorly designed buildings and projects have crime rates as much as three times higher than those of adjacent projects housing socially identical residents at similar densities.

Considering the needs of low-income families, there is no rationalism to the design of most high-rise residential developments, other than the

FIG. 6. Pruitt-Igoe, St. Louis, Missouri. View of vandalism to windows of public access galleries serving upper levels of the buildings. (Photo by Bob Williams)

narrow dictates of investment economics. Once built, they prove dangerous to live in and costly to maintain. The economic argument which led to their initial construction is reversed exactly. Their cost of operation is surpassed only by the social costs borne by the inhabitants. High-rise apartment developments are a new genre, with us little more than a hundred years. As a means for housing low- and middle-income American families, most date back to the early fifties. They are not the result of a careful application of the knowledge employed in housing the few, transferred to the problems of housing the many. Their form evolved in response to pressures for higher densities, with no reference to previous traditions and no attempt at understanding the range of need to be answered in human habitat. Beyond an occasionally successful composition, there is little evidence of any genius and now, in this period of high crime rates, they have become containers for the victimization of their inhabitants. This book presents an alternative—housing of medium density which through its physical design enables residents to control their living environment rather than become its victims.

Defensible space design returns to the productive use of residents the public areas beyond the doors of individual apartments: the hallways, lobbies, grounds, and surrounding streets—areas which are now beyond the control of inhabitants. Four elements of physical design, acting both individually and in concert, contribute to the creation of secure environments.

The territorial definition of space in developments reflecting the areas of influence of the inhabitants. This works by subdividing the residential environment into zones toward which adjacent residents easily adopt proprietary attitudes.

The positioning of apartment windows to allow residents to naturally survey the exterior and interior public areas of their living environment.

The adoption of building forms and idioms which avoid the stigma of peculiarity that allows others to perceive the vulnerability and isolation of the inhabitants.

The enhancement of safety by locating residential developments in functionally sympathetic urban areas immediately adjacent to activities that do not provide continued threat.

Defensible space can be made to operate in an evolving hierarchy from level to level in the collective human habitat—to extend from apartment to street. It is a technique applicable to low-density row-house groupings as well as to developments composed of high-rise apartment buildings. The small cluster of apartments at each floor of a multi-story building is the first level beyond the apartment unit where occupants can be made to extend the realm of their homes and responsibilities. The

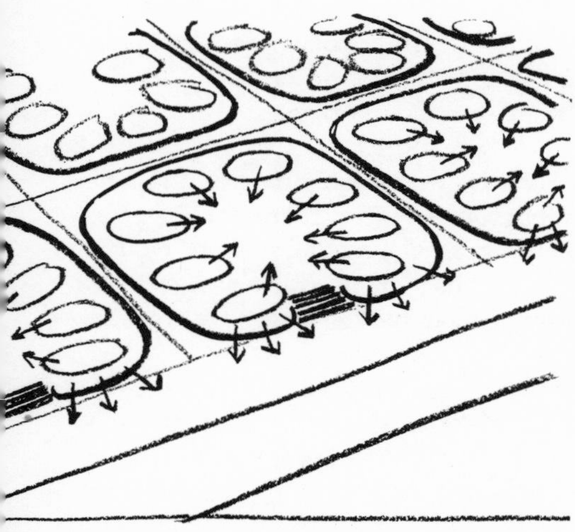

FIG. 7. Defensible Space. Schematic sketch illustrating territorial definition reinforced with surveillance opportunities (arrows).

FIG. 8. Hierarchy of Defensible Space. Schematic diagram illustrating evolving hierarchy of defensible space from public to private. Arrows indicate entries at different levels of the hierarchy.

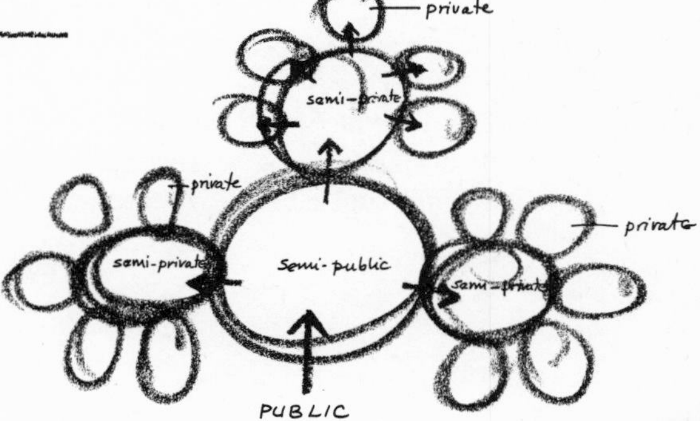

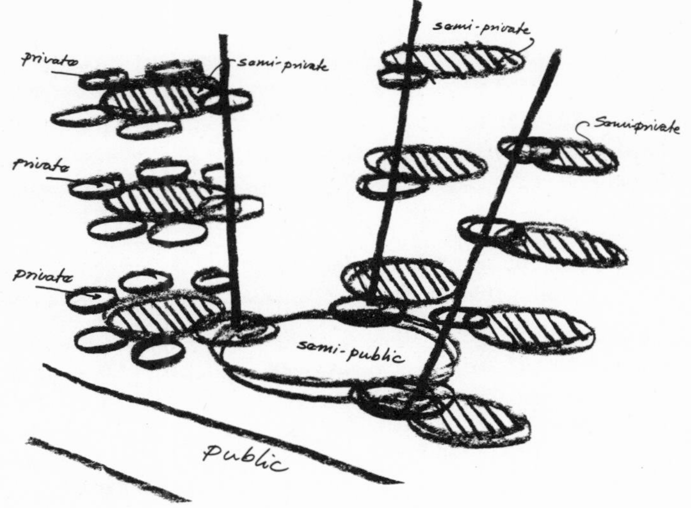

FIG. 9. Defensible space hierarchy in multi-level dwelling.

second level is the common entry and circulation paths within their buildings. The third level is the clustering of buildings which define a project's grounds and its entry. The final level in the hierarchy occurs when the housing development stakes its claim on surrounding urban streets.

In our examination of developments in every major city in the country, an effort was made to study the housing of all income groups for the purpose of comparison. A variety of study techniques were employed, including interviews with inhabitants, project managers, and police who serve these developments. Where recorded data on crime, vandalism, and maintenance costs was available, it was incorporated into the analysis. In New York City the analysis has been most extensive and detailed. The New York City Housing Authority is responsible for 150,000 units of public housing located in its five boroughs. This represents approximately 19 percent of all public housing in the country. The Housing Authority keeps computerized files on all its tenants, their incomes, the ages of each of the members of a family, their backgrounds, etc. In addition, the Housing Authority has its own sixteen-hundred-man police force who in turn keeps data on the occurrence and reporting of crime. The unique aspect of the Housing Authority Police data is that it also pinpoints the place of the crime. Specific buildings and interior locations are recorded along with the nature of the crime, victim, and offender. This resource allows us to consider the function of every physical variable and its effect on crime.

The results of our findings from three years of study apply to residential design for most income groups. In all instances, the physical mechanisms suggested to create safety and improve upkeep are tools of "self-help." The designs catalyze the natural impulses of residents, rather than forcing them to surrender their shared social responsibilities to any formal authority, whether police, management, security guards, or doormen. In a sense, this study takes its place as a partner in the political movements calling for the return of participation and control to the local level. However, it must be said that the ideas in this book, when initially presented to police, housing officials, and tenants often met with disbelief. Residents who live in hourly terror pointed at their scarred steel-plated doors and suggested that the author was wonderfully naive. Police officers—turning their attention from bands of teen-agers and addicts who do not appear to seriously weigh the consequences of being caught—pointed out the high costs of physical modification compared to increased police manpower. Ghetto leaders and social scientists have challenged us in our belief that crime, born of a poverty of means, opportunity, education, and representation, could be prevented architecturally.

Some of this skepticism is well-founded—particularly that of a low-income resident who does not believe physical change is likely to occur, regardless of the new-found knowledge. However, the skepticism is based on the assumption that a particular building prototype and project design represents the only available solution to a particular set of density and cost restraints. Most people do not know that different residential building prototypes are available to do the same job. The 150 New York families trapped in apartments that open onto the double-loaded corridors of a seventeen-story high-rise building—whose elevators, fire stairs, hallways, and roofs are freely roamed and ruled by criminals—find it hard to believe that the project across the street, composed of three- to six-

FIG. 10. Aerial Photo of two adjacent projects of equal density. The one in the foreground consists mostly of walk-ups; the other mostly of high-rises. (Courtesy of New York City Housing Authority)

story buildings in which two to three families share a hallway and six to twelve an entrance, actually accommodate people at the same densities and could be built at the same cost. The families in the seventeen-story building are continually aware of the fact that they are the constant prey of criminals and are equally aware that things are a lot better across the street. They find it incomprehensible that both projects house families at equal densities, and that the design differences between the two projects are predominantly the result of the whims of each designer. Examples of adjacent housing projects which differ dramatically in their crime vulnerability are detailed in subsequent chapters. It seems unforgivable that high-rise projects would have been designed to make their inhabitants so vulnerable, when projects across the street were able to avoid these problems simply by not creating them in the first place.

Society may have contributed to the victimization of project residents by setting off their dwellings, stigmatizing them with ugliness; saying with every status symbol available in the architectural language of our culture, that living *here* is falling short of the human state. However, architecture is not just a matter of style, image, and comfort. Architecture can create encounter and prevent it. Certain kinds of space and spatial layout favor the clandestine activities of criminals. An architect, armed with some understanding of the structure of criminal encounter, can simply avoid providing the space which supports it. In discussing our tenant surveys with police, they were surprised to discover that residents of alternate building prototypes have radically different attitudes toward representatives of formal authority, and policemen in particular. These varying attitudes are strongly reflected in the varying rates of reported crime. In the two adjacent projects already mentioned, residents with identical social characteristics hold quite different views of the police. In one high-rise project—a labyrinthine profusion of corridors, fire stairs, and exits—police report great difficulty in locating apartments, to say nothing of pursuing criminals. Officers responding to calls meet tenant indifference if not open hostility. It is not uncommon for tenants to angrily attempt to drive off police responding with well-intentioned assistance. Tenants are skeptical of police effectiveness and fearful of police officers and of police intentions. Records show that only very serious crimes are brought to police attention. A comparison of tenant interviews with police reports shows that only one crime in four is ever reported. The obverse is true as well. In anonymous, crime-ridden high-rises, police officers—whether out of fear or because they respond negatively to the apparent anonymity of the environment—are often dictatorial, arbitrary, and unrespecting of the tenants' rights and needs.

Yet across the street in a development mixing walk-ups and low, elevator buildings, the same policemen behave like polite, conscientious civil servants. Tenants respond positively. Police move easily and familiarly through the project, and tenant-police relations are much better. Tenants in these buildings not only report more of the crimes they are involved in or witness, they make a practice of reporting loitering strangers and potentially threatening situations. In interviews, their trust in the efficacy of police intervention was found to be stronger, possibly not unrelated to their ability to keep police in hand in their own buildings.

The adoption of defensible space design in new building or the modification of existing buildings may well pay for itself in terms of the increased level of police efficiency. Although police expenditures are unlikely to go down in the near future, new projects constructed along defensible space guidelines can help curb an otherwise necessary expansion of police control and budget. If we are ever to lower the expenditures and profile of police in our cities, it will be through measures such as these. In federally supported housing, security personnel—always considered a luxury by the Federal Housing Administration—are increasingly expensive and difficult to support from overextended city and housing authority budgets. In New York it has been demonstrated that because of fringe benefits and time off, making one additional patrolman evident costs the equivalent of the annual salary of ten policemen.[2] The cost of security personnel is beginning to compete with the cost of building maintenance, while the effectiveness of increased manpower is in serious question.

The root causes of inner city and ghetto crime lie deep in the social structure of our nation. Criminal and victim alike come from that strata of the population without the power of choice. In the United States, the correlation of criminal and victim with poverty is unmistakeable.[3] To both, access to institutions which lead out of their condition has been denied. Our social and educational systems have not adapted to admit the minority groups who largely make up this population. In a disturbing percentage of the inner city and ghetto population, the one institution normally most resistant to social disruption, the family, is crumbling. Lee Rainwater, in his article "Fear and the House-as-Haven," about his study of Pruitt-Igoe, defines security as the most important need to be satisfied in a residence for low-income groups.[4] Feelings of insecurity about one's residential environment often lead to the adoption of a negative and defeatist view of oneself, to ambivalence about job finding, and to expressions of general impotence in the capacity to cope with the outside world. The secure residential environment—understood by a resident as a haven and interpreted by outsiders as the expression of the inhabitants' egos—may be one of the most meaningful forms of social rehabilitation available to the family and to society. The way in which community attitudes toward security and insecurity act as social causes is still to be studied. Children who live in high-rise buildings seem to have a poorly developed perception of individual privacy and little understanding of territory.

There may be evidence that the physical form of a residential environment plays a significant role in shaping the perception of children and in making them cognizant of the existence of zones of influence and, therefore, the rights of others.

It is difficult to isolate the various mechanisms which have been producing the high crime rates we are presently experiencing in our urban core areas. Some contributory causes can be assumed: the concentration of the disadvantaged in these areas; the attraction of criminals to an urban environment which is at the same time increasingly anonymous and decreasingly self-protective; and the evolution of an urban physical form and residential environment which encourages and fosters criminal behavior. The poor are most vulnerable to crime in any setting. But in anonymous buildings which facilitate their victimization, we have the makings of a situation of crisis proportions.

No one has met these problems with conscious solutions. The poor are unable to choose alternatives. Low-middle-income populations that have not succumbed to apathy have fled. The exercise of choice in the housing market has glutted the suburbs with newly transplanted families, who at times feel cut off from the social life of their original neighborhoods, from the convenience of place of work, shopping, entertainment, and friends—but are safe. How quickly suburbs will slide into the same insecurity that plagues the city is open to speculation. For the time, suburban families have avoided the problem for themselves. The problem remains, however, and evasion has its social costs.

Some middle-class families have not fled to the outskirts, but have withdrawn into high-rise security-guarded fortresses of semiluxury. This introversion and intentional isolation inevitably occurs at the expense of adjacent surroundings. But mental and physical withdrawal from the social order and its problems has at least three dangerous attending characteristics. First is the indifference to the problem once it has been evaded. Second—and this follows on the first—is the relegation of the problem of security, the traditional responsibility of the citizenry, to formally designated authority. It is no doubt impossible to imagine a modern city without a functioning police force, although their advent is as little distant as the introduction of the "Bobbys" of London in 1840. But the function of police has traditionally been to apprehend criminals. Fear of apprehension and ensuing speedy prosecution is, of course, a deterrent to criminal behavior. But police alone can in no major way create or foster security. Society, in the persons of citizens, must adopt this function. An apathetic, detached citizenry far too often limits its participation to bitter criticism of police for not accomplishing work which rightly must be undertaken by the citizenry itself. The well-off citizen, by isolating himself in a secure fortress, by restricting his own ventures into the streets, and by demanding that authority assume all responsibility for ensuring the safety of streets, has effectively set the stage for the defeat of his own demands. The street, without the continued presence of the citizen, will never be made to function safely for him. Without the continued presence, focused demand, and responsibile overview of the citizen, the police become lackadaisical, their commitments distorted, and they fall easy prey to corruption.

The third characteristic of withdrawal from urban life is the resultant physical design of the buildings of our cities. To provide security by means of a guard or doorman requires that entry to a building complex be restricted to one location. This usually means walling off a two- to ten-acre housing complex from the surrounding neighborhood. By this action, thousands of feet of street are removed from all forms of social and visual contact. A natural mechanism providing safety to our streets has been sacrificed to insure the security of the residents of the walled-off complex.

On the other hand, it is possible to design a multi-family housing complex in which as low a number of units as possible share a common entry off the street. Designers can position units, windows, and entries, and prescribe paths of movement and areas of activity so as to provide inhabitants with continuous natural surveillance of the street and project grounds. The street comes under surveillance from the building, the building entries and lobbys under the surveillance of the street. As with the fortress, this design also provides security. But instead of relegating the responsibility to others, it is assumed by the residents in the natural flow of their everyday activities. Moreover, the building complex and the residents are integrated into the community. The complex protects the street as well as itself. The street life helps, in turn, to protect the complex. Instead of being an act of withdrawal, this design reinforces residents in their expression of concern for their own domain and for the streets and activity areas to which it is tied. In this way, residents do not achieve internal security at the expense of the surrounding area, but by insuring that the surrounding area is equally secure. Their concerns are in harmony with those of the community. This is defensible space design.

For urban residential settings, for low- and moderate-income populations in particular, defensible space design is imperative. In many cases, withdrawal is not an option open to them. Four million people live in federally subsidized low-middle-income housing. For them there is effectively no choice to exercise on the housing market. The same factionalizing of our society which is expressed in middle- and upper-class withdrawal has, moreover, infected the design and structure of their environment. The stigma of poverty and minority group membership has been stamped onto public housing. It has been made to appear as different as possible from its surroundings; it has been marked off as clearly as if by quarantine. It is not our concern here to unravel the social forces which have influenced the architectural form and symbolism of contemporary low-income America, but to offer an alternate model of design. Because of the location of their residences, because of their social position, and because of the design of their housing, the poor are the most consistently victimized of our urban population.[5]

Even those who have fled the old neighborhoods often find they have purchased a transitory security. Thinking they left the victims behind, they have often designed themselves into a victimization which, if it has not yet arrived, is nonetheless on the way. In September 1970, a fifty-thousand-unit housing development, built privately for cooperative ownership, was completed in an outlying area of the Bronx, New York. It was occupied almost overnight, predominantly by an older middle-class population fleeing an adjacent area of the Bronx only a few miles away. Many see that their new homes and environment are inferior to the area they have abandoned. Their apartments are smaller, shopping is inconvenient and expensive, television provides most of the available enter-

FIG. 11. Aerial view of Co-op City. (Courtesy of Skyviews Survey Inc.)

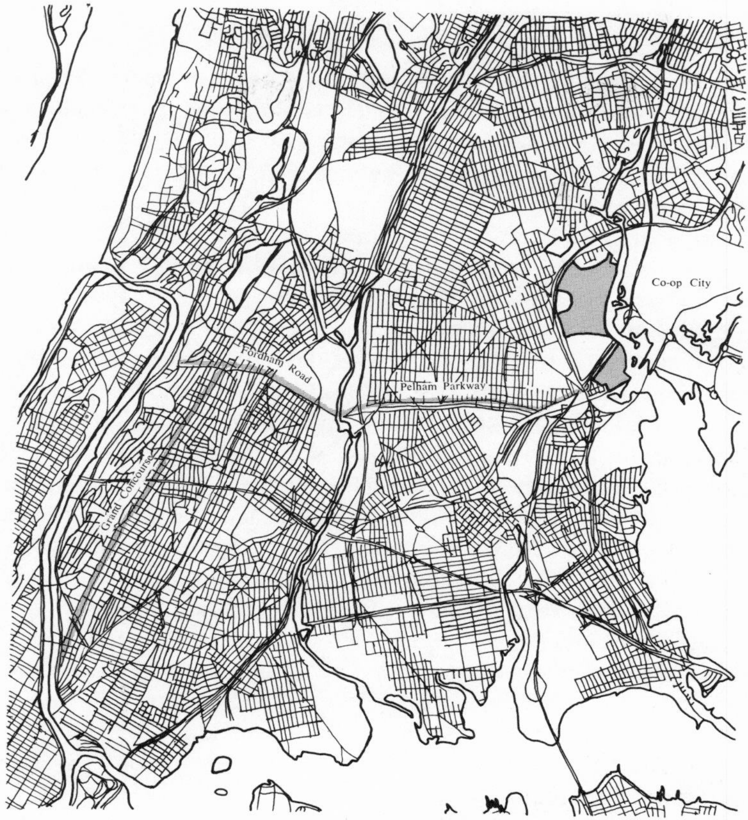

FIG. 12. Map of Upper Manhattan and The Bronx, locating Co-op City, Grand Concourse, Fordham Road, and Pelham Parkway.

tainment. They have left behind them friends and institutions—a way of life.

Many of these deficiencies will be remedied as the project is completed and the area becomes more heavily populated. Yet the new residents spend little time complaining. In a sense they are pleased with the costs and faults. These are, after all, a small and necessary price to pay for what they most crave—security. They have escaped from a once-friendly environment, which had come to terrify them. Muggings, burglaries, and assaults had made life in their "old neighborhood" impossible for a generation of elders. In a random interview, almost all those questioned admitted that in their abandoned neighborhood they had long ago stopped going out in the evening. All had either experienced robberies or had close friends who had. This is no new story. What is fascinating and fearful is the way this population chose to solve its problems. They fled *en masse* and segregated themselves within a new middle-class ghetto —an isolation of their own making, one which fits their image of the social order. In Co-op City they live among their own kind—45 percent of the adult population is over 50, 65 percent is Jewish, and the average wage earner makes between seven and ten thousand dollars a year.[6] Once a heterogenous, gregarious, active, and culturally involved community, the new residents of Co-op City now are segregated by income and ethnicity and only desire to breathe more easily. Those who fled to this haven would be shocked to know that the buildings and residential settings they now occupy are much less defensible than those they abandoned. The onslaught of only a small percentage of the criminals they fled is all that would be required to make their dream world evaporate.

Co-op City works now because it is far from the site of crime. But, how long before the project is recognized as vulnerable—before the criminal extends his range and mobility? The developers of Co-op City recognized that by ensuring a uniform middle-class population they could ensure a low crime rate. So long as all the families in Co-op City are exclusively white, middle-class, and elderly, the crime rate will stay down. The appearance of anyone else sends out a danger signal as obviously as an alarm bell. But already there are young families moving into Co-op City—black families, Puerto Rican families—seeking the same security and using the same means to achieve it. As the population becomes mixed, the success of this strategy will diminish.

An important principle of defensible space design is that subdivision allows residents to distinguish neighbor from intruder. In Co-op City this is accomplished not through design but by isolating a large, uniform population. Unfortunately, this is only a temporary respite for a small, privileged segment of the population. It employs statistics and segregation as weapons for keeping out those who are already the chief victims of crime—the poor. It will not work for very long, and it is repellent by virtue of the racism and prejudice it practices. It will not, in any way, contribute to the redemption of our cities.

The lesson to be learned from Co-op City is that crime control can be achieved by creating a situation in which it is possible for the potential victim to recognize in advance the potential criminal. A criminal will rarely commit a crime in a building in which he knows he will be easily recognized. Design can facilitate the process of recognition. Rather than the device of uniformity of population, such a design enables a varied and mixed population to know and control its own territory, to distinguish who (in an apparently complex and anonymous urban space) is neighbor and who intruder, and to do this at the level of the building as well as at the individual and communal level.

Subtle difficulties arise in attempting to improve the security of low-income, as compared with middle-income housing; these are mainly a function of the social characteristics of the resident populations. The social characteristics of the middle class greatly facilitate the task of providing them with a secure environment. Middle-class people have developed a refined sense of property and ownership; they have a measure of self-confidence and pride in their personal capabilities. Their everyday experiences reinforce their social competence; they can retain some control over the forces that shape their lives; and they recognize alternatives among which they can choose. These positive social controls give them a feeling of potency in protecting and enforcing their rights within a defined sphere of influence; for instance, they are well-practiced in their demand for and use of police protection.

Security design for a low-income population is very difficult. This is not only because of the economic restraints on cost and the higher concentration of criminal and victim. Daily social experience reinforces among the poor the sense of their own impotence and removes to a level of fantasy the thought of altering or improving the conditions of their lives. Closed out of the game financially, politically, educationally, and in virtually every other way, those among the poor who have not accepted the image of their own impotence are rare. In this light it may be unrealistic to expect an individual to assume positive social attitudes and influence in one sphere of his life—his family and residential environment—when he has learned clearly and consistently in the other facets of his existence that he has no such power.

Defensible space, it may be charged, is middle-class thinking. The poor have their own culture. They don't want the peaceful, secure, dull life of the middle class. They don't want property. They don't want the values middle-class society wishes to foist upon them. Violence, it is contended, is part of their culture. So, apparently, is communality. They don't want walls, whether real ones, or the ones you place in their minds by the design of space.

This romantic view of the poor is without foundation. Interviews with hundreds of low-income housing residents reveal that most hold the goals and aspirations of the middle class. The desire for security is not limited to the middle class. The desire for a living environment over which one has personal control is part and parcel of the desire for a life which one controls. The creation of communities able to keep themselves free of crime—and to keep their members from becoming criminals—is the task of every society. Anonymous, stigmatized high-rise projects are neither the work of nature, nor the free choice of their inhabitants. They do, however, prove to be important contributors to crime. If it is "middle class" to wish to escape this fate, then the overwhelming majority of

FIG. 13. Aerial Perspective of Tilden Houses in Brooklyn, New York. (Courtesy of New York City Housing Authority)

lower-class people hold middle-class goals and aspirations which are very dear to them.

NOTES

1. The total number of crimes reported in the first nine months of 1971, as compared with the same period in 1970, indicates that crime rose nearly three times as fast in suburban areas as in cities with populations over one million—11 percent as compared with 4 percent. Overall, crime in the suburbs rose nearly twice as fast as in the nation as a whole (*Uniform Crime Report*, Federal Bureau of Investigation, as reported in the *New York Times*, 30 January, 1972, p. 1).

2. *New York City Criminal Justice Coordinating Council Report* (New York, 1971), p. 34.

3. *To Establish Justice, to Insure Domestic Tranquility: Final Report of the National Commission on the Causes & Prevention of Violence* (New York: Bantam Books, 1970), pp. 20–21.

4. Lee Rainwater, "Fear and the House-as-Haven in the Lower Class," *AIP Journal* 32 (January 1966):23.

5. *To Establish Justice*, p. 24.

6. Jane Krause, "Co-op City: Beauty or the Beast?" (Paper, New York University Graduate School of Public Administration, January 1972 [from an interview with Don Phillips, quoting in-house publication, "Projection Completion," of the Office of Cooperative Education, Co-op City, Bronx, N.Y., December 16, 1971]).

2

THE PROBLEM

Before embarking on a detailed discussion of how the various characteristics of building design and project layout combine to produce a defensible space environment, it would be useful to examine the general design characteristics of typical housing projects suffering high crime rates. There are five or six physical characteristics that reinforce criminal behavior, and these occur both in developments built for low- and middle-income occupancy. The projects are usually very large, accommodating over a thousand families, and consist of high-rise apartment towers over seven stories in height. The sites are usually an assembly of what was previously four to six separate city blocks, amalgamated into one giant superblock, closed to city traffic. The buildings are positioned on the site in a rather free compositional fashion. The grounds are designed as one continuous space, moving freely among the buildings and open to the surrounding streets. In the detailed site design, there is seldom any attempt at differentiating the grounds so as to make portions relate to a particular building or cluster of buildings.

The buildings themselves are commonly slab or cruciform towers, housing from 150 to 500 families. They are generally designed with a single lobby which faces onto the interior grounds of the development. The lobby itself contains a mailbox area and a waiting space for a bank of two to four elevators. A typical floor consists of a long central corridor with apartments lining both sides, which is designated in the building profession as a "double-loaded corridor." The elevator bank is located at the center of this corridor.

To furnish sufficient exits in fire emergencies, two, and occasionally four sets of emergency stairwells are provided, running the full height of the building. Sometimes two sets of stairs are grouped together behind the elevators in what is called a scissors-stair configuration; at other times the emergency stairs are located at the ends of the corridors. (Location requirements are determined by local building codes.) Every set of stairs requires its own exit at the ground level. One or two exits may be allowed to be located within the lobby. A high-rise tower, depending on its size, will have from one to four exits in addition to the main entry.

What has just been described will no doubt be seen as a common enough phenomenon, well within the experience of most urbanites. The only difference between a low-income and a high-income development is the presence of fences and guards in the upper-income project, or a doorman provided for each of its buildings. These slight but expensive additions, however, are what make the one a workable habitat and the other not. The same urban high-rise residential developments for low- and

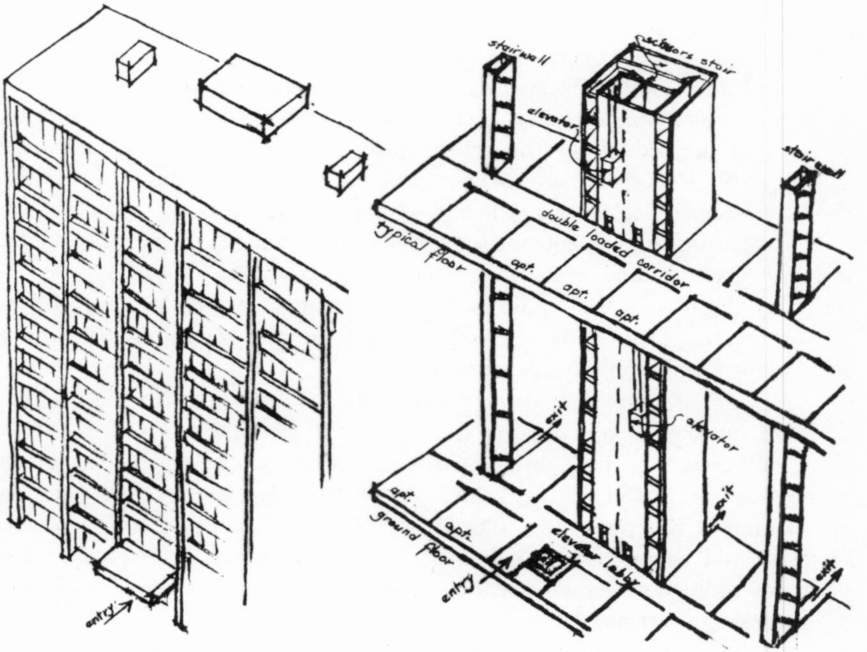

FIG. 14. Typical Double-Loaded Corridor Apartment Building. The view at left is of an apartment building as it is typically seen. At right the building is seen in an x-ray view to illustrate how the horizontal and vertical circulation elements are disposed.

middle-income families, devoid of the doormen, guards, and resident superintendents, become pasturelands for criminals.

The following pages explain just how each of these common physical characteristics facilitiates the victimization of the development's inhabitants. While many of these architectural forms were produced in response to economic dictates, many others are the unfortunate by-products of well-intentioned architectural and planning philosophy.

Middle- and upper-income families who choose to live in high-rise buildings in cities, rather than in single family suburban houses, are able to compensate in a variety of ways not open to the poor, they get away for vacations, send the kids to camp or recreation clubs, and take off by subway or car to the large regional parks serving the city. Most of these options are simply beyond the means of low-income families. Knowledgeable planners and architects, aware of the needs but limited resources of low-income children, and inheriting the decision of the urban renewal and housing agencies to build housing at high densities, find they have two choices open to them: to build walk-up apartments so densely packed together as to have limited land left free of building; or to build high-rise elevator apartment buildings and thereby free a large portion of the project grounds for the required open space and recreation. The second alternate has always been seen as holding more promise. To most planners, recreation and open space are still reckoned in terms of the square footage of available grounds. This notion, coupled with the inherited imagery of the model for the future ideal city pictured by Le Corbusier in his *Ville Radieuse*, and mastered in architectural school, inevitably produce a decision in favor of the high-rise in an open setting.

It was difficult, of course, for the well-intentioned planners to predict that the grounds and recreation space they provided would seldom see use; that the towers they built to create open space would prove too dangerous to send children through alone; that the gap separating apartment from playground would never be bridged.

Another pet concept of the planner was to contribute to the undoing of these housing developments: the notion of the automobile-free superblock. Whenever a site consisting of four to six blocks of existing urban fabric was assembled, it was taken for granted that in the new plan the intervening streets would be closed off. The closing of streets produces more ground which can then be used in the calculation of density and so produces more housing units for a particular site—and more open space. This thinking is erroneous on three accounts.

Firstly, as the plan will be built at the same density regardless of the size of the site, there will be no net increase in open space resulting from street closing. Secondly, had the streets not been closed, the amount of building which could have been accommodated on the site would have been appreciably less, and the streets would still have been there to provide space and light between buildings—and a very useful form of recreation space for all age groups. Lastly, and most significantly, streets provide security in the form of prominent paths for concentrated pedestrian and vehicular movement; windows and doorways, when facing streets, extend the zone of residents' territorial commitments and allow for the continual casual surveillance by police in passing cars. Jane Jacobs in her *Death and Life of Great American Cities* contends that the surveillance provided by the casual passerby on foot or in a car is important as a deterrent to criminal activity.

Streets also provide security according to the positioning of a building's entry lobby relative to the street. In large superblock housing projects, the interior grounds are usually left open and are freely accessible from the street. More often than not, the planners face the lobby entries of buildings onto the interior grounds. An inhabitant returning home must leave the public street and wind his way through the undefined and anonymous grounds of the project to reach the front door of his building. He would have been much safer had be been able to go directly from street to front door, and safer still if the front door and lobby of his building faced directly onto the street. When lobby crime and elevator muggings in housing projects whose building entries face the street were compared with those whose building entries face the interior grounds, the differences were found to be significant.

In apartment towers, the forced disassociation of the life in the apartments from the play and recreation activity areas of the project grounds below, is a further contributant to the anonymity and potential danger of these spaces. Their lack of security results eventually in total nonuse and accompanying withdrawal, all of which serves to make them more dangerous still.

It is the apartment tower itself, however, that is the real and final villain of the piece. It is inconceivable that one genius alone could have been responsible for its creation. High-rise, elevator-serviced, double-loaded corridor apartment buildings for the use of low- and middle-income families have proven disastrous. Their provision in many cases is the result of a set of circumstances now common to most inner city developments: land costs driven up by land speculation; zoning increased by city planning departments so as to provide more housing; pressed housing officials; harried Federal mortgage financiers; and indifferent architects. No one person would have dared so much. The evolution of this building prototype could only have been conceived by a group of anxious men following the barest thread of rationalism: the search for the most economical solution; a way of housing the most within the least.

The high-rise apartment tower is primarily a by-product of the need to build at higher densities to justify inflated land costs. Where, at under sixty units to the acre, a variety of building prototypes are still available

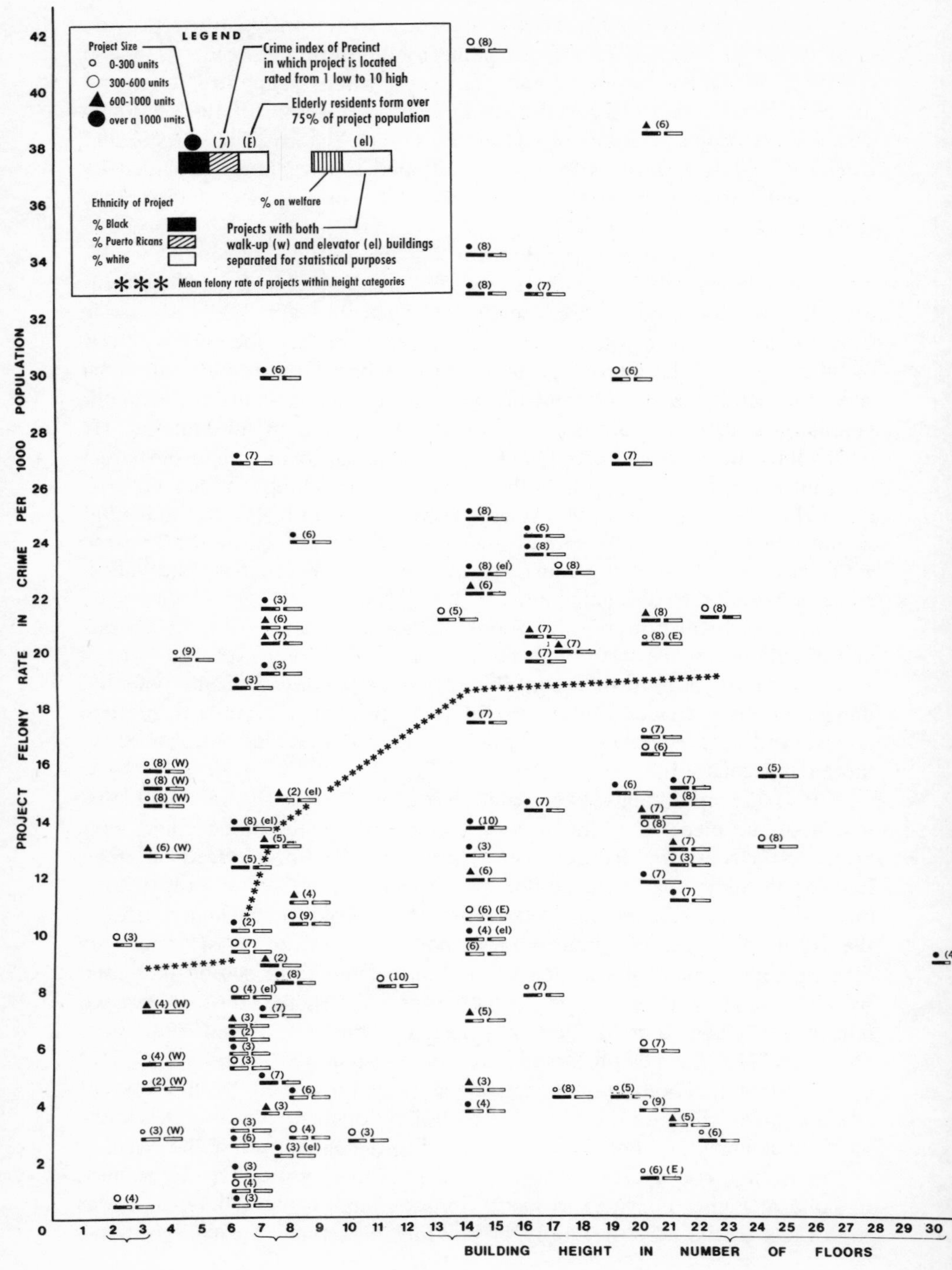
LEGEND
Project Size
0-300 units
300-600 units
600-1000 units
over a 1000 units
Crime index of Precinct in which project is located rated from 1 low to 10 high
Elderly residents form over 75% of project population
(7) (E)
(el)
Ethnicity of Project
% Black
% Puerto Ricans
% white
% on welfare
Projects with both walk-up (w) and elevator (el) buildings separated for statistical purposes
*** Mean felony rate of projects within height categories
PROJECT FELONY RATE IN CRIME PER 1000 POPULATION
BUILDING HEIGHT IN NUMBER OF FLOORS

for use by a housing designer, once seventy-five units per acre is reached, the high-rise slab becomes about the only option open. Crime rate has been found to increase almost proportionately with building height, as illustrated by figure 15.

Project size has also been found to affect crime rate. If the two variables of building heights and project size are coupled, the probability of crime increases to the extent that it is possible to guarantee a higher crime rate in virtually all projects of excessive height and size. In New York City, 95 percent of the Housing Authority's projects greater than six stories in height and larger than a thousand units in size have higher crime rates per thousand population than those which are both smaller and lower.

In a high-rise, double-loaded corridor apartment tower, the only defensible space is the interior of the apartment itself; everything else is a "no-man's-land," neither public nor private. The lobby, stairs, elevators, and corridors are open and accessible to everyone. But unlike the well-peopled and continually surveyed public streets, these interior areas are sparsely used and impossible to survey; they become a nether world of fear and crime.

The investigation of the relationship between building height and crime was begun with the basic hypothesis that a positive correlation exists between the two; that as building height increases, so does crime. Recognizing the fact that height alone was not the reason for such a connection, we took into account the various other factors that usually attend high buildings: a larger number of apartment units and people using a single lobby, entry, and elevators, with resulting anonymity; more interior public space hidden from view and so on.

From the computer tapes of the New York City Housing Authority Police, the 1969 crime records for 100 projects were examined. These projects were selected to meet the following criteria: (1) buildings throughout an individual project had to be of uniform building type, and (2) the project had to be seen as a separate entity from the surrounding community. Projects were divided into two groups, those with buildings six stories or less, and those with buildings seven stories or greater. In addition, these projects were divided by size, those under 1000 units and those greater than 1000 units. Population can be substituted for units to indicate project size. An examination of data revealed a linear correlation between the two, allowing such interchangeability. The crime rate for a project was found by taking the total number of felonies, misdemeanors, and offenses occurring in 1969 and dividing it by the project population. An analysis of variance was performed on the subsequent data, and the results are shown in table 1.

FIG. 15. Felony rate by building height, with population, project, and neighborhood characteristics. Based on New York City Housing Authority Police data for 1969.

TABLE 1

Project Size and Building Height versus Crime

		BUILDING HEIGHT	
		Equal to or Less Than 6 Stories	*Greater Than 6 Stories*
Project Size	Equal to or Less Than 1000 Units	N = 8 M = 47 SD = 25	N = 47 M = 51 SD = 23
	Greater Than 1000 Units	N = 11 M = 45 SD = 26	N = 34 M = 67 SD = 24

NOTE: N = number of cases; M = mean number of crimes per thousand; SD = standard deviation

The apparent effect of building height on crime is quite evident. In both project size categories, the mean or average crime rate jumps significantly when one compares low buildings with higher buildings. But what is most interesting is the fact that in buildings of six stories or less, the project size or total number of units does not really make much difference. In fact, projects of 1000 units, but under six stories in height, have a lower crime rate than smaller-sized projects of similar height. In terms of our hypothesis, larger projects encourage crime by fostering feelings of anonymity, isolation, irresponsibility, lack of identity with surroundings, etc. Our evidence indicates that low buildings seem to offset what one may assume to be a factor conducive to high crime rates. In the higher buildings, a significant increase in average crime rate is seen when one compares the smaller-size project category with the larger. The fact that projects greater than 1000 units, with buildings of seven or more stories, have the highest rate, indicates that it is not large size alone, but large size in combination with higher buildings that contributes to a more criminally active situation. It seems that one can still maintain high density (size) and not encounter higher crime rates, as long as building height remains low.

Total felonies were compiled for all qualifying projects over a period of one year, including those exterior crimes that occurred near a building as well as interior building crimes. When this data, in the form of a ratio of crimes (felonies) per thousand population, was arranged in five building-height categories and examined, a dramatic increase occured: from a mean of 8.8 for three-story buildings, the rate rose to 20.2 for buildings sixteen stories and over. The reason the rate of increase appears to level off in buildings over thirteen stories in height is that burglaries of apartments occur most frequently in ground-floor apartments, (four times as often) and in top-floor apartments (two times as often). The higher the building, the proportionally fewer ground-floor and top-floor apartments, and hence fewer burglaries per apartment occur. Another factor that might explain the apparent leveling off is the unwillingness of criminals to repeatedly "hit" the same building (see figure 15).

Robbery (muggings) occurring in interior public spaces (elevator, hallway, and stairs) was investigated, and once again this data was examined by building height (see figure 16). From a rate of 2.6 per 1000 people for six-story buildings, crime rose to a high of 11.5 per 1000 people for buildings with nineteen or more floors.

The relationship of height to crime was also analyzed in terms of location, that is what percentage of a project's crime occurs in the interior public spaces, as opposed to the grounds and apartments. The results strongly supported the crime rate data. High-rise projects not only experience a higher rate of crime within the buildings, but a greater proportion of the crime occurs in the interior public spaces of these buildings as compared with lower buildings. Table 2, Location of Crime—All Projects, was compiled from the 1969 data of the New York City Housing Authority Police. This data encompasses 150,000 units of public housing in the five boroughs of New York. For our purposes, it constitutes a dossier on the nature and location of crime in housing projects.

Unlike other police departments, the New York City Housing Authority Police keep records localizing the place of occurrence of a crime committed within a project. Crimes ranging from serious felonies to minor misdemeanors are all recorded, and complaints are noted, even when they have not led to apprehensions or arrests. Police reports also separate

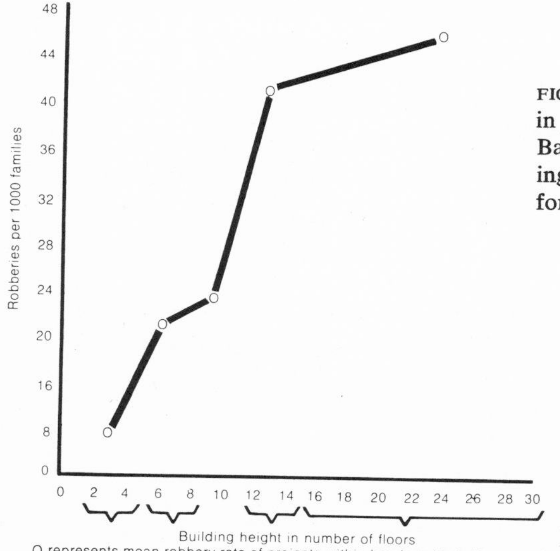

FIG. 16. Frequency of robberies in buildings of different heights. Based on New York City Housing Authority Police statistics for 1969.

TABLE 2

*Location of Crime—All Projects**

General Space Category	*Exact Location*	*Total Crime*	*Total FMO's†*	*Total Felonies*	*Assault*	*Burglary*	*Murder*	*Rape*	*Robbery*	*Lingering*	*Mailbox (all incidents)*	*Drugs (all incidents)*	*Malicious Mischief (all incidents)*
Interior Private Space	Apartment	21680	5692	2321	54	2087	7	16	62	29	22	195	2561
Interior Public Space	Lobby	9746	4103	682	18	7			591	3321	2267	207	828
	Elevator	5451	2165	1549	10	1		13	1490	58		12	537
	Stairway	4572	2129	347	14		1	14	286	1460	1	230	1568
	Hallway	7379	2419	817	40	3	1	5	718	1720	6	185	1263
	Roof and Landing	1395	396	72	3	3		39	7	446	3	210	143
	Other Inside	3894	1351	319	14	197		2	73	309	4	80	777
	Subtotal	32437	12563	3786	99	211	2	73	3165	7314	2281	924	5116
Non-Tenant Space	Social Facility	1639	610	227	2	213			3	32	1	5	271
	Commercial Facility	285	144	55		38			15	11	1	1	41
	Subtotal	1924	754	282	21	251			18	43	2	6	

Exterior Project Public Space	Project Grounds	15031	4649	1990	107	3	2	8	1419	719	7	660	432
Exterior Nonproject Public Space	Contiguous to Project	763	358	229	11		1		175	4		67	3
	Off-Project and Other	24	7	3		2			1	1		1	1
	Subtotal	787	365	232	11	2	1		176	5		68	4
Total		71859	24023	8611	273	2554	12	97	4840	8110	2312	1853	8425

* All incidents reported to NYCHA Police in 1969, excluding intrahousehold incidents.
† Felonies, misdemeanors, and offenses.

crimes committed on project grounds from those committed inside buildings and within apartments proper. Because place of occurrence is significant information to the Housing Authority, we have been able to learn where the recurring danger areas in housing projects and buildings are, and to measure the extent to which physical design is a statistically significant contributing factor in the frequency of occurrences.

Perhaps the most revealing fact is that of all recorded crime taking place in housing projects, 79 percent occurs within the buildings proper. This includes nearly all categories of serious crime: robbery (muggings), burglary, larceny, rape, and felonious assault and leads to the inevitable conclusion that the buildings themselves, rather than the project grounds, are the most unsafe areas. It follows, too, that a criminal probably perceives that the interior public areas of buildings are where his victims are most vulnerable, and where the possibility of his being seen or apprehended is minimal. Statistics on apprehension reveal that proportionally more than twice as many criminals are caught committing crimes on project grounds than are caught committing crimes within buildings (see table 3).

TABLE 3

Apprehension by Location

Robbery	*Percent Apprehended Same Day*	
Apartment	3.2	3.4 Percent Average
Lobby	5.8	
Elevator	1.9	
Stairway	2.4	
Hall	3.6	
Grounds	7.6	

Much of the free-wheeling accessibility to the interior areas of public housing may be the result of the Federal policy that states that projects, by law and tradition, are open to all members of the urban community. The interior of project buildings and grounds suffer the unique distinction of being public in nature and yet hidden from public view. Consequently, they are unable to benefit from the continual surveillance to which the public areas of our cities are normally subject (see figure 17). The numbers in figure 17 and table 2 further reinforce this conclusion.

Three-story buildings have limited interior public spaces com-

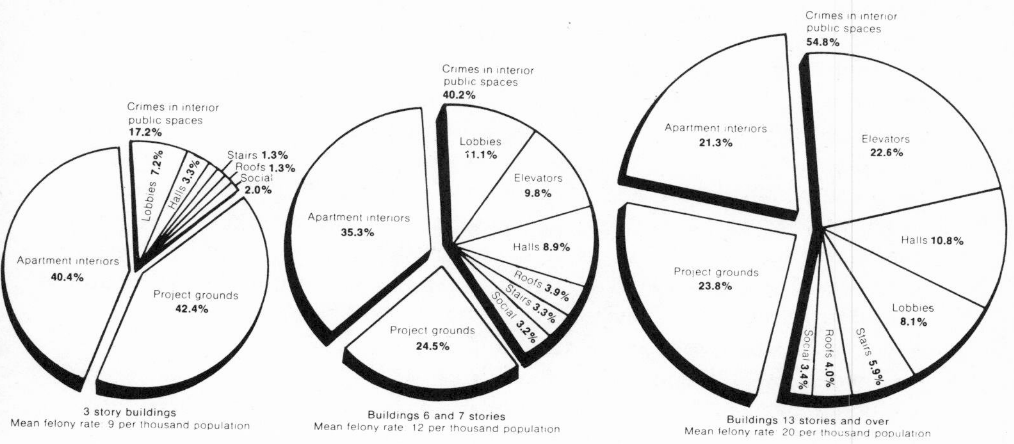

FIG. 17. Place of Occurrence of Crimes in Buildings of Different Heights. Based on New York City Housing Authority Police 1969 data (felonies).

pared with six- and seven-story buildings and buildings thirteen stories and over. Note that in the pie chart for the highest category of buildings almost 55 percent of the project crime takes place in these interior common spaces. This diminishes to 40 percent for six- and seven-story buildings, and to 17 percent for the three-story walk-ups. Muggings form 95 percent of crimes committed in the interior public areas where burglaries form 90 percent of apartment interior crime. Note that not only does the area of location change, but the total number of felonies in each category goes from nine per thousand in three-story buildings to twenty per thousand in buildings thirteen stories and over.

The specific area within a high-rise building that is most vulnerable —the elevator—is a prime example of an area lacking surveillance. Thirty-one percent of all robberies (muggings) in all housing projects occur within elevators. The victim may then be moved at the threat of force to the apartment, or in the case of rape, to the sealed-off fire stairs or roof landings, where traffic and observation are rare (see table 2).

Evidence indicates that those spaces which people must use on a continuing basis to get from the public area outside the project to the safety of the interior of the apartment are particularly dangerous if screened from natural observation and from formal patrol. In this light, the elevator is a space public in nature but totally screened from all observation. For the interval of the ride, it provides the optimum situation for a criminal and is so understood by the tenants.

Entrance lobbies are not much safer and account for 12 percent of all robberies. This is very often the result of the peculiar design convolutions of the lobby layout. The elevator bank is usually required to be located at the center of the corridor of the typical apartment floor. In answering this requirement, architects sometimes have difficulty resolving the positioning of elevators at the ground level. It is not uncommon for them to produce circuitous passageways and hidden double turns in linking up the entry-lobby to the elevators. These configurations produce screened-off elevator waiting areas and mailbox positions hidden from direct street view. As previously mentioned, the limited visibility of lobby entrances has been found to contribute to high crime rates.

There is still another problem area worth singling out for special discussion: the fire stairs and secondary exits. Because of the multitude of fire stairs required in servicing large, double-loaded corridors, and because the fire code requires they be designed as vertical concrete boxes with little or no windows, they are continually used by criminals as places to waylay or bring victims. More importantly (and this is not a phenomenon which appears in the statistics) the profusion of fire stairs and exits, plus the difficulty of keeping activities within them under surveillance, makes pursuit of a criminal next to impossible. There are so many potential evasion routes open, and so many different possible exits, that it would take a contingent of policemen to apprehend a criminal, even if they knew for sure that he was within a particular building. More important than apprehension, however, is the fact that a criminal casing a scene will perceive at a glance the number of escape options open to him and realize his risks are minimal. A building, through its basic design, can make evident to criminals either that they will be seen everywhere they go and have only one avenue of escape, or, as in the case of the double-loaded corridor, high-rise, elevator building that they will be out of sight continually and have a virtual maze in which to hide and escape. Most public housing projects built in the fifties are identical to the physical format already described, with a few additional aggregates to provide a final *coup de grace*. They are totally devoid of any embellishments or amenities which might give the buildings or site a sense of scale or humanity, and they are located in the highest crime areas of our cities.

The distinctive form of high-rise, publicly assisted housing is immediately recognizable. The barren, red-brick towers stand out as prominent landmarks in all our cities—well-built monuments to a halfhearted attempt at benevolence. It would be unjust, however, to suggest that the politicians, bureaucrats, planners, and architects responsible for these projects were callous or maliciously motivated. The end result of their efforts may now appear inadequate and irrational, but they were well-

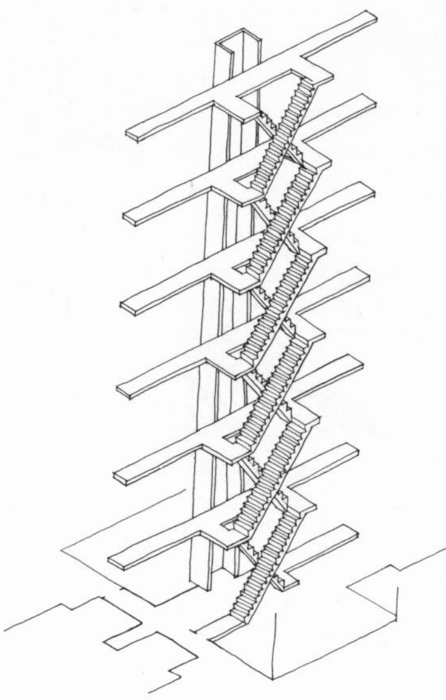

FIG. 18. Exploded view showing function and location of "scissors fire stairwell"

The physical arrangement of the scissors stairway is rather complex: two separate landings, accessible from the hallway, are located in the same position on every floor of a building. Each landing is joined by straight-run stairs to the "opposite" landings on the floors just above and just below, such that access to the next higher or lower floor is possible via either of the two landings on a floor. The total pattern is such that adjacent floors are connected by two straight-run stairs which form a criss-cross or "x" pattern (hence the name scissors stairs).

Each of the two landings on a floor forms a part of one of the separated stair systems that comprise a total scissors stair. The circulation pattern in a scissors stair might be described as that of two "squared" spiral stairways, intertwined around one another but not connected to each other. Two persons can enter the two landings on a floor at the same time and descend the stair system at the same rate, without seeing or hearing each other: there is a fire wall between each. Each pair of "criss-cross" stairs, and the two landings at each floor are unconnected, and one must leave the stairway and walk along the hall to reach the other landing.

intentioned. Unfortunately, the process of development, from a project's inception to its completion, involves a series of low-level, compartmentalized decisions which may each represent the best solution to a particularized problem, but together produce a very banal and bleak reality.

The location of low-income housing projects does not help appreciably. The Report of the President's Commission on Law Enforcement and Administration of Justice, 1968, in attempting to understand the nature of the current crime problem, was able to isolate the prevalence of crime and found it to be concentrated in inner city areas.

> Of 2,780,015 offenses known to the police in 1965—these were index crimes—some two million occurred in cities, more than half a million occurred in suburbs, and about 170,000 occurred in rural areas.[1]

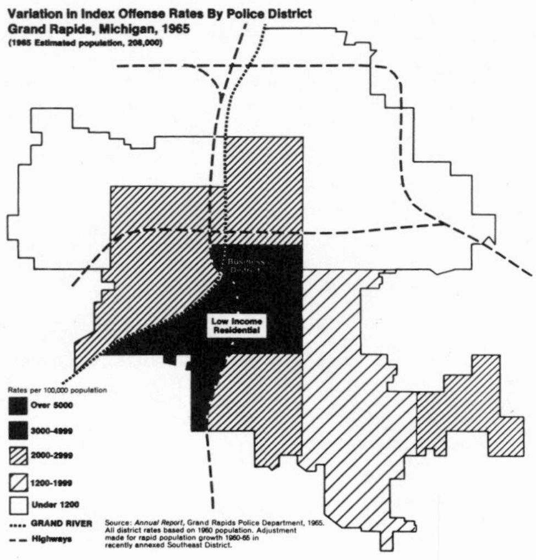

FIG. 19. Variation in index offense rates by police district in Grand Rapids, Michigan, 1965. (Courtesy of U.S. Government Printing Office)

> Crime rates in American cities tend to be highest in the city center and decrease in relationship to the distance from the center. This typical distribution of crime rates is found even in medium sized cities such as the city of Grand Rapids, Michigan.[2]

Too often public housing is seen as housing of last resort. It is the result of a Federal program which came into full flower in the fifties and which committed the government to the responsibility of providing adequate housing for the poor and the aged who could not afford it. That we should have donned this mantle of responsibility thirty to a hundred years after other Western countries is only a small additional testament to our late blooming as a welfare state. In many respects, the decision to house the poor and the old together in large public housing ghettos followed naturally. For one thing, no middle-class community really wanted the poor around. A housing program committed to the use of many, small, in-fill sites located in middle-class neighborhoods was, and still is, unthinkable. Large sites at the periphery of existing urban ghettos were the only solution in the past and are likely to remain the only solution.

To a significant degree, the large numbers to be housed were the by-product of another form of belated Federal enlightenment—the Urban Renewal Program. In many of our older cities this last-ditch effort to save commercial investment in the urban core from its dispersal into suburbia required the large-scale clearance of slums bordering the central business districts. The hope was to coax new business and middle-class housing back to town. The successes of urban renewal, seen twenty years later, are modest indeed. However, the testing of the notion required a commitment to the grand-scale destruction of low-income tenements in every major American city.

Our purpose is not to discuss the merits or faults of the Federal Urban Renewal Program, but only to recognize its contribution to our heritage of large, high-rise, low-income housing projects. The destruction of densely occupied, semideteriorated urban ghettos to create cleared land for new business and middle-income housing, in turn, created the need for replacement housing for the poor. The question was where to put this housing? The middle-class communities in other areas of the cities would have none of it. Beyond the occasional availability of peripheral urban sites adjacent to and previously zoned for industry, the only other large-scale land available was the cleared urban renewal land itself, deep in the inner city. However, embarking on a program of filling up this land with new housing to replace what was being torn down to create new land for commerce would not have been too sensible. It was then realized that if the new, low-income housing was built at five to ten times the density of the old, the poor could be housed on small, out-of-the-way, portions of the cleared land, usually at the periphery of remaining ghettos.

The fact that large, low-income families had never been placed in high-rise elevator buildings before, in this or any other country, did not deter the solution seekers. For one thing, there was evidence of some middle-income families successfully living in high-rise buildings. For another, placing federally sponsored housing of high density on urban renewal land insured that a higher price per acre could be paid by a city's housing agency to a city's urban renewal agency. This would show as an important plus in the accounting ledger of the renewal agency which, meanwhile, was finding that the rest of its newly freed land was not selling too well. These accounting procedures were, of course, the flimsiest of self-deceptions—an instance only of one agency of government charging another agency of government high prices so as to show a paper profit.

Current renewal and housing programs are claimed to be more enlightened. The Model Cities Program was heralded as a federal effort that would give more community input and guidance to renewal. It was intended to provide additional funds for allied social programs that would supplement old deficiencies. There is little to look at in what is being accomplished that gives much evidence of this. New federal housing programs, Turnkey, 235, 236, and state financing efforts, were all intended to replace or expand on public housing and 221D3 efforts. Their major accomplishment, however, has been the reorganization of financing procedures. Despite the HUD guidelines, new financial and organizational opportunities, the old design mistakes continue to be built. The excuse that no other options are available is still accepted. Even some of the inspired low-middle-income housing programs are proving failures because they bring people together in environments which do not allow them to exercise their proprietary inclinations and concerns.

In the following pages, a comparison is made of two housing projects which are identical in every respect except the physical. One has three times the robbery rate of the other. This comparison will serve to give the reader an overview not only of how physical design characteristics operate independently, but of how they combine to produce a safe or unsafe environment.

There are many factors contributing to crime rates in housing projects other than the physical characteristics of the buildings and the nature of their grouping. Housing developments are often located in high crime precincts, and New York City Housing Authority Police statistics indicate that a housing development's crime rate usually reflects the crime rate of the surrounding community. Similarly, but for very different reasons, the greater the percentage of elderly in a project, and the greater the percentage of teen-agers, the greater the crime rate. The elderly tend to be easily victimized and so suffer a greater number of crimes than members of middle-aged families.[3] As long as records on crime rates have been kept, they have shown that the ages between twelve and twenty are the most prone to crime. Projects with more teen-agers therefore tend to have more crime.

In attempting to isolate the significance of physical design alone in affecting crime rate, it is necessary to take into account the effect of these other factors and endeavor to weigh them out. There are various statistical techniques available for doing this. Analysis of Variance and Multiple Regression Analysis are two techniques which have been employed and

FIG. 20. Comparison of Van Dyke Houses and Brownsville Houses. Van Dyke Houses (left) and Brownsville Houses (right) are located across the street from one another in the Brownsville section of Brooklyn. Both projects are almost identical in overall size, density, and population characteristics. (Photo by author)

are discussed at length in Appendix B. Still another method, Comparison of Coupled Projects, was commonly used in our study and of all three; it is perhaps the one most graphically comprehensible.

Statistical comparison of coupled projects involves finding two housing projects in which all the variables which could affect the crime rate are identical, except for the projects' physical design characteristics. For a start, both projects have to be located within the same crime-rated area. Similarly, the percentage of teen-agers and elderly persons living in the two projects should not vary significantly. For true comparison to be made, a list must be compiled of all factors which are known to affect crime rate, along with those factors which many believe should affect crime rate. Comparisons must be made of the ages of tenants, their incomes, the number of years living in the project, the number of broken families or families without a male head of house, the number of families on welfare, the percentage white, black, Puerto Rican and so on. It was important that two additional physical characteristics, other than location, be kept identical: the project size (number of acres) and the housing density (number of persons per acre). It was considered likely that these last two variables might have an important contributing effect on a project's crime rate.

Coupled projects meeting all of the necessary characteristics proved scarce and difficult to locate, but a few were found. As an example of the method employed in making comparisons and as an illustration of significant findings, the Brownsville and Van Dyke projects in New York City will be discussed and explored in detail.

• *A Tale of Two Projects*

Brownsville and Van Dyke are strikingly different in physical design, while housing comparatively identical populations in size and social characteristics. The high-rise towers at Van Dyke are almost totally devoid of defensible space qualities, while the buildings at Brownsville are comparatively well-endowed with such qualities. It should be mentioned, even before beginning the comparison, the Brownsville, the better of the two projects, is still far away from answering all defensible space design directives.

Review of the objective data on the physical characteristics of the two projects reveals many striking parallels. The projects are almost identical in size, each housing approximately 6,000 persons, and are designed at exactly the same density: 288 persons per acre. Major differences arise in the composition of buildings and the percentage of ground-level space they occupy. Brownsville buildings cover 23 percent of the available land, whereas Van Dyke buildings cover only 16.6 percent of the total land

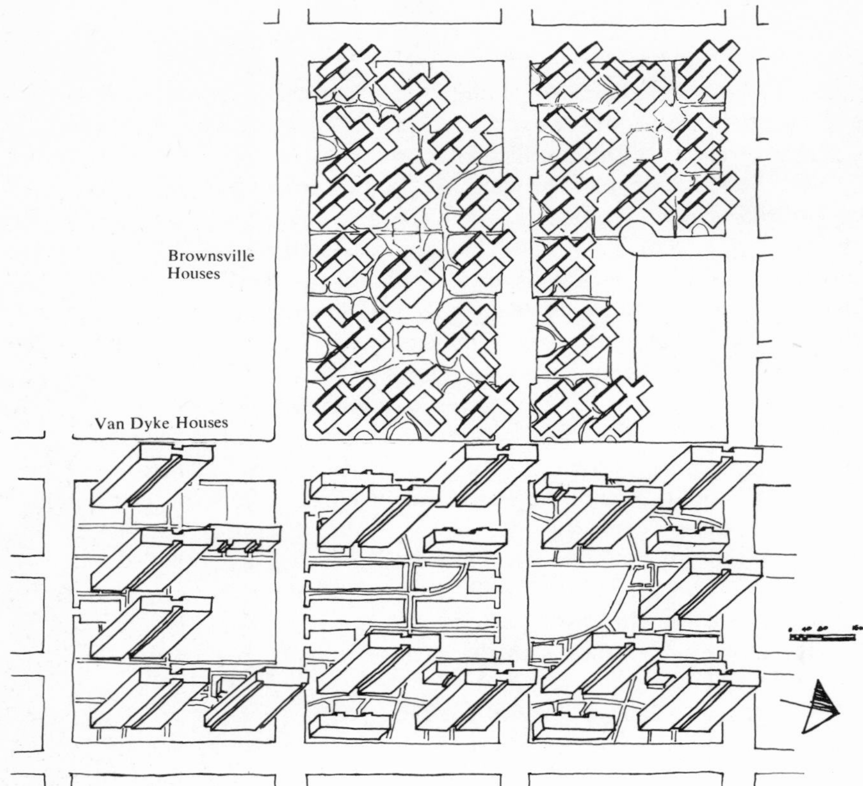

FIG. 21. Site plan of Brownsville and Van Dyke Houses

area—including nine, three-story buildings which occupy a large percentage of space but house only 24 percent of the total project population. In addition, the two projects differ in design (see figure 21) in that Brownsville is comprised of low, walk-up and elevator buildings, three to six stories, while the latter is comprised of a mix of three-story buildings and fourteen-story high-rise slabs (87 percent of the apartment units at Van Dyke are located in the high-rise slabs). The two projects are located across the street from one another and share the same Housing Authority police and New York City police services.

Differences in physical design of the Brownsville and Van Dyke projects are apparent even to the casual observer. Van Dyke Houses has the appearance of a large, monolithic project. The most dominant buildings are the thirteen, fourteen-story slabs. In less evidence are the nine, three-story structures. Each of the buildings at Van Dyke sits independently on the site, with large open spaces separating it from its neighbors. At the center of the project is a single, large open area, used for a Parks

FIG. 22. Central Grounds of Van Dyke Houses. The buildings were intentionally designed tall so as to free the grounds for recreation, but the grounds go unused because they are anonymous and too distant to allow supervision from the typical apartment. (Photo by author)

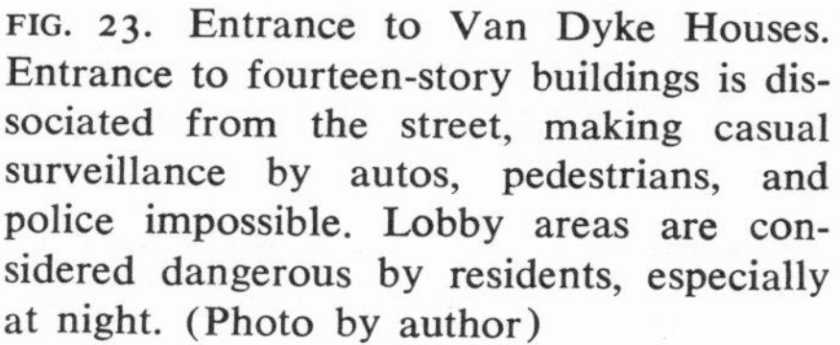

FIG. 23. Entrance to Van Dyke Houses. Entrance to fourteen-story buildings is dissociated from the street, making casual surveillance by autos, pedestrians, and police impossible. Lobby areas are considered dangerous by residents, especially at night. (Photo by author)

Department playground and for automobile parking. By means of its design, this large open area has been distinctly separated from and is unrelated to the surrounding buildings.

None of the buildings at Van Dyke may be entered directly from the public street. Entrance requires that tenants leave the public street and walk onto project paths that wind into internal project areas, blind to street surveillance. The only areas of the project grounds which relate somewhat to buildings are the small seating areas in the channel of space between the double row of buildings. The functional entrance to the high-rise buildings is a small door shared by 112 to 136 families. This door is located directly off the project paths, with no gradation or distinction indicated by the design of the grounds in front of the building lobby.

Two low-speed elevators carry families to their living floors in each of the high-rise buildings. Elevators are placed directly opposite the building entrances, as mandated by the Housing Authority, to improve surveillance from the outside. Full benefit is not derived from this arrangement, however, since entrances face the interior of the project rather than the street.

The housing floors of the high-rise buildings are each occupied by eight families. The elevator stops in the middle of the corridor, and the apartment units are reached by walking left or right down a dead-end corridor with apartments positioned on both sides (a double-loaded corridor).

In contrast, Brownsville Houses presents the appearance of being a smaller project, due to the disposition of units in smaller and more diverse clusters of buildings. It might be said that the buildings and the way in which they were placed on the site has been used to divide the project into smaller, more manageable zones. The ground areas have been humanized through their relationship with the individual residential buildings. Activities that take place in small project spaces adjoining buildings have become the business of the neighboring residents, who assume a leading role in monitoring them.

All residents and police who have been interviewed at Brownsville perceive the project as smaller and more stable than Van Dyke. All intruders, including police and interviewers, feel more cautious about invading the privacy of residents at Brownsville. By contrast, their attitude toward the invasion of the interior corridors at Van Dyke is callous and indifferent.

This emphasis on space division carries over into the design of the building interiors of Brownsville Houses. Individual buildings are three- and six-story structures with six families sharing a floor. The floor is

FIG. 24. Brownsville Houses. Oblique view shows dense coverage and subdivision of grounds into areas defined by and associated with buildings. Each wing of the six-story buildings contains three apartments on a floor clustered around a common vestibule. (Photo by author)

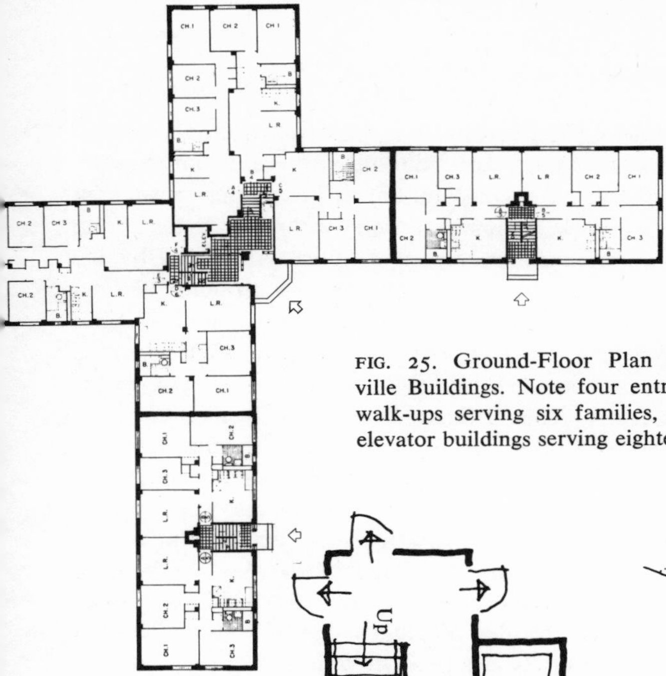

FIG. 25. Ground-Floor Plan of Brownsville Buildings. Note four entries—two to walk-ups serving six families, and two to elevator buildings serving eighteen families.

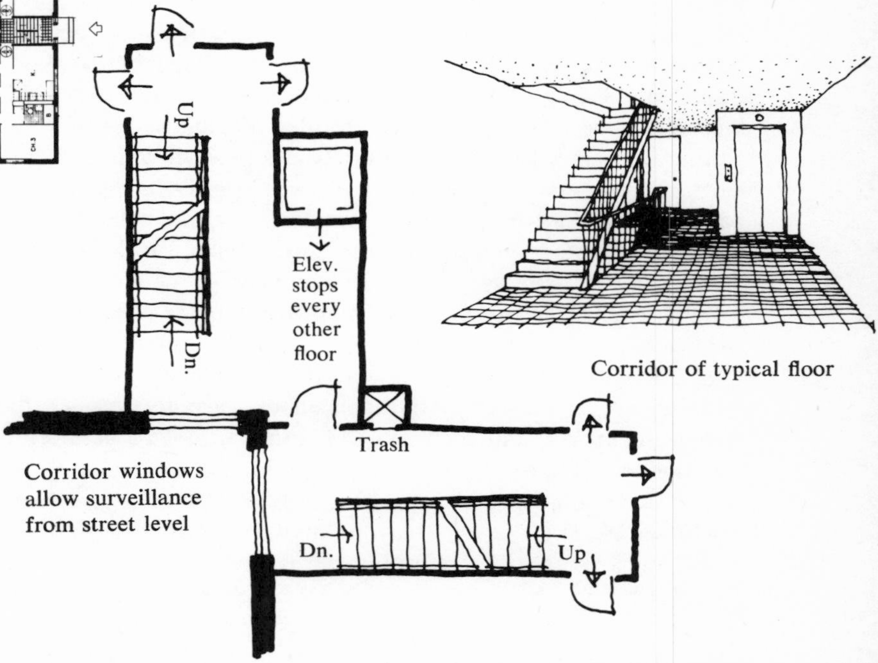

Up

Elev. stops every other floor

Dn.

Corridor of typical floor

Trash

Corridor windows allow surveillance from street level

Dn.

Up

FIG. 26. View of Interior Corridor of Brownsville Houses. Corridor plans show clustering of apartment entries around open stairwells.

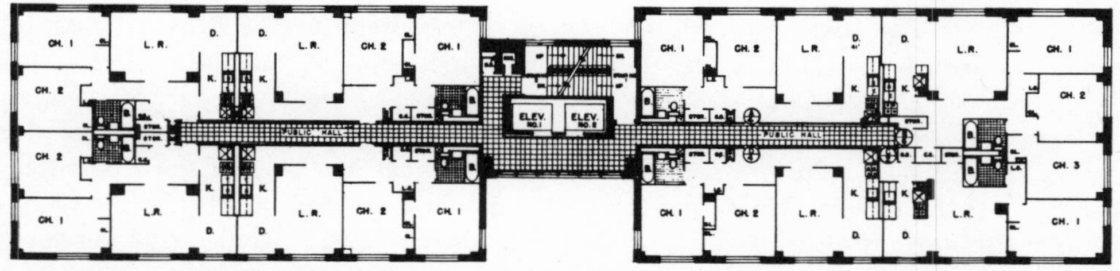

FIG. 27. Floor Plan of Van Dyke Houses. Floor plan shows the location of elevator and scissors fire stairs with respect to the individual apartments on a typical floor in Van Dyke high-rise buildings. This separation occurs on all floors.

further divided, by an unlocked swinging door, into two vestibules shared by three families each. In the six-story buildings there is an elevator which stops at odd floors, requiring residents of upper stories to walk up or down one flight, using an open stairwell around which apartment doors are clustered. Vertical communication among families is assured by this relationship of elevators to apartments, and also by the presence of open stairwells connecting the floors.

At the ground level, the building lobby leads up a short flight of stairs to several apartments that maintain surveillance over activity in this small entryway. On all floors, tenants have been found to maintain auditory surveillance over activity taking place in the halls by the device of keeping their doors slightly ajar. These features of the building have allowed occupants to extend their territorial prerogatives into building corridors, hallways, and stairs. Those mothers of young children at Brownsville who allow their children the freedom to play on landings and up and down the stairwells monitor their play from within the apartment. A mere interruption in the din of children at play was found to bring mothers to their doors as surely as a loud scream.

By contrast, most young children at Van Dyke are not allowed to play in the corridors outside their apartments. The halls of Van Dyke and other high-rise buildings are designed solely for their corridor function and are inhospitable to the fantasy-play of children. In addition, too many families utilize a typical high-rise hall for a mother to comfortably leave her child there unsupervised. For the same reason, mothers are reluctant to leave their door ajar for surveillance—too many people, including strangers and guests of neighbors, wander through the Van Dyke halls unchecked and unquestioned. Finally, to give children real freedom in the use of the building would require their using the elevator or fire stairs to gain access to other floors. But both these areas are frightening and would take the children out of the surveillance zone of the mother and other tenants. The elevator cab is sealed by a heavy metal door that cannot be opened manually. The fire stairwells are designed to seal floors in the event of a fire. A by-product of their fireproofing is that noises within the stairwells cannot be heard in the corridors outside. Criminals often force their victims into these areas because the soundproofing feature and low frequency of use make the detection of a crime in progress almost impossible.

The sense of propriety which is apparent in the way tenants of Brownsville Houses use their halls to monitor and maintain surveillance over children and strangers appears to have carried over to the grounds adjacent to building entrances. Because of the unique construction of the buildings, there are areas on the ground level just outside the front door of the building where parents can allow their children to play, while maintaining contact with them through their kitchen windows. Interviews

FIG. 28. Brownsville Houses from Street. The buildings dispositions at Brownsville create triangular buffer areas which are used for play, sitting, and parking. These areas are easily observed from the street and from apartment windows. Entry to buildings is typically from the street through these buffer zones. Residents regard these areas as an extension of their own buildings and maintain active surveillance over them. (Photo by author)

have revealed that the range of spaces into which young children are permitted to roam is greater in Brownsville than in Van Dyke.

Finally, where entries to Van Dyke high-rise buildings serve 130 families, Brownsville buildings are entered through different doors, each serving a small number of families (nine to thirteen). The ground area adjacent to these entries has been developed for use by adults, and for play by young children. Parents feel confident about allowing their children to play in these clearly circumscribed zones. Frequently, these entry areas are located just off the public street, and serve to set off the building from the street itself by acting as an intervening buffer area. The placement of entrances just off the street avoids the dangers created at Van Dyke: forcing tenants to walk along blind interior project paths to get to their buildings.

Inspection of tables 4 and 5, reveals that the tenants of Bownsville and Van Dyke are rated similarly on overall indexes of socio-economic status, family stability, and ethnic, racial, and family composition. It is also clear that these rough similarities are consistent from year to year. Comparison of demographic data over the period 1962 to 1969 (see Appendix B) reveals few exceptions to this overall pattern of identity between the projects.

It was a widely held belief that many so-called "problem families," displaced by the Model Cities renewal programs, were among recent move-ins to Van Dyke. Many people drew an immediate correlation between the higher crime rate at Van Dyke and this change in population.

TABLE 4

Tenant Statistics

Characteristic	*Van Dyke*	*Brownsville*
Total population	6,420	5,390
Average family size	4.0	4.0
Number of minors	3,618 (57.5%)	3,047 (57.8%)
Percent families black	79.1%	85.0%
Percent families white	5.6%	2.6%
Percent families Puerto Rican	15.3%	12.4%
Average gross income	$4,997	$5,056
Percent on welfare	28.8%	29.7%
Percent broken families	29.5%	31.7%
Average number of years in project	8.5	9.0
Percent of families with two wage earners	12.2%	11.0
Number of children in grades 1–6	839	904

SOURCE: New York City Housing Authority Records, 1968.

TABLE 5

A Comparison of Physical Design and Population Density

Physical Measure	*Van Dyke*	*Brownsville*
Total size	22.35 acres	19.16 acres
Number of buildings	23	27
Building height	13–14 story 9–3 story	6-story with some 3-story wings
Coverage	16.6	23.0
Floor area ratio	1.49	1.39
Average number of rooms per apartment	4.62	4.69
Density	288 persons/acre	287 persons/acre
Year completed	1955 (one building added in 1964)	1947

SOURCE: New York City Housing Authority Project Physical Design Statistics.

Information was therefore obtained on a representative sample of families who have moved into the two projects over the past three years. Sample data on one of every five move-ins reveal no striking differences in the social characteristics of residents in both projects.

The total number of move-ins in the past three years in any case constituted fewer than 5 percent of the project population in both Van Dyke and Brownsville. To blame problems of the Van Dyke project on a small number of "bad seeds" is clearly gratuitous. However, to insure that these mean figures were not misleading, frequency distributions were plotted for each variable which permitted such treatment. For example, the frequency of each family size varying from one to fifteen was plotted separately for Brownsville and Van Dyke and reveals no apparent reason to doubt the representativeness of these summary statistics (see Appendix B).

Crime and vandalism are major problems at both Van Dyke and Brownsville Houses. The problem has become serious over the past ten years, with the decline of the old Brooklyn community and the failure to create renewal opportunities. The area surrounding both projects is severely blighted; store owners conduct business in plexiglass booths to protect themselves from addicts. The local library requires two armed guards on duty at all times. The local hospital claims it records fifteen teen-age deaths per month due to overdoses of drugs.

Table 6 presents data on major categories of crime for both projects as collected by housing police. Data are presented on specific crimes, including robbery, possession of drugs, and loitering. A comparison of 1969 crime incident rates (see table 6) and maintenance rates (see table 7) for the two projects was quite revealing. In summary, Van Dyke Homes was found to have 50 percent more total crime incidents, with over three and one-half times as many robberies (384 percent), and

TABLE 6

Comparison of Crime Incidents

Crime Incidents	*Van Dyke*	*Brownsville*
Total incidents	1,189	790
Total felonies, misdemeanors, and offenses	432	264
Number of robberies	92	24
Number of malicious mischief	52	28

SOURCE: New York City Housing Authority Police Records, 1969.

TABLE 7

Comparison of Maintenance

Maintenance	*Van Dyke (constructed 1955)*	*Brownsville (constructed 1947)*
Number of maintenance jobs of any sort (work tickets) 4/70	3,301	2,376
Number of maintenance jobs, excluding glass repair	2,643	1,651
Number of nonglass jobs per unit	1.47	1.16
Number of full-time maintenance staff	9	7
Number of elevator breakdowns per month	280	110

SOURCE: New York City Housing Authority Project Managers' bookkeeping records.

64 percent more felonies, misdemeanors, and offenses than Brownsville. Another measure of security can be understood from examination of the rate of decline of facilities. Even though Brownsville Houses is an older project, beginning to suffer from natural decay, Van Dyke annually required a total of 39 percent more maintenance work. It is interesting to note that the average outlay of time and funds for upkeep of Van Dyke is significantly higher than that of Brownsville. Not only is there less need of repair at Brownsville, but tenants themselves play a greater role in seeing to the cleanliness of buildings either through insistence on the upkeep of janitorial services or by individual effort.

One of the most striking differences between the two projects concerns elevator breakdowns. The far greater number of breakdowns at Van Dyke is primarily a function of more intensive use. However, more breakdowns are due to vandalism at Van Dyke than at Brownsville. This form of vandalism is especially diagnostic, showing that adolescents who tamper with Van Dyke elevators do not have a sense of identity with the people they inconvenience.

As a measure of tenant satisfaction, Brownsville Houses, with smaller room sizes in similarly designated apartment units, has a lower rate of move-outs than Van Dyke Houses. To avoid historical accident and subsequently limited conclusion, results were tabulated annually over an eight-year period, including sampling of move-ins to the two projects. These data have provided additional confirmation of the differences in crime and vandalism between the projects that cannot be assigned to differences in their tenant populations. These are discussed at greater length in Appendix B.

It is unwarranted to conclude that this data provide final and definitive proof of the influence of physical design variables on crime and vandalism. It is equally misleading to assume, as management officials initially did, that the differences can be explained away by variations in tenant characteristics in the two projects. The project manager assumed that Van Dyke Houses had a larger number of broken families and that these families had a larger number of children than those at Brownsville. The statistics do not bear out this assumption, but the image described by the manager and other public officials suggests the extent of the problem and may in turn contribute to it.

There are some elementary differences in the physical construct of the projects which may contribute to the disparity of image held by officials. Police officers revealed that they found Van Dyke Houses far more difficult to patrol. To monitor activity in the enclosed fire stairs requires that a patrolman take the elevator to the upper floor and then walk down to the ground level, alternating at each floor between the two independent fire-stair columns.

Police express pessimism about their value at Van Dyke Houses. About Brownsville they are much more optimistic and, in subtle ways, respond to complaints with more vigor and concern. All these factors produce a significant positive effect in Brownsville. At Van Dyke the negative factors of anonymity, police pessimism, pessimism about police, and tenant feelings of ambiguity about strangers (caused by large numbers of families sharing one entrance) conspire to progressively erode any residual faith in the effectiveness of community or official response to crime.

In summary, it seems unmistakable that physical design plays a very significant role in crime rate. It should also be kept in mind that the defensible space qualities inherent in the Brownsville design are there, for the most part, by accident. From a critical, defensible space viewpoint, Brownsville is far from perfect. The comparison of the crime and vandalism rates in the two projects was made using gross crime data on both projects. Twenty-three percent of the apartments at Van Dyke consist of three-story walk-up buildings serving a small number of families. It is likely that comparative data on crime rates in the low buildings versus the towers at Van Dyke would reveal significant differences. This would make the comparison of crime rates between Van Dyke and Brownsville even more startling.

• *Four Characteristics of Defensible Space*

The following three chapters describe in detail how different features of the physical design of housing reinforce inhabitants in their ability to control their environment. There is always a danger in categorical subdivision in that it may suggest that any one of the mechanisms can operate independently. Whereas some are independent, others are rendered almost meaningless if used alone. As an example, the definition and assignment of territorial areas to groups of inhabitants has been found to operate most effectively where occupants have also been given visual control of the defined area. Equally, improving visual surveillance opportunities may be a pointless task if the resident is viewing activity taking place in an area he does not identify with. Therefore, in the discussion of each defensible space mechanism, continuous cross-reference will be made to other categories where the two act in tandem or symbiotically.

Many of the housing projects described in the following chapters as significant accomplishments in "defensible space" design were born of a different historical era. For a variety of reasons—some economic, some social, some relating to evolving building and fire codes—they would be difficult to reproduce today. However, the same social and psychological benefits could be achieved through the use of contemporary physical and electronic means.

The four major categories created for the discussion of defensible space in the following chapters are:

1. The capacity of the physical environment to create perceived zones of territorial influence: mechanisms for the subdivision and articulation of areas of the residential environment intended to reinforce inhabitants in their ability to assume territorial attitudes and prerogatives. (Chapter 3)

2. The capacity of physical design to provide surveillance opportunities for residents and their agents: mechanisms for improving the capacity of residents to casually and continually survey the nonprivate areas of their living environment, indoor and out. (Chapter 4)

3. The capacity of design to influence the perception of a project's uniqueness, isolation, and stigma: mechanisms which neutralize the symbolic stigma of the form of housing projects, reducing the image of isolation, and the apparent vulnerability of inhabitants. (Chapter 5)

4. The influence of geographical juxtaposition with "safe zones" on the security of adjacent areas: mechanisms of juxtaposition—the effect of location of a residential environment within a particular urban setting or adjacent to a "safe" or "unsafe" activity area. (Chapter 5)

NOTES

1. The President's Commission on Law Enforcement and Administration of Justice, *The Challenge of Crime in a Free Society* (New York: E. P. Dutton, 1968), pp. 66–67.

2. *Ibid.*, pp. 130–132.

3. The elderly are 9.7 percent of all tenants in New York City Housing Authority projects, but experience 29.9 percent of all the robberies and 19.6 percent of all felonies, misdemeanors, and offenses. Source: New York City Housing Authority Police, 1969.

3

TERRITORIALITY

- *The Capacity of the Physical Environment to Create Perceived Zones of Territorial Influences*

TERRITORIAL DEFINITION

Historically the intactness of the family living unit and the territorial zone of the cluster of family units has always been given architectural expression. The single-family house set on its own piece of land, isolated from its neighbor by as little as six feet, has been the traditional expression of arrival in most every Western culture. It is the symbolic token of having a stake in the social system; it is deeply rooted in notions of proprietorship and belonging to the establishment. To many it represents the reaching of maturity and the achievement of success and potency. In certain cities and states in our nation, home ownership brings with it special rights and responsibilities which relate to participation in legal processes, and the opportunity to reinforce existing societal values. In our interviews with public housing tenants, we have found that expression of territorial feelings correspond strongly with a concern for the maintenance of law and belief in the possibility of its enforcement.

By its very nature, the single-family house is its own statement of territorial claim. It has defined ownership by the very act of its positioning on an integral piece of land buffered from neighbors and public street by intervening grounds. At times the buffer is reinforced by symbolic shrubs or fences, and in other cultures by high walls and gates. The

FIG. 29. Semidetached Housing, The Bronx, New York, circa 1930s. The integrity of the single-family unit is still very much intact: the defined front walk, porch, and lawn and the fenced-off rear yards. (Photo by author)

positioning of lights and windows which look out upon the buffering grounds also act to reinforce this claim.

As one moves to denser and denser agglomerations—to row houses, walk-up flats and high-rise apartments—opportunity for individual and collective efforts at defining territory become increasingly difficult.

The pathetic jerry-built row-house grouping (see figure 30), for all its anonymity, bears testimony to the depth of the need to pursue the life style and gain the social status of the territorially intact single-family house. But what of the apartment unit embedded somewhere in a 300-family high-rise building on a thirty-acre project site? What recourse have its occupants? What avenues exist for self-assertion, or opportunities for an even limited form of collective identification or territorial association?

At present, most families living in an apartment building experience the space outside their apartment unit doors as distinctly public; in effect they relegate responsibility for all activity outside the immediate confines of their apartments to public authority. The question is whether there are physical mechanisms which can be employed to extend the boundaries of these private realms: to subdivide the public space outside the private apartment unit so that larger dominions come under the sphere of influence and responsibility of the apartment dweller.

Examination of some better functioning housing developments indicate that through exterior site planning and interior building design, it is possible for an architect to subdivide a high-density project so that occupants and outsiders will perceive various portions of it as being under the sphere of influence of particular groups of occupants. It is further possible to structure this subdivision hierarchically so that at the level of housing projects, the grounds are subdivided into building clusters, and at the level of the apartment units, three or four apartments share a commonly defined entry area.

We have found that such physical subdivisions, if clearly defined and related to access paths, amenities, and entries, encourage occupants to adopt proprietary attitudes and to exert potent territorial prerogatives which serve as natural and significant deterrents to crime.

The following pages define the various mechanisms which can be employed to break down high-density residential agglomerations into territorial, subdivided, and identifiable subunits. These mechanisms succeed in providing both resident and outsider with a perceptible statement of individual and group concern over areas of buildings and grounds. More importantly, in so doing, they allow occupants to develop a heightened sense of responsibility toward care of the environment and control of its penetration by outsiders.

Mechanisms for the subdivision of housing developments to define the zones of influence of particular buildings

SITE DESIGN

It is our hypothesis that high-rise buildings, sited so that the grounds around them are defined and related to particular buildings, serve to create a territorially restricted area. These defined areas, outside otherwise anonymous high-rise towers, strongly indicate to residents and

FIG. 30. Jerry-built Row Housing, The Bronx, New York, circa 1965. (Photo by author)

strangers alike that the grounds, and hence the building, are for the private use of residents. This definition of grounds can be made to occur naturally when high-rise apartments are built on vest-pocket sites, that is small sites surrounded by the medium-density fabric of the existing city. It should be noted that a single high-rise building perceived as a unit defined by its exterior walls is itself a form of subdivision and territorial identification. Reinforced with symbolically defined grounds, and with sufficient space around it to be recognized as an entity, it can become a potent form of territorial expression.

Breukelen Houses in New York, a medium-density project built in 1952, is an excellent example of such grounds differentiation. The buildings are L-shaped and are positioned so as to touch the street at the two extreme points of the "L." The area enclosed by the right angle is defined as a semiprivate territory onto which two to four entries to the building open. The use of this area for recreation, through the provision of play equipment for young children and seating areas for adults, reinforces its territorial restriction. The location of such activities in this area facilitates its recognition as an extension of the semiprivate building zone of residents. The fact that children play and adults sit in these areas serves to increase residents' concern with the activity taking place there. Inter-

FIG. 31. Site Plan of Breukelen Houses, Brooklyn, New York. Built in 1952, consisting of a mix of three- and seven-story buildings. Contains 1,595 apartments at a density of 21.3 dwelling units per acre.

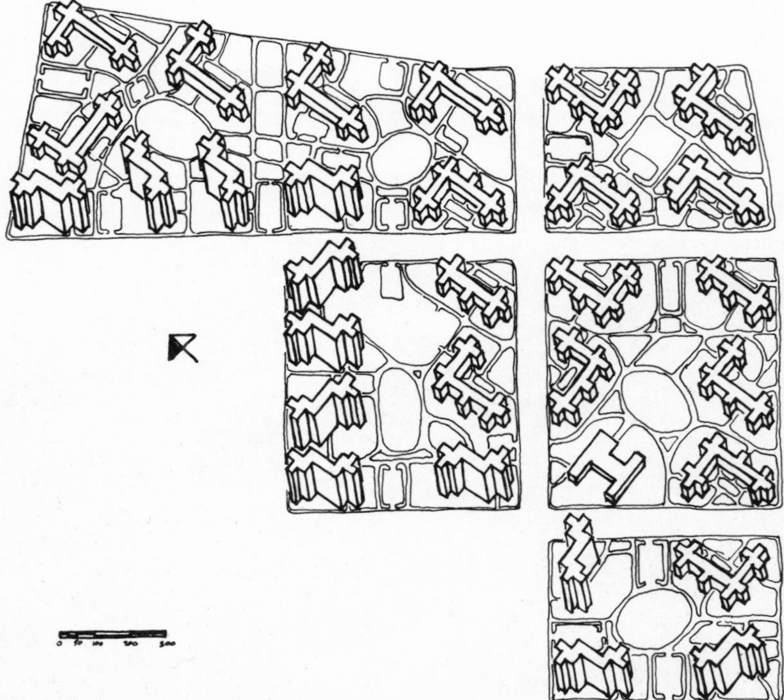

FIG. 32. Street View of Breukelen Houses. The L-shaped block forms a play and sitting area, creating a buffer zone for the four separate entries within the one building block. (Photo by author)

views show that residents know most other building residents who share this space with them. Strangers are easily recognized, and their activity comes under observation and immediate questioning. Building residents have no right, under the laws governing public housing, to evict anyone from these grounds; but at Breukelen they go to great lengths to assure themselves that strangers represent no threat. If not so assured, they readily call Housing Management or the police.

Entry to all buildings at Breukelen is through these semiprivate zones, which for the most part face directly onto existing city streets. Al-

FIG. 33. View of the Interior Grounds at Breukelen. The interior grounds were designed to be open to public access from surrounding streets. They do not relate to particular buildings and house few defined activities. Residents view these interior areas as the most dangerous in the project. (Photo by author)

though the grouping of these L-shaped buildings partially seals off the interior grounds of the project from neighboring streets, this has not been done with conviction sufficient to achieve territorial integrity; the interior grounds at Breukelen remain open and accessible from many directions. In interviews, residents have identified these interior grounds as the most dangerous of the project. Had the interior grounds been fenced off from all access other than from the buildings proper, their success as grounds for resident use might have been greater.

As a means of implementing their policy that project grounds contribute to the amenity of neighboring communities as well as their own, housing authorities prefer to keep them open. The result is that these areas are seldom used either by residents or by the surrounding community.

In contrast to the subdivision and territorial definitions in Breukelen are most of the now typical examples of high-rise public housing. The early fifties produced a series of large-scale projects across the country. Born of that period were Pruitt-Igoe in St. Louis, Columbus Homes in Newark, Van Dyke in New York, and Rosen Houses in Phliadelphia. Every city has its own claim to notoriety. It was common practice, in developing the site plan for these projects, for the architects to close off the existing streets in the four to twelve blocks they acquired, thus freeing additional grounds to be turned into either recreation areas or off-street parking. It was common, too, in the design of these superblocks, to position the high-rise towers freely, with little attempt at assigning particular areas of grounds for the use of specific buildings. The Pruitt-Igoe project in St. Louis consists of large high-rise slabs sited on grounds intentionally left open for use by both the resident population and the surrounding community. Each building is entered directly from the public grounds, onto which the elevator doors open. As a result, areas which should be recognized as territorially restricted have remained public in nature.

A stark remedy to the problems created by high-rise towers being scattered randomly on project grounds occurred by chance at Pruitt-Igoe in St. Louis. During one of the many salvaging operations attempted in the series of crises it has faced, an endeavor was made to provide some new play equipment and seating areas adjacent to one building. For the period of construction, the area around one building was fenced off (except for a gate opposite the building entry) to reduce the pilferage of materials and to prevent accidents. Residents of this building subsequently asked that the fence be left in place. They found that incidents of crime and vandalism had been reduced significantly during the six-month construction period. Two years later, the fence is still there; the crime and vandalism rate in this building is 80 percent below the Pruitt-Igoe norm. This building, like others in Pruitt-Igoe, has no security guard. It is the only building in which residents themselves have begun to show

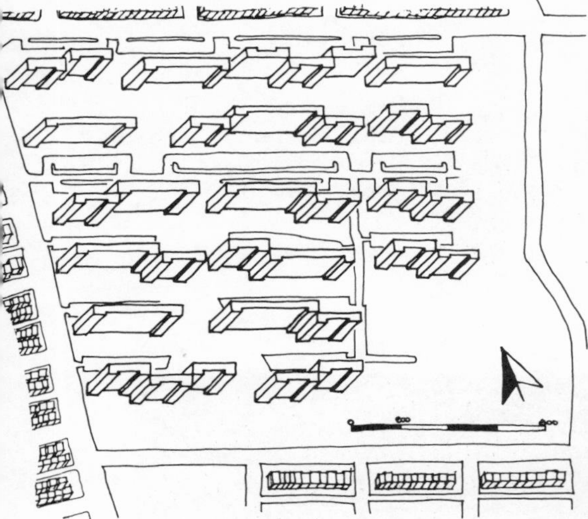

FIG. 34. Site Plan of Pruitt-Igoe, St. Louis, Missouri. Built in 1955; eleven-story buildings; 2,764 apartments; fifty dwelling units per acre. This drawing illustrates the marked contrast between project buildings and surrounding residential community.

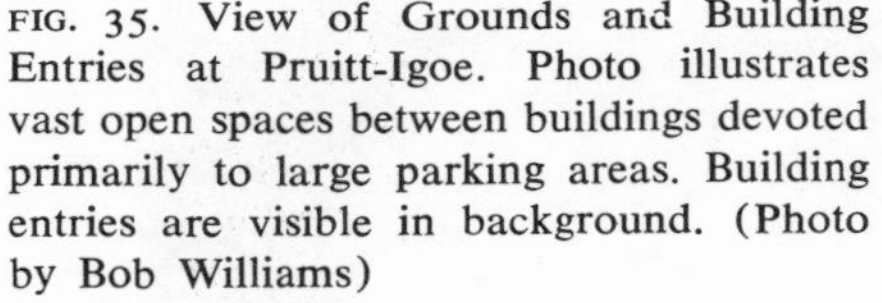

FIG. 35. View of Grounds and Building Entries at Pruitt-Igoe. Photo illustrates vast open spaces between buildings devoted primarily to large parking areas. Building entries are visible in background. (Photo by Bob Williams)

FIG. 36. View of Retained Construction Fence and Breezeway Entry at Pruitt-Igoe. Note residents sitting in the breezeway and making use of this now semiprivate defined space. The gate is locked with only tenants of this building having keys. (Photo by author)

FIG. 37. Pruitt-Igoe gallery area, as seen in 1951 artist's rendering. (Drawing by the architect)

FIG. 38. Actual View of Pruitt-Igoe Gallery Area. View of what was intended by the architects to be highly-used public gallery (see fig. 37). These corridors are not juxtaposed with apartment units and so are feared by residents and unused. The open doors lead to what were once laundry rooms. (Photo by author)

signs of concern about the maintenance of the interior: picking up litter, sweeping the corridors, and replacing light bulbs. The vacancy rate in this building varies from 2 percent to 5 percent, in contrast with the overall vacancy rate for Pruitt-Igoe of 70 percent.

This is an extreme example of territorial definition and is certainly not one which we are advocating. But its accomplishments are significant in the light of the Pruitt-Igoe failure. The question to be asked is how does one initially achieve thoughtful building groupings rather than having to resort to barbed-wire fences and locks after the fact.

FIG. 39. Public Gallery in Fenced-In Pruitt-Igoe Building. Although vandalism has been curbed by restricting access to this building, the galleries are still not used as gathering and sitting areas because they are dissociated from apartment unit entries. The exit sign marks the elevator area. (Photo by Bob Williams)

THE COMPOSITIONAL VERSUS THE ORGANIC APPROACH

Examination of the design methodologies employed by architects of Breukelen and Pruitt-Igoe reveals two fundamentally different approaches, each with its own accompanying evaluative criteria for successful design. The design approach which produces projects in the Pruitt-Igoe mold has its root in a "compositional" commitment and orientation: the architect was concerned with each building as a complete, separate, and formal entity, exclusive of any consideration of the functional use of grounds or the relationship of a building to the ground area it might share with other buildings. It is almost as if the architect assumed the role of a sculptor and saw the grounds of the project as nothing more than a surface on which he was endeavoring to arrange a series of vertical elements into a compositionally pleasing whole. Little effort was expended in developing relationships between buildings and ground activities; in fact, separation was most desired. Success in building disposition was thought to be achieved through strict adherence to compositional dictates; therefore concern with function on the part of the designer would only serve to muddy this design approach. Only when the composition of buildings was completed were access paths, play equipment, and seating areas located to serve the buildings.

This compositional approach to the form and positioning of buildings has serious repercussions when one confronts the problem of apartment unit design and location within the building proper. In this approach, the primary concern in the disposition of individual apartment units within the building is the effect the individual unit will have in giving form to the building as seen from the outside. The relationship of individual units to one another and the provision of functionally useful and shared space at each level become secondary considerations.

The design approach which produces a territorially intact project, as exemplified by Breukelen Houses, begins by viewing buildings and grounds as an organically interrelated whole. In this approach, a major design concern is the way in which buildings themselves serve to define and break up the grounds on which they sit. The relationship of building entrances to territorially defined grounds, and of vertical access systems to entry areas, also receive primary consideration in the site plan. The disposition of the apartment units follows organically the results of the initial site plan and is directed at framing relationships between units and creating areas of shared entry, much as the building itself defines the use of the ground on which it sits.

STREET DESIGN

In a similar way, it is possible to subdivide the existing fabric of city streets in order to create territorially defined blocks and areas. We have learned of instances in which associations of private homeowners have restricted parts of the city street system for predominant use by residents of a single block. The two instances we will discuss here—the St. Louis private streets and St. Marks Avenue in Brooklyn—do not totally restrict vehicular access, but rather interrupt the existing geometric traffic pattern and so discourage easy vehicular through-access by requiring intentionally circuitous movement. It is important to note that in both instances vehicles were not excluded but rather their movement restricted. This is an important distinction in that vehicular access provides a form of continuous natural surveillance, as well as an opportunity for formal patrol by a policing authority.

The St. Louis private street system was a device initially developed by wealthy residents occupying large single-family houses at the periphery of municipal St. Louis. The residents contracted with the city to take on the responsibility of road and street-light maintenance for a slight rebate of city taxes. Through this arrangement they gained the right of closing a one- to two-block stretch of street at either end. Access was provided from the central cross streets.

We have not yet measured the full success of this endeavor in reducing crime, vandalism, and maintenance costs. It is also a high-income area, and the resources available for the upkeep of the street and its general welfare makes an objective analysis difficult. However, five years ago, residents of an adjacent middle-income neighborhood formed a street association and closed their streets in the same way. These residents feel that there has been an appreciable reduction in crime. Most importantly, however, the residents claim that their street is now used very differently: children play in the central roadway; most everyone claims to know, or at least recognize people up and down the block; strangers to the street are greeted by questioning glances and a cacophony of barking dogs.

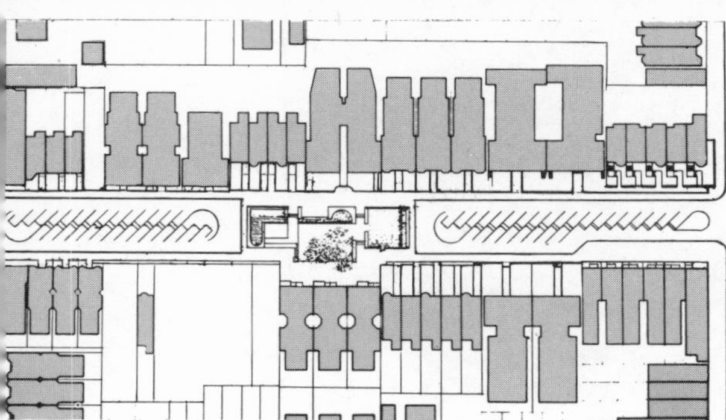

FIG. 40. Site Plan of Saint Marks Avenue, New York City. Plan shows modifications to vehicular circulation and parking and provision of play and sitting areas.

FIG. 41. Pedestrian Area, St. Marks Avenue. View of play equipment and parking area. The rear portion of the street is not open to through-traffic. The only visible sign of vandalism is the broken concrete piling which was hit by a city sanitation truck. (Photo by author)

Modifications to St. Marks Avenue in the Bedford-Stuyvesant section of Brooklyn, New York, completed only one and a half years ago, involve no major street closings. The street has been shaped to slow traffic, and symbolic portals have been located at each end. A portion of the central area of the street has been completely closed to traffic and has been turned into a play and communal area. Residents claim that street crime has been almost eliminated, that their residences are burglarized much less frequently, and that drug addicts noticeably avoid the area. On their own initiative, residents have begun to plant gardens and define the areas immediately adjacent to their houses. Concern for the maintenance and safety of the street appears to be universally shared by residents. Every Saturday morning a different group of residents gather to give the street a thorough cleaning.

FIG. 42. Community use of St. Marks Avenue. (Photo by Bob Williams)

FIG. 43. Parking Area, St. Marks Avenue. View of St. Marks Avenue showing solution to parking which frees other half of street from all traffic. (Photo by author)

Interviews with inhabitants and with the president of the block association found expressions of a new cohesiveness among the people living on the street and a parallel active interest in the maintenance of physical surroundings and in social activities. The staying power of these attitudes and activities remains to be measured over a longer period of time.

Mechanisms for creating boundaries which define a hierarchy of increasingly private zones—from public street to private apartment

SYMBOLIC VERSUS REAL BARRIERS

There is a language of symbols which has come to be recognized as instrumental in defining boundaries or a claim to territory. These boundary definers are interruptions in the sequence of movement along access paths and serve to create perceptible zones of transition from public to private spaces. Many of these symbols have been mentioned in our previous discussion of the mechanisms for defining territory or zones of influence. Some represent real barriers: U-shaped buildings, high walls and fences, and locked gates and doors. Others are symbolic barriers only: open gateways, light standards, a short run of steps, planting, and changes in the texture of the walking surface. Both serve a common purpose: to inform that one is passing from a space which is public where one's presence is not questioned through a barrier to a space which is private and where one's presence requires justification.

These symbolic barriers are also found to be identified by residents as boundary lines in defining areas of comparative safety. Because they force an outsider to the realization that he is intruding on semiprivate domain, symbolic barriers prove very effective in restricting behavior within the defined space to that which residents find acceptable. For example, almost any type of behavior can occur on a city street: loitering, dancing to a transistor radio, leaning against cars, and begging. Within the confines of an area, defined if only by a change in surface texture or grade level, the range of possible behavior is greatly reduced. It is, in fact, limited to what residents have defined as the norm. All other behavior is incongruous and is so understood and dealt with. An intruder who does not know the rule system, or hesitates in making his intentions clear, is easily spotted as not belonging. He arouses suspicion which leads to the circumvention of his activities.

Different from symbolic zone definers, real barriers have the further capacity of requiring that prior to entry, intruders possess a key, a card, or some other means of indicating their belonging. That is, access to a residence through a real barrier is by the approval of its occupants only, whether in person, through their agent, or by electronic signal. The success of the symbolic versus real barrier in restricting entry hinges on four conditions: (1) the capacity of the intruder to read the symbols for their intended meaning; (2) the evident capacity of the inhabitants of the internally defined space, or their agent, to maintain controls and reinforce symbolic space definition through surveillance; (3) the capacity of the internally defined space to require that the intruder make obvious his intentions—that is, the space must have a low tolerance for ambiguous use; and (4) the capacity of the inhabitants or their agent to challenge the presence of the intruder and to take appropriate subsequent action if need be. It is obvious that these conditions work in concert, and that a successful symbolic barrier is one that provides the greatest likelihood of all of these components being present. By employing a combination of symbolic barriers, we have found it possible to indicate that one is crossing a series of boundaries in the transition from public access paths and spaces to sequentially more private areas, without employing literal barriers to define the spaces along the route.

When moving through a sequence of territorially defined areas—from project grounds to dwelling unit cluster—one experiences these symbolic barriers and portals as a matter of course. Behavior and expectations are changed accordingly, even without the sharp divisions created by locked gates and doors. These tools for symbolically restricting space usage assume particular importance in the case of projects which simply do not allow themselves to be subdivided into territorially intact zones. Where it is still the intent to make space obey semiprivate rules and to fall under the influence and control of tenants, symbolic elements along paths of access can serve this function without actually prohibiting entry.

The opportunities for the use of real and symbolic barriers to define zones of transition are many. They occur in moving from public street to the semipublic grounds of the project; in the transition from outdoors to indoors; and finally in the transition from the semipublic space of a building lobby to the corridors of each floor. The use of literal barriers, e.g., locks, gates, and electronic interview systems, must be viewed as one component of a hierarchy of means of defining space which also includes a wide range of suggestive and persuasive symbolic elements.

A good example of a housing project which employs symbols to define boundaries, or zones of transition, but does not literally delimit specific territorial areas, is First Houses, located in a relatively high-crime area in the Lower East Side in New York City.

Figure 45 shows the low walls and entry portals to the project set four feet back from the line of the street. This four-foot setback of sidewalk defines the first step in the transition from public to private. The walls and portals then define the semiprivate nature of the project interior. Further territorial restrictions are symbolized by the steps and porch shared by both of the five-story buildings. The design of the building interiors continues to reinforce this symbolic system, indicating a progression to more private space through the use of stairs and landings, leading

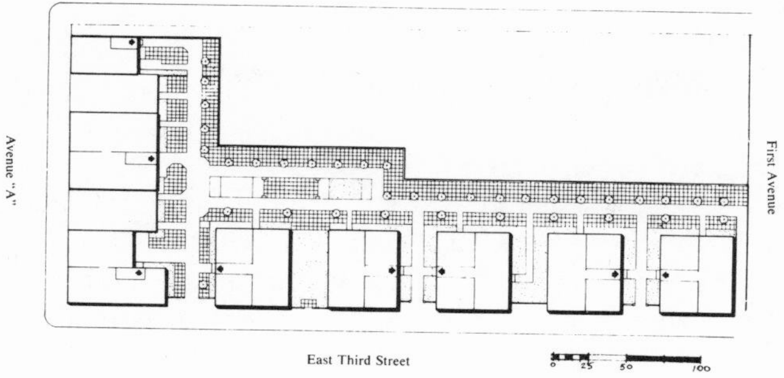

FIG. 44. Site plan of First Houses. (Courtesy of New York City Housing Authority)

FIG. 45. First Houses, Manhattan. View showing relation of entrances to street. Note the large number of symbolic barriers: walls, piers, stoops, hedges. The courtyard area serves as a symbolic transition zone and barrier to the project grounds beyond. The defining zones are reinforced with many opportunities for visual surveillance. Note that there are bars on ground-floor windows facing the street, but not on windows facing the court. (Photo by author)

eventually to the apartment proper. Figure 45 also shows two elderly residents of the project who have chosen to move their lounge chairs onto the semipublic portion of the public sidewalk. The feeling of security they display is evidence of how well these symbolic indicators can work to enhance the sense of safety.

What ingredients are responsible for making the presence of strangers obvious in a zone which is private? The decisive element is the degree of ambiguous behavior a zone will tolerate. As was briefly mentioned, intensely public streets are places which will tolerate a wide variety of behavior: people can choose to walk by, stand and chat, sit on the hood of a car; in some neighborhoods singing, dancing, screaming, and soliloquizing are common street activities that are not challenged. This activity, which is accepted by residents if it takes place on adjacent sidewalks, is rejected when carried beyond the symbolic portals of First Houses into the defined semipublic space of the project. This is a space that is merely an extension of the public sidewalk but here such behavior is perceived by residents and public actors as intolerable. Within this defined zone, activity must have an acceptable purpose or intent; if it is unusual, it is dangerous. While no attempt is made to question the presence of, or to identify, individuals on a public sidewalk, individuals within a territorially restricted zone are required to efficiently pursue a goal or purpose; lingering becomes a privilege available only to recognized residents following proscribed rituals.

It is noteworthy that buildings which consistently have the highest crime and vandalism rates: Pruitt-Igoe in St. Louis, Columbus Houses in Newark, and Van Dyke in New York, have little in the way of these transitional differentiating elements, either literal or symbolic. For the most part, public space in these projects flows uninterrupted from the bordering streets onto the project grounds; from the lobby and corridors of a high-rise building right up to the door of the individual apartment unit. The Pruitt-Igoe project in St. Louis is perhaps the most notorious example of this phenomenon, and its present state of devastation bears full witness to the potential seriousness of breakdowns in the social system resulting from the spatial design of high-rise buildings.

FIG. 46. Breezeway at Pruitt-Igoe, St. Louis. Typically vandalized breezeway entry to a high-rise building. Destruction of public areas around mailboxes, elevators, and stairwells at Pruitt-Igoe is systematic and complete. (Photo by author)

Mechanisms for the subdivision of building interiors to define the zones of influence of clusters of apartment units

When economic considerations become the paramount criteria in high-rise building design, the result is usually the production of high-rise slab buildings in which many individual apartment units are served by long, double-loaded corridors. The physical configuration of this corridor results in an overwhelmingly large and anonymous public space, devoid of opportunities for the assumption of territorial prerogatives which subdivision would provide.

Alternatively, the interiors of high-density buildings can be designed so that peculiar groupings of units and shared, vertical-access stairs provide the opportunity for inhabitants to develop territorial concern for the space immediately adjacent to their dwellings. A good example is the interior stair system and corridor at Breukelen. The L-shaped buildings at Breukelen are subdivided to allow each building two to five entries, each serving from six to nine families. This subdivision has created an entire network of small social groups whose members cooperate to maintain a mutually beneficial environment. The lobby and stair area of each entry is understood by the families who share it to be their corporate responsibility. Our interviews show that residents can all recognize one another, although the extent of their relationships varies from nodding acquaintance to fast friendship.

At each floor of an entry level, two to four families share a common corridor area. The doors to the apartment units are grouped around this common corridor, and access to it from the stairwell is screened by a

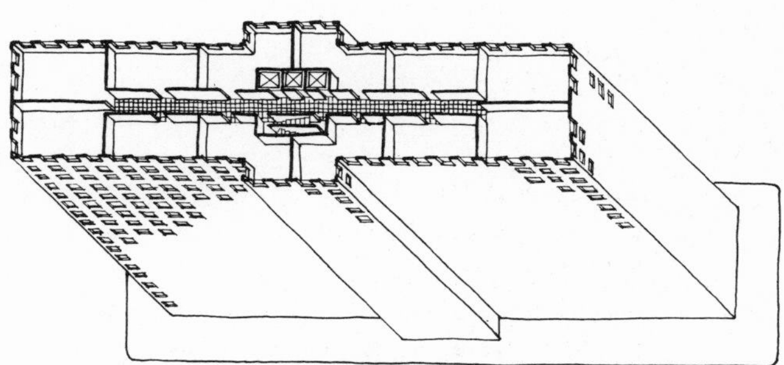

FIG. 47. Double-Loaded Corridor Apartment Building. Exploded view of a typical floor of a high-rise double-loaded corridor building. Note position of elevator and scissors stairwell.

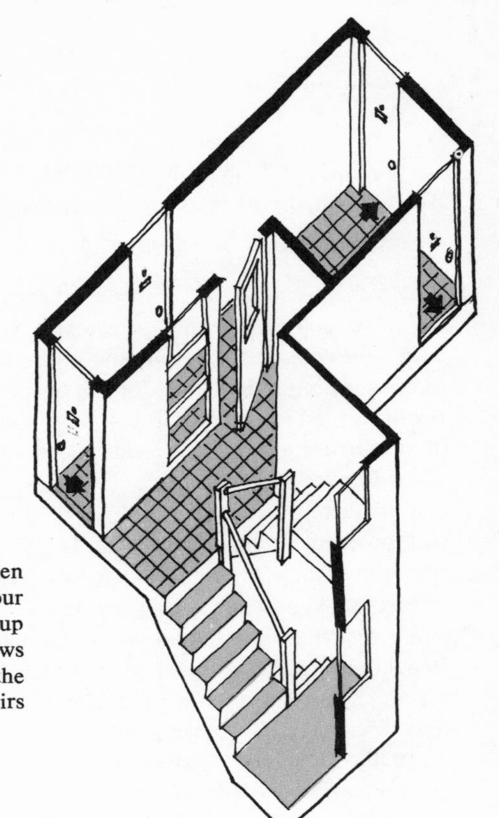

FIG. 48. Interior Corridor at Breukelen Houses. Common corridor shared by four apartments in Breukelen Houses, a walk-up apartment building. The corridor follows this configuration so as to provide the necessary separation from the access stairs to meet fire codes.

glazed partition to satisfy fire regulations. The net effect is that the residents of the floor have adopted the corridor as a collective extension of their dwelling units. Management informs us that although the tenants are not required to maintain this area, they see that it is kept scrupulously clean and well lighted. Further subtlety appears in the design of the seven-story units at Breukelen. The entrance lobby is two steps lower than the corridor serving the ground-floor apartments. These steps serve to differentiate the more public lobby from the semiprivate corridor on the ground floor serving two to four families.

It is probable that neither these steps nor the glass partitions previously mentioned are the result of a conscious attempt on the part of the architects to define territorial zones within the building. Each was built in response to other demands: the wired-glass partition is a form of fire wall, isolating the stairwell. The three-step transition from the common lobby area to the ground floor apartments is a device often used to raise the windows of these apartments eight feet above the outside grounds to discourage burglaries. Both, however, are perceived by tenants as building components which clearly define zones within their building. Very young children are permitted to play in the common corridor and are

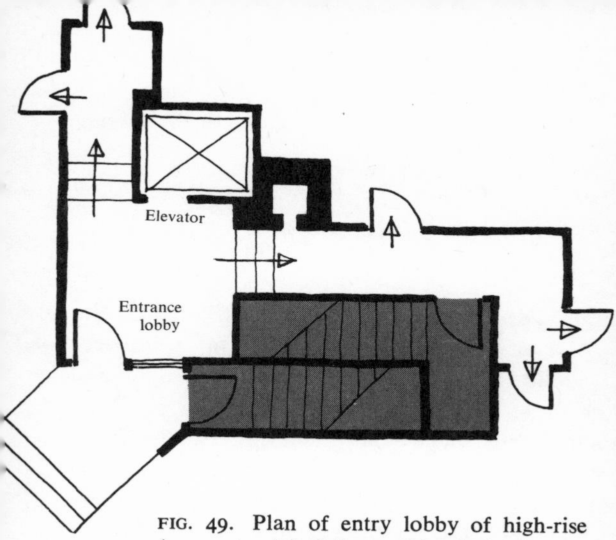

FIG. 49. Plan of entry lobby of high-rise (seven-story) buildings at Breukelen.

FIG. 50. Entry Lobby at Breukelen. View of entrance lobby showing a portion of the elevator door and the two steps which separate the lobby from the corridor serving the ground-floor units. (Photo by author)

cautioned not to go beyond the steps or outside the glass wall. As in Brownsville Houses, the doors to the apartments are usually kept slightly ajar in order to allow the mothers to monitor the activity in these spaces. The screening of strangers in these spaces and, by extension, in the more public lobby and stairwell is an additional beneficial result.

In order to measure the extent to which crime rates increased with the number of families sharing a hallway, the total number of felonies, misdemeanors, offenses, and lingering crimes committed in hallways was compared for every housing project in New York City. Examination of the results, as seen in figure 51, reveals that smaller halls (defined as those with two–five apartments) have a much lower crime rate average than larger corridors.

Rate of crime in hallways (felonies, misdemeanors, and offenses per thousand population).

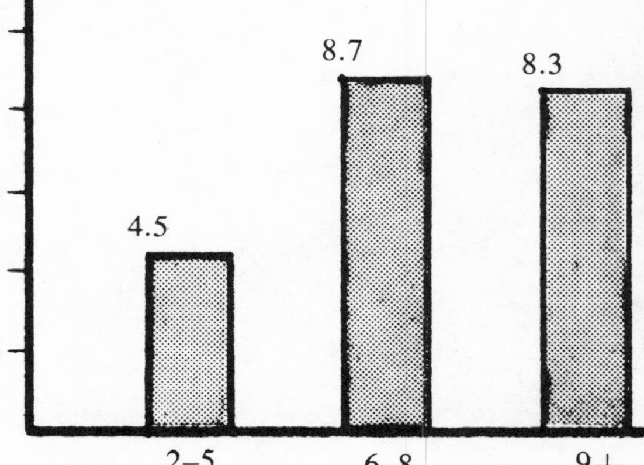

FIG. 51. Influence on crime rate of number of families sharing a hallway

The incorporation of amenities and facilities within defined zones of influence which answer to occupants' needs

The subdivision of areas within housing projects to define the zones of influence of groups of residents receives significant reinforcement as defensible space if facilities directed to the needs of intended sharers are located within these zones.

Our observations have shown that very young children (ages two to five), when playing out-of-doors, limit their field of play to the area immediately adjacent to the entry door of the apartment buildings. If these entry courts are further enhanced by play equipment and surrounded by benches, the areas will become an important focal point and screening device for the use of building residents. Breukelen Houses is a particularly good example of a project with building entry areas that are reinforced by the incorporation of amenities.

The location within territorially assigned grounds of amenities such as play and sitting areas, washer-dryer facilities, and automobile repair facilities will tend to give an area a higher intensity of use and further support any initial claim of territory. The presence of residents involved in various activities, individual or communal—children at play, women chatting or doing a wash, or men talking over the best way to tackle a

FIG. 52. Entry Buffer Area at Breukelen. View of entry to seven-story buildings—sitting and play area create semiprivate transitional zones which are further strengthened by sloped walk leading to entry doors. (Photo by author)

faulty carburetor—brings these areas under casual surveillance by concerned members of the family and further reinforces its defensible space attributes. If these areas are juxtaposed to building entrances, then still another means has been created for facilitating the screening of possible intruders.

The significance of "number" in the subdivision of buildings and projects

Reducing the number of apartment units grouped together to share a collectively defined territory, and limiting the number of buildings that comprise a housing project, are extremely important factors in the successful creation of defensible space (see table 8).

At various scales of subdivision—from number of apartments per hallway, apartment units per building, and number of buildings per project—there appears to be a rule which says that the lower the number, the better. We are by no means certain that we can identify the magical number beyond which the grouping of units at each of the identified scales becomes critical. We have, however, been able to find various situations where a specific number has proven quite effective.

In the design of walk-up buildings there is usually no economic conflict in choosing to either design the building as a single entity (running a central corridor down the full length of it—positioning stairs every hundred feet or so as fire codes dictate) or to distinctly subdivide the building mass internally so that stairs serve only a limited number of units. There are economies in both designs. In the second case, each stair serves only a small number of families (two to four at each level) and a maximum

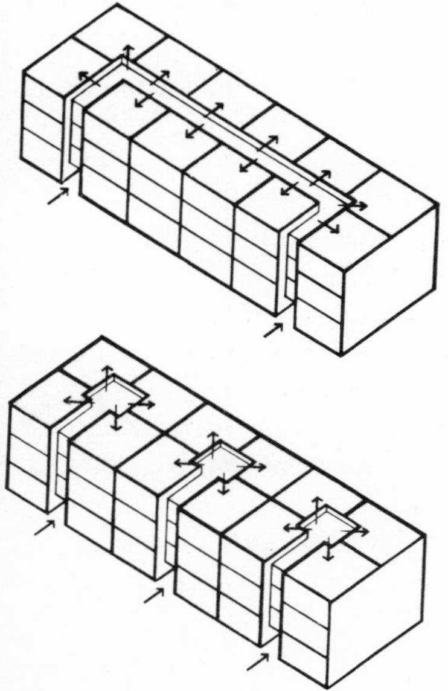

FIG. 53. Alternate designs and access arrangements for three-story walk-ups. Both buildings were designed within the same three-dimensional envelopes, but their internal subdivisions produce radically different environments.

A. All thirty-six units in the building are accessible from the two entries and the double-loaded corridors. Twelve units share a hallway at each level.

B. Each of the three separated entries serves its own twelve units. Only four units share a hallway at each level. Residents are easily able to extend their territorial claims to include the hallways and the entry to their particular sub-building.

TABLE 8

Project Size and Building Type versus Crime

		BUILDING TYPE	
		Point Block	*Double-Loaded Corridor*
Project Size	1000 Units or Less	N = 6 M = 54 SD = 31	N = 41 M = 51 SD = 22
	More Than 1000 Units	N = 4 M = 72 SD = 15	N = 30 M = 66 SD = 25

NOTE: N = number of cases examined; M = mean, crimes per thousand; SD = standard deviation

In studying the effect of size on crime, projects were divided into two groups: those with 1000 units or more, and those under 1000 units. It was hypothesized that larger projects would most likely experience higher rates of crime, due to their impersonality as perceived by both tenants and potential criminals and that residents of large projects would be less likely to be able to identify fellow tenants or develop associations of mutual benefit. Such isolation breeds anonymity and alienation—two factors that make projects attractive to criminals.

When a two-way analysis of variance was performed on project size and building type, those projects that were under 1000 apartment units in size had a significantly lower crime rate in both of the building types examined than those of over 1000 units. There was no statistically significant interaction between type and size.

of six to twelve families for the full three stories, rather than connecting to a common corridor that serves all units at each level. In the former instance, there are many entries to the building, each serving a limited number of families.

We have found that where buildings have been subdivided in the second fashion, residents have adopted a very clear proprietary attitude toward what they can identify as their sub-building, its internal corridor, landings, stairwells, entry, lobby, and the grounds immediately outside the entry door. Brownsville Houses and Breukelen Houses in Brooklyn are examples of this phenomenon. The St. Francis Square development discussed in chapter 7 is an example of a three-story slab building divided into independent vertical subunits.

Two operating mechanisms make "number" significant.

The capacity for people to distinguish or recognize by sight the members of the families sharing a building and entry with them. The lower the number, the more quickly and easily this capacity is established.

The value of a facility shared with others decreases with the number of people involved in the sharing. We have found that an outside play and sitting area, if it is intended for the exclusive use of twelve families, has greater significance for each family than a larger area shared by proportionately more families.

These two mechanisms operating in concert seem to play a very important role in facilitating residents' adoption of territorial attitudes and prerogatives.

Elevator apartment buildings, unlike walk-ups, do not readily allow themselves to be subdivided. Depending on the type of elevator employed, economics dictates a very specific ratio of apartments-per-floor to be serviced by each elevator. Buildings four to six stories in height can usually be served by an inexpensive hydraulic elevator. In such instances, one elevator can serve as few as four or five units per floor. High-rise buildings over seven stories in height, however, require expensive high-speed elevators, which economy dictates must serve a large number of apartments, both per building and per floor.

To reduce elevator waiting time and installation costs, it is common practice for two to six elevators serving a building to be grouped into a single bank. This practice of grouping improves the performance time of

FIG. 54. The photograph shows a 540-unit housing project in Minneapolis (with one common lobby) following the plan of alternate A, shown in figure 54a. (Photo by author)

FIG. 54a. Alternate access and circulation plans for 520-unit high-rise building

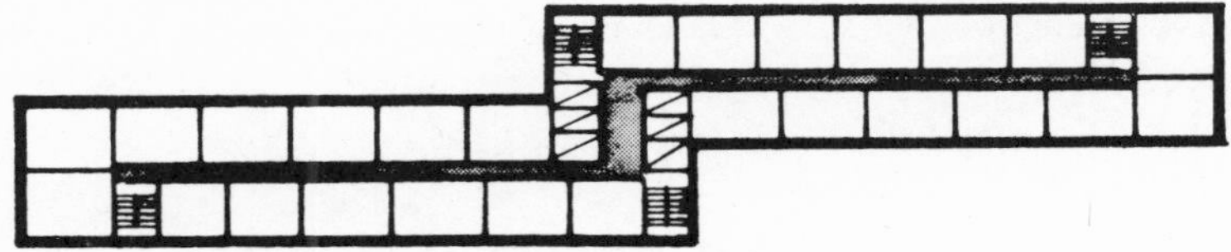

A. Plan of a twenty-story building housing 520 families who share one entry lobby and a bank of six elevators

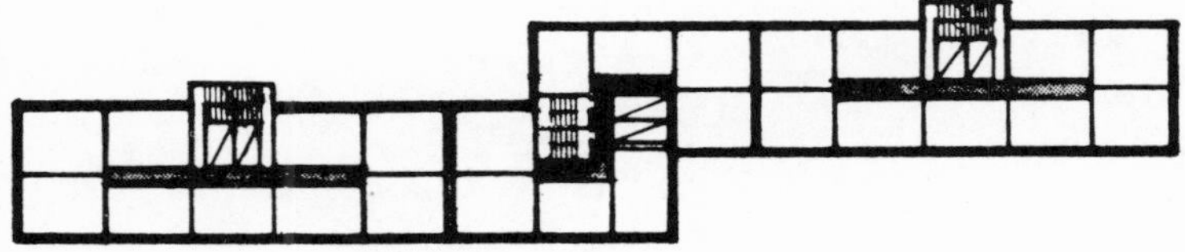

B. Assuming the building configuration is fixed by the site and the desire to hold the building's peripheral walls to a minimum, it is still possible to divide the building into three distinct segments. Each would have its own entry and two elevators serving 160 to 180 families. This plan requires additional sets of fire stairs but saves space by reducing the length of corridors.

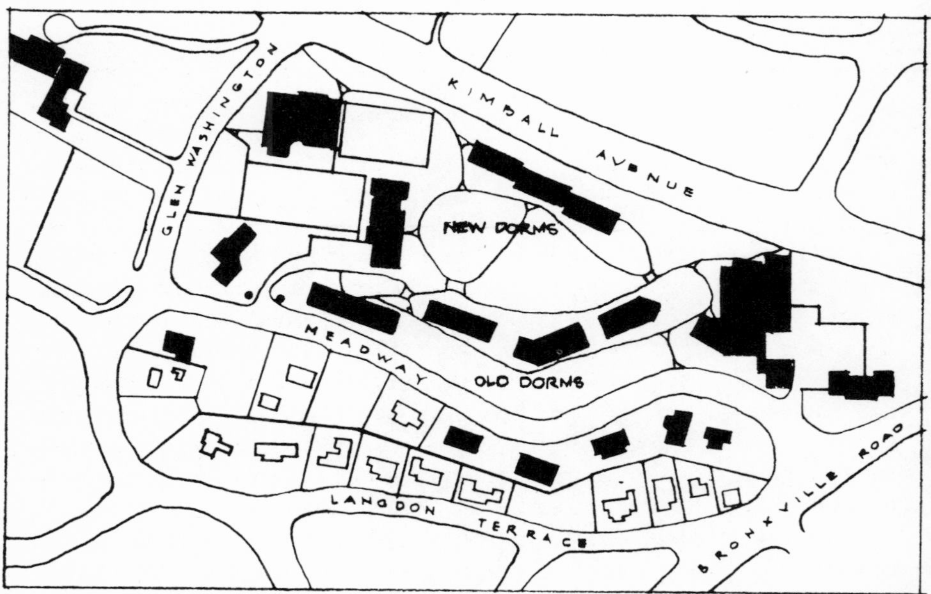

FIG. 55. Site Plan of Sarah Lawrence College, Bronxville, New York. Dormitories are situated on either side of the main campus commons. Old dorms: MacCracken, Lawrence, Titsworth, Gilbert. New dorms: Rothschild, Carrison, Taylor. (Courtesy of Sarah Lawrence College)

elevators, and produces in corridors 200 to 600 feet long, many with L- and T-shape configurations. Following the requirements of fire-safety codes, emergency stairs must be located every 150 feet along the corridor. The combination of frequent fire stairs and long corridors which serve as many as twenty to thirty apartments results in a highly anonymous interior public spaces. This can be remedied, at the expense of increased waiting time, by separating the elevators so that each serves only four to eight apartments per floor.

Perhaps the most fascinating example of the phenomenon of "number" at work was provided by a comparative analysis of two sets of dormitories situated on either side of the main campus commons at Sarah Lawrence college. Both sets of dormitories house approximately the same number of students. The one to the west is a new building, consisting of one long slab served by an interior, double-loaded corridor and four sets of stairs. On the eastern side of the Commons is the older set of dormitories, consisting of three detached buildings, each with its own internal hall and stairways. The three buildings are in the style of an old English manor. Each has two entrances and a small internal corridor. The entries are small and cramped, with narrow halls and stairs and low ceilings. The individual rooms in both old and new buildings are very small.

In interviews with students in both sets of buildings, and with student counselors, the following story emerged. Whereas there is a strong communal sense in each of the old buildings (called "houses"), it is nonexistent in the new buildings. Student residents in the new buildings have resisted any and all attempts by counselors and other students to shape them into social groups. Almost universally, they have adopted a loner's attitude, conducting their lives within the confines of their individual rooms, and seeming unconcerned with the other residents of the building.

The new building also suffers from a high incidence of vandalism and a general disregard, on the part of students, for the maintenance and cleanliness of corridors and furnishings provided in the common lounges. By contrast, students in the older set of dorms feel that they are very much members of an individual house, and that its property, furnishings, and image are theirs for their period of stay at the college. They form strong social entities which define norms or orders of behavior. As a result, the corridors and common areas in the older dorms are meticulously cared for by the students.

Two other problem areas facing most dormitory colleges across the country also trouble Sarah Lawrence. The way in which the two dormitories deal with them is very revealing. There is a much lower frequency of drug abuse and problems stemming from the occasional use of drugs in the individual houses than in the large dormitory. Student counselors explain this as being the result of (1) the greater ease with which strangers from outside the campus can frequent the new building, (2) the fact

FIG. 56. New Dormitories, Sarah Lawrence College. The new dorms are tied together in one long double-loaded slab structure, not unlike a motel. Students in the new dorms feel isolated without any sense of community. It is claimed by college counselors that the students easily fall into patterns of antisocial behavior. (Photo by author)

FIG. 57. Old Dormitories, Sarah Lawrence College. The old dorms are divided into separate buildings which resemble old manor houses. Students in each dorm have a strong sense of identity and communal responsibility. (Photo by author)

that girls in the new building feel they are isolated and on their own, and (3) lack of group moral pressure to respond to situations which get out of hand.

Since the adoption of a new open-door policy at the college, students are allowed to have occasional overnight guests. In some instances, this policy has resulted in boyfriends from the surrounding community using the opportunity to find a place to stay for longer stretches of time. Such guests have occasionally grown unruly, too dependent, or have otherwise proven to be a problem for a girl, and she has found it necessary to evict him. In the new dorms, a pattern has emerged wherein the rejected boy has simply moved down the corridor, or to another floor in the building, and thus succeeds in extending his stay for weeks at a time. By contrast, a boy evicted by a girl living in one of the older dormitories also finds himself evicted from the house and finds it extremely difficult to ingratiate his way into another such house. (The studies of Pruitt-Igoe and other similar large-scale projects housing welfare mothers identified a parallel phenomenon—a similar floating male population—among the Aid-to-Dependent-Children mothers.)

The reputation of the new dormitory building has now become legend at Sarah Lawrence, and every freshman scrambles to be rehoused elsewhere for her sophomore year. This has resulted in the new dorms being assigned primarily to unsuspecting freshmen—further aggravating the situation. So insurmountable are the problems of the new dormitory that the college has entered into negotiations with the State, under whose dormitory program the building was constructed, to persuade them to allow the college to purchase it back and turn it into classrooms and offices. It is now the intent of the college authorities to construct new dormitories similar in form to its more successful older buildings.

In summary, it should be pointed out that project sites containing only a few (two to four) high-rise buildings have been found to have appreciably lower crime rates than projects containing many buildings. It is possible that this is due to the radical reduction in the housing project image. It is improbable that residents are able to distinguish intruders more readily in a grouping of a few high-rise buildings than in one with many, but it is possible that intruders may feel that they can. In either case, there appears to be much less freedom of movement in the public spaces of the smaller high-rise projects. Unlike buildings in large developments, every building of a small grouping usually has an entrance directly off a public street. They more closely resemble middle-income high-rise developments and look more private and impenetrable.

4

NATURAL SURVEILLANCE

- *The Capacity of Physical Design to Provide Surveillance Opportunities for Residents and their Agents*

SURVEILLANCE AND TERRITORIALITY

Improvements in surveillance capacity—the ability to observe the public areas of one's residential environment and to feel continually that one is under observation by other residents while on the grounds of projects and within the public areas of building interiors—can have a pronounced effect in securing the environment for peaceful activities. An additional benefit, of possibly greater import, is that surveillance has a demonstrable effect in reducing irrational fears and anxieties in inhabitants. This may have some self-fulfilling attributes in that residents, feeling that an area is secure, will make more frequent use of it and so further improve its security by providing the safety which comes with intensive use.

However, experience has shown that the ability to observe criminal activity will not, in and of itself, impel the observer to respond with assistance to the person or property being victimized. The decision to act will also depend on the presence of the following conditions:

> The extent to which the observer has a developed sense of his personal and proprietary rights and is accustomed to defending them.

The extent to which the activity observed is understood to be occurring in an area within the sphere of influence of the observer.

Identification of the observed behavior as being abnormal to the area in which it occurs and therefore warranting response.

The observer's identification with either the victim or the property being vandalized or stolen.

The extent to which the observer feels he can effectively alter (by personal or collective response) the course of events being observed.

Physical means for furthering the development of proprietary feelings and extending the zone of identification were discussed under mechanisms for the definition of zones of territorial influence.

The Kitty Genovese incident, perhaps one of the most widely known examples in which the many observers of a crime were incapable of mounting an effective response, has been the subject of many studies, some involving in-depth interviews with witnesses. The common excuses given for inaction were that the victim was unknown to the observers, and that the incident occurred on a public street. These two factors, it seems, precluded intervention. This and other similar incidents happening in urban areas point out a serious breakdown in traditional social values and responsibilities.

The provision of surveillance should not be interpreted as a universal panacea for a complex problem. It is necessary to reinforce the point that the *effectiveness* of increased surveillance depends on whether the area under surveillance is identified by the observer as falling under his sphere of influence. Improved surveillance operates most effectively when linked with the territorial subdivision of residential areas, allowing the resident to observe those public areas which he considers to be part of his realm of ownership and hence responsibility. A further operating factor has also been introduced which will be more fully discussed later—the recognition of or identification (on the part of the observer) with the victim. This implies an ability to distinguish strangers and has been found to be closely related to the number of families sharing a particular defined area at each level of a development's subdivision. The unilateral success of surveillance capacities as a mechanism of crime control is, therefore, by no means implied.

The following set of mechanisms are directed to the design of the grounds and internal semipublic areas of housing developments to facilitate natural visual and auditory monitoring of activities taking place within them.

Most crime in housing occurs in the visually deprived semipublic interiors of buildings: the lobbies, halls, elevators, and fire stairs. However, it is possible, through the relative juxtaposition of apartment windows with stairs and corridors, as well as with the outside, to ensure that all public and semiprivate spaces and paths come under continual and natural observation by the project's residents.

It is our hypothesis that the provision of such surveillance opportunities is a significant crime deterrent that markedly lessens the anxiety of inhabitants, and serves to create an overall image of a safe environment. Most important, this image is also perceived by the potential criminal, who is deterred from initial consideration of this area as an easy hit.

THE GLAZING, LIGHTING, AND POSITIONING OF NONPRIVATE AREAS AND ACCESS PATHS, IN BUILDINGS AND OUT, TO FACILITATE THEIR SURVEILLANCE BY RESIDENTS AND FORMAL AUTHORITIES. (ACCESS PATHS REFER TO VERTICAL PATHS AS WELL AS HORIZONTAL ONES AND INCLUDE STAIRS, ELEVATORS, CORRIDORS, AND LOBBIES, ALONG WITH THE MORE OBVIOUS OUTSIDE PATHS.)

EXTERNAL AREAS

Following the directives of early planning manuals, many housing projects have been intentionally designed to look inward on themselves, with the result that residents cannot view bordering streets. In medium-density, row-type housing projects, only the ends of buildings meet adjacent streets; their entrances and windows face the interior of the project. As a result, these bordering streets have been deprived of continual surveillance by residents and have proven unsafe to walk along—for both project residents and the members of the surrounding community. Residents often find that the nighttime journey from the bus stop to the project interior assumes harrowing proportions. Many project residents choose to remain at home rather than use these streets in the evening, further adding to the lack of path surveillance and to feelings of insecurity.

Formal motor patrol of the interior areas of these projects is made impossible. This difficulty has been somewhat overcome in New York City projects through the use of motor scooters by housing police. Nevertheless, the opportunity for the informal supervision provided by passing cars and pedestrians is lost. Similarly, it is impossible for city police to include the internal grounds of such projects in their normal routes.

The traditional row-house street is considered by both residents and police to be superior in design to the superblock configuration most often

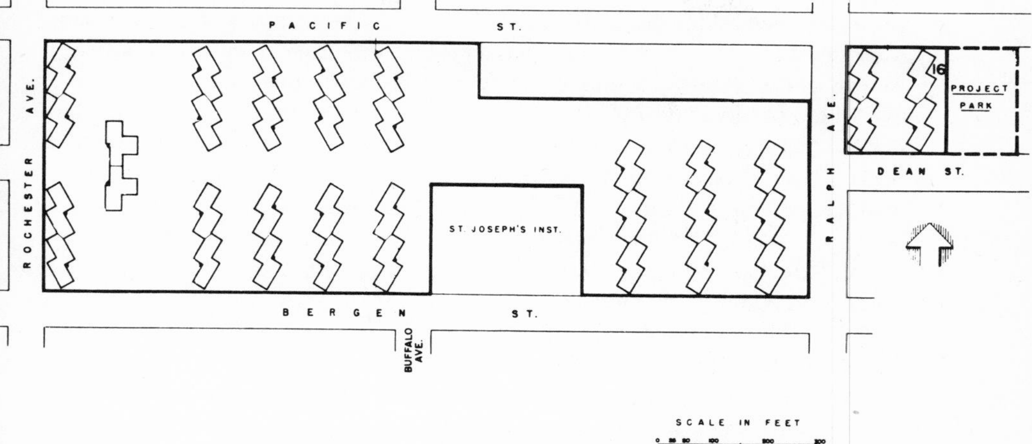

FIG. 58. Site Plan of Kingsborough Houses, Brooklyn, New York. Because the project buildings are oriented inward, the streets surrounding the project are considered unsafe. The activity along Pacific and Bergen streets cannot be observed by residents from their apartment windows.

FIG. 59. View of a portion of a row-house street.

employed in medium- and high-density residential developments. The front entrances of the row-house units are easily surveyed by patrolling automobile. Well-lit front-door paths, with individual lights over the entrances, allow cruising police to spot at a glance any peculiar activity taking place on a row-house street. The positioning of front entrances along the street provides them with continuous natural supervision by passersby;

the residents within their houses, in turn, provide these passersby with protective surveillance. The New York City Housing Authority Police consider projects with buildings having entrances facing the street superior to those with entrances facing the interior project grounds.

The random positioning of high-rise towers on housing sites has produced systems of access paths which are filled with sharp turns and blind corners. Circuitous paths of movement through the interior of large projects are a recurring complaint of residents, especially in projects where the main building entries face interior project grounds rather than public streets. Woodhill Estates in Cleveland, Baruch Houses in New York and Columbus Homes in Newark are examples. Winding access paths provide many opportunities for muggers to conceal themselves while awaiting the arrival of a victim. The circuitous access route to building entries is made even more dangerous by the common practice of positioning shrubs exactly at the turn in a path. Compositionally satisfying as this practice might be, such visual barriers provide natural hiding places and vantage points for potential criminals.

Regardless of how well-lit these areas are, residents express strong fears about turns in the path system connecting the street to the building lobby. This problem does not of course arise in the traditional row-house pattern where buildings are set back only a few yards from the street. Nor does it occur in projects such as Breukelen and Brownsville (discussed in chapters 2 and 3) where the entry is only slightly set back from the street. In these projects, residents are able to scan the terrain they are about to use; they move in a straight line from the relative safety of the

FIG. 60. Aerial view of Baruch Houses, New York. (Courtesy of New York City Housing Authority)

public street to what they can observe to be the relative safety of the well-lit lobby area in front of their building.

The design of such projects as Columbus Homes in Newark, Pruitt-Igoe in St. Louis and Baruch in New York requires residents to leave the comparative safety of the neighborhood street and enter the project grounds without knowing what lies ahead. Access to the building entry requires entering the project interior, circumnavigating a few corners, and finally approaching a point from which they are able to observe the lobby of their own apartment building.

To test the soundness of our theories on building location and its effect on crimes, existing New York City housing projects were divided into three categories:

Those with buildings facing and within fifty feet of the street.

Those with buildings facing and within fifty feet of the street and with good lobby visibility (large window area)—a subcategory of (1).

Those with less than 30 percent of the buildings facing and within fifty feet of the street.

The total number of felonies, midsdemeanors, and offenses was calculated for all projects, as well as for those in the three categories, and a rate per thousand population was determined.

The lowest crime rates were recorded for the second category (optimum surveillance possible). The highest rates occurred in the third category, where most buildings had poor surveillance potential. Evidently, the orientation of a building to the street and the open design of its lobby have a direct effect on the attractiveness it possesses to criminal elements. A project with buildings facing and close to a street, with lobbies visible to passersby, is decidedly less likely to experience as much crime as one where these factors do not interplay. (See table 9.)

As a further test of the effect of visibility on crime rate, the same projects were divided into two groups according to type of lobby entry. Those projects with buildings having little or no definition were labeled "poor" and those with significant or precise entry definition were, labeled "good." (See figure 61 design criteria.)

In addition, the same projects were also divided into two groups, "good" and "bad" according to quality of lobby visibility, from the outside primary door. Those projects that fell into "good" design categories, for both entrance definition and visibility, were labeled "Category I"; those that qualified as "good" on only one design criterion formed Category II; and finally, those projects in which buildings were rated "poor" on both criteria were listed under Category III. Felonies, misdemeanors, and

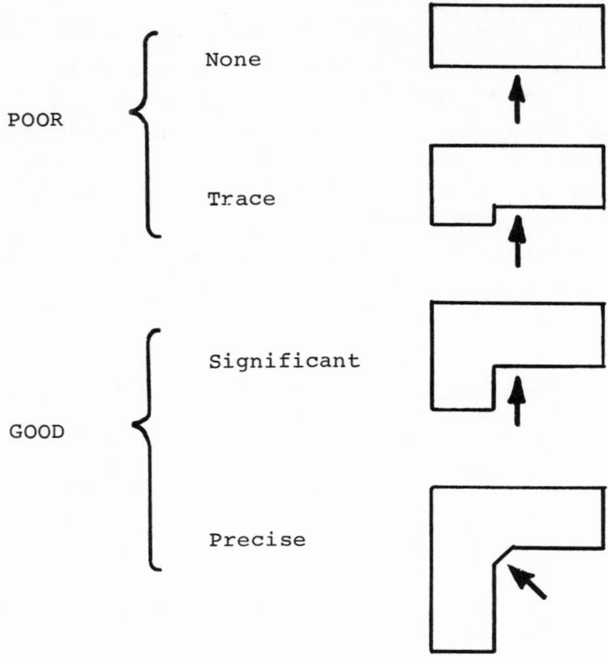

FIG. 61. Extent of definition of lobby entry as formed by shape of building.

TABLE 9

Surveillance (Building in Relation to Street)

FMO's in Lobby*	*All Projects*	*(a) Projects Where All Buildings Are Facing and within 50 feet of Street*	*(b) Projects Where All Buildings Are Facing and within 50 feet of Street and Having Good Lobby Visibility*	*(c) Projects Where Less Than 30% of the Buildings are Facing and within 50 feet of Street*
Rate per 1000 Population	7.5 (140 projects)	5.3 (22 projects)	4.4 (12 projects)	9.7 (21 projects)

* Felonies, misdemeanors, and offenses.

offenses occurring in both lobbies and elevators were totaled for all projects concerned.

The results, shown in table 10, underline the importance of the effect of design on discouraging crime.

TABLE 10

Effect of Lobby Visibility and Entry Design On Crime Rate

			Crime Rate (FMO's) per 1000 Population	
			Lobby	*Elevator*
Category I		good visibility/good entry definition	7.3	3.8
Category II	(*a*) or (*b*)	poor visibility/good entry definition or good visibility/poor entry definition	7.8	4.5
Category III		poor visibility/poor entry definition	8.6	4.6

Category I projects, in which buildings were rated "good" on both counts, had a comparatively lower crime average. Category II had slightly higher crime rates. The highest rates were recorded for Category III, where both design factors were considered "poor."

When separate scores were calculated for both parts of Category II (see table 11), it was discovered that for both the elevator and lobby, crime rates were higher in buildings with poor visibility, clearly indicating that of the two design factors, visibility seems to be the determining one for crime rate and *not* entry definition.

TABLE 11

Breakdown of Category II

			Crime Rate (FMO's) per 1000 Population	
			Lobby	*Elevator*
Category II	(*a*)	poor visibility/good entry definition	8.9	4.9
	(*b*)	good visibility/poor entry definition	7.2	4.1

A final indication of the relationship between visibility and crime was discovered when robberies occurring in elevators were examined (elevator robberies were the most numerous of the major crimes in 1969). The annual rate per thousand population for elevators judged not visible from outside the main entrance was 65 percent higher than for elevators that were visible (3.8 compared to 2.3).

INTERNAL AREAS

The internal areas of high-rise buildings contain many zones devoid of any opportunity for surveillance. Lobbies, elevators, hallways, and fire stairs are, by definition, public rather than private spaces and are intended for use by all building residents. Yet, these zones differ from other public areas, like city streets, in that they exist without benefit of continual observation by either patrolling officers, residents, or passersby. It would have been preferable to design all these internal public areas so that activities within them could be readily observed from outside the building.

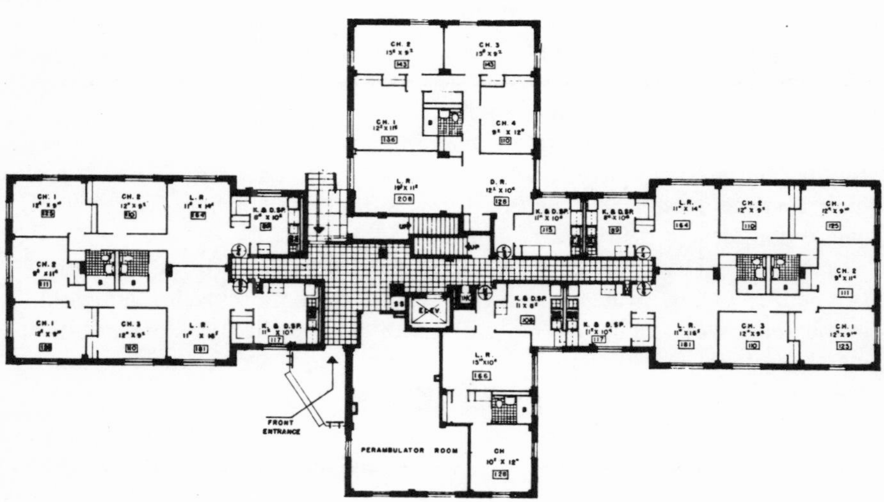

FIG. 62. Ground-Floor Plan of Bronxdale Houses, The Bronx, New York. Note that the elevator waiting area in the lobby is hidden from outside view. Residents must enter the building with no foreknowledge of what may be awaiting them. If molested here, they are under no surveillance.

FIG. 63. Entry at Bronxdale. The elevator waiting area is around a bend in the lobby and totally hidden from the view of someone entering the building. (Photo by author)

Lobby

Lobby design is easily provided with surveillance from outside a building, and it is possible and preferable to design the lobby so that internal activity—getting mail, waiting for the elevator, using the pram room, or, as the case may be, purse snatching or drug dealing—is observable from the streets and exterior grounds of the project. As an example of how poorly lobbies can be designed, the entrance of the Bronxdale Houses project in The Bronx, New York, requires one to make a double turn before reaching the elevator waiting area. Residents of Bronxdale are required to enter the building "blind" with no foreknowledge of what awaits them; once inside they are completely isolated from visual or auditory observation by persons within the apartment units or outside on the project grounds.

By contrast, the design of the lobby of Highbridge Gardens is clearly preferable. In these buildings, elevators are located directly opposite the entry doors which were designed as a part of a large window wall. Similarly, at Edenwald Houses in The Bronx, the lobby is glazed, well-lit, and open to visual observation from as far away as fifty yards. Figure 65 compares crime location in Bronxdale and Highbridge with an average of twenty projects. Where allover crime rates are three-fourths the average at Bronxdale and two-thirds at Highbridge, lobby crime at Bronxdale is 52 percent higher than the average, while at Highbridge, it is 33 percent below the average.

FIG. 64. Ground-Floor Plan of Highbridge Houses. The elevator waiting area is located directly opposite the entry. Residents can screen the lobby before choosing to enter. While inside the lobby, they are under continuous surveillance by people using the outside paths.

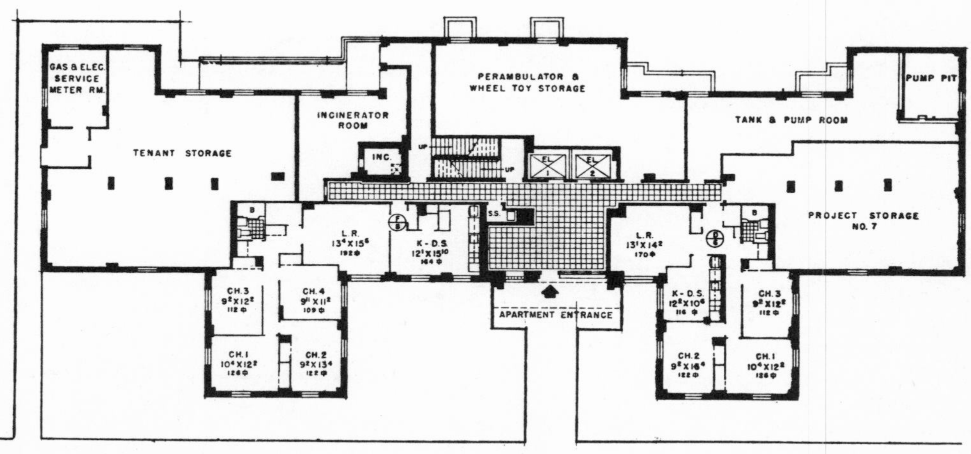

CRIME* LOCATION PROFILE

SOURCE : N.Y.C.H.A. POLICE STATISTICS—1970

* FELONIES, MISDEMEANORS & OFFENCES

BRONXDALE

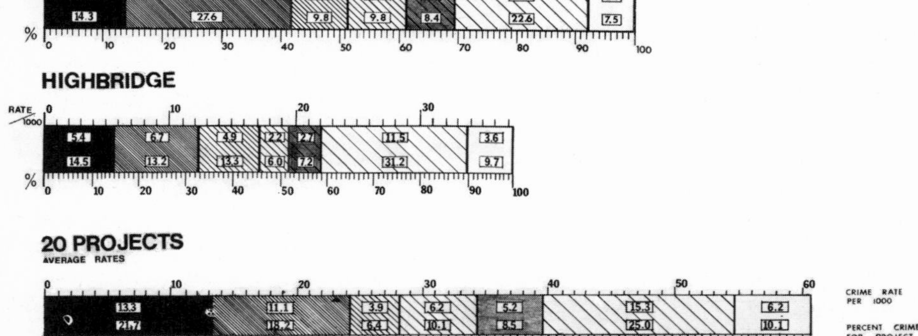

FIG. 65. Crime Location Profile for Bronxdale, Highbridge, and twenty average projects

Fire Stairs

Another area of high-rise buildings devoid of both visual and auditory surveillance opportunities is the fire stair system. Because of changes in fire code regulations, fire stairs in elevator buildings must be enclosed in fireproof wells. These regulations have resulted in the widespread adoption of the scissors-stair design. This solution has precipitated a wide range of allied problems.

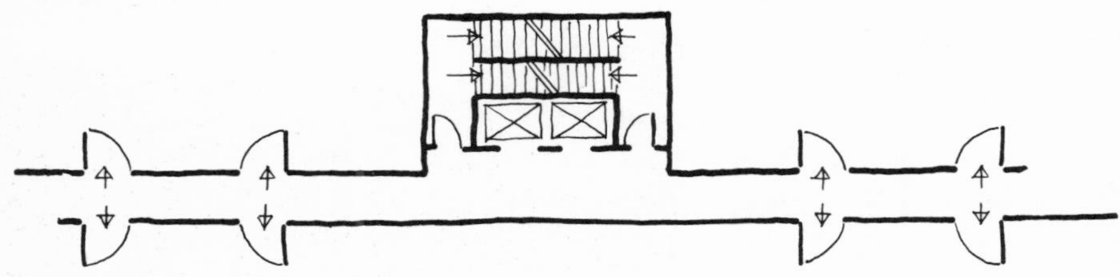

FIG. 66. Plan of Typical Floor, Double-Loaded Corridor Apartment Building. Scissors stairs positioned behind a bank of elevators in a double-loaded corridor building.

Due to fire code requirements, the stairs are virtually sealed off from heavily traversed areas of the buildings they serve. The stairwells are commonly constructed of concrete, with access provided through heavy, fireproof steel doors in which the only opening is a one-foot-square area of wired glass. This arrangement effectively precludes the possibility of visual or auditory monitoring of activity in the stairwells. Consequently, most residents rarely make use of the stairwell for entry and exit, thereby increasing its isolation.

A disproportionate amount of crime has been found to occur on these stairs. It is common practice for criminals to accost their victim in a more heavily used public area of the building—the lobby, elevator, or corridors—and then move him or her, by threat or force, to the sealed fire stairs. Not surprisingly, fire stairs are the area in which a high percentage of the rapes occur, and in which narcotics addicts congregate.

In older buildings and projects, fire stairs were constructed with glass areas larger than contemporary fire codes permit. For example, at Breukelen Houses the landing areas and a good portion of the stairs are surveyable both from the interior corridors and from the grounds and street. Large windows at the stair landings flood the internal stair with daylight. Users of these well-trafficked stairwells feel that they are under observation by other residents and that in an emergency they can call out to people in the street below.

FIG. 67. View from Inside Scissors Stairs at Breukelen. Photo shows landing and end wall composed of glass-block window. This glazed end wall, and its positioning adjacent to the street and entry area to the apartment building, provide an important degree of contact between persons in the stair and those outside. It also facilitates police patrol of the stairs, providing an important degree of visual surveillance. A removed stairwell light is usually read as a danger signal by patrolling police and is investigated. (Photo by author)

Effective formal police surveillance is a difficult task in high-rise buildings with scissors stairs. Housing police patrol the interior of a building of double-loaded corridor design by taking the elevator to the top floor and descending one fire stair after another, observing activity in the corridors at each floor level as they go down. In addition to being burdensome and boring this method is not particularly effective; it is difficult to see more than a few yards ahead, and it is impossible for a man to cover more than one stair at a time. Conversely, evading a patrolman is very easily done. A criminal can hear a patrolman coming three floors away, by the sound of his footsteps and the opening of doors at each level. Eluding pursuit by police is further facilitated by the double, scissors-stair configuration which produces an exit door on each side of the building. Police officers may be going down one of the staircases while the intruder slips down and out of the other.

Members of the staff of the Project for Security Design accompanied officers of the New York City Housing Authority Police in their nightly and daily patrols and witnessed the comparative ease of formal patrol of buildings which have features such as (1) windows in the fire-stair walls, (2) lobbies and mailbox areas that are well lit and easily viewed from the

FIG. 68. Tilden Houses, Brooklyn, New York. The positioning of windows at the end of the corridor on each floor and at the stairwell landings allows a patrolling officer on the street to observe activity in these public interior spaces.

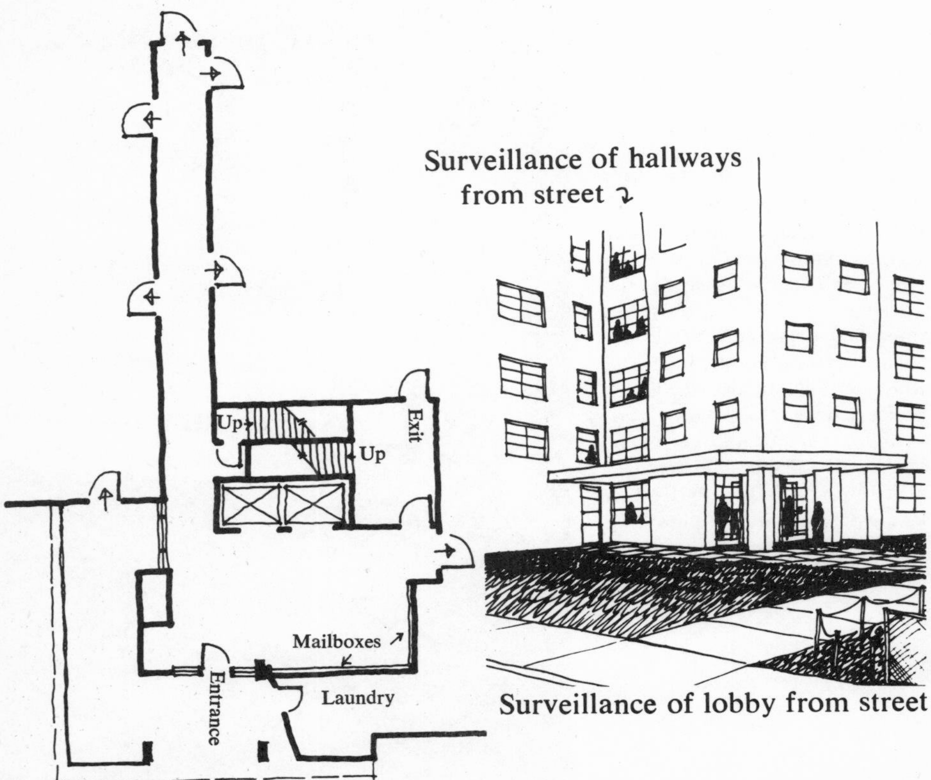

street; and (3) elevator waiting areas at each floor which can be seen from the street below. These areas can be surveyed from the ground at a glance. Trouble spots in buildings can be pinpointed easily from the street. Someone moving down a set of stairs can be observed in progress. Dark landings resulting from smashed or unscrewed light bulbs provide a warning that some activity may be taking place there.

Tilden Houses illustrates the increased surveillance opportunities made possible by simple modification of what is otherwise a standard floor plan: windows were inserted at the end of the corridor on each floor and at each landing of the fire stair. As a result, the patrolling officer on the street can observe much of the activity in the public interior space of the building.

Roof landings (the last landing of the fire stair before exit onto the roof) have presented a similar surveillance problem, because they are used by addicts as a gathering place. At Brownsville Houses, two kinds of roof landings are employed: one set of landings is dark, and one has windows and is well lit. Drug addicts are seldom found in the second, but the first is the location of numerous arrests on narcotics charges.

The juxtaposition of activity areas in apartment interiors with exterior nonprivate areas to facilitate visual surveillance from within

Design that facilitates the surveillance of outside areas from within the apartment can be accomplished in many ways. This involves designing apartments so that people *within* them will naturally view the communally used paths, entries, play, and seating areas of a project during their normal household activities.

Breukelen Houses, discussed in the previous chapter, has employed this technique. The result is very little crime, or fear of crime, on its grounds. The architects of Breukelen located kitchen windows in each apartment so that they face the building entries, and then incorporated play areas and parking lots adjacent to these entries. As adult occupants spend a good portion of their time in the kitchen-dining area, they easily and naturally observe their children at play outside, while at the same time monitoring the comings and goings of residents and strangers.

Surveillance of the public areas of building interiors from the apartments can be provided for equally well. Apartment buildings of "single-loaded corridor" design provide ready opportunity for natural surveillance of their corridors from within the apartment. "Double-loaded corridors" are, by contrast, devoid of surveillance opportunity except where ten-

FIG. 69. Transitional Path at Breukelen Houses. View of the transitional path leading from the common play area of the buffer zone to one of the entries and stairwells within the L-shaped building. This area is considered to be sufficiently defined as semiprivate (serving only the nine families in the building) so that a baby can be left in a pram alone beside the entry. Note, however, that the kitchen windows of the apartment units on both sides of the entry and at each level are immediately adjacent to the entry and stairwell and look out upon this area. (Photo by author)

FIG. 70. Transitional Buffer and Parking Area at Breukelen. The transitional zones formed by the L-shaped buildings at Breukelen at times include parking. This combination of parking, seating, and play space adjacent to the multiple-entry buffer serves to create a well-peopled and well-watched-over semiprivate outside zone serving the apartment building. In this L-shaped building, five entries share a common buffer area and parking lot. Each entry, in turn, has its own transition zone leading from the common buffer area. (Photo by author)

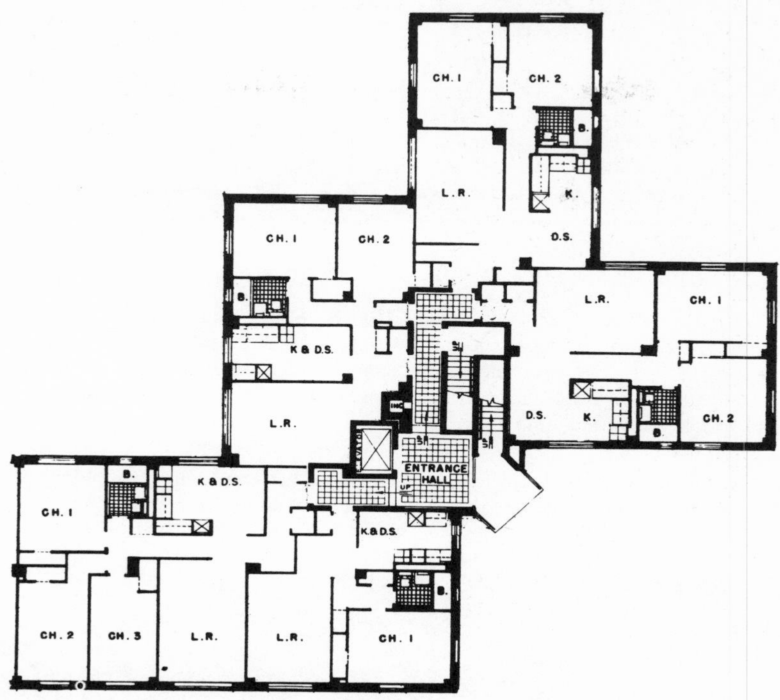

FIG. 71. Ground-Floor Plan of Breukelen Houses. The design of the apartment units facilitates surveillance. Kitchen windows face out on front entries, allowing parents to observe the movements of children and passersby.

ants choose to use the peepholes in their doors. As was described earlier, a double-loaded corridor denotes a building designed with apartment units positioned on either side of a central corridor; "single-loaded" corridor designates a building design in which apartment units are located exclusively on one side of the corridor and face an exterior wall which is glazed or, in mild climates, left open to the weather. The open corridor allows designers to locate windows in the apartment wall facing the corridor to achieve cross-ventilation of the apartment unit. The provision of windows allows as well for excellent surveillance opportunities. Cross-ventilation of units in a double-loaded corridor design is, of course, impossible. The setting of windows in the corridor wall is further precluded by fire regulations and the lack of privacy that would result from the close proximity of windows in the facing apartment.

An example of single-loaded corridor design in a public housing project is Stapleton Houses in Staten Island, New York. Here, the corridor approaching an apartment unit can be monitored by residents through both their kitchen-dining room and their living room windows. These cor-

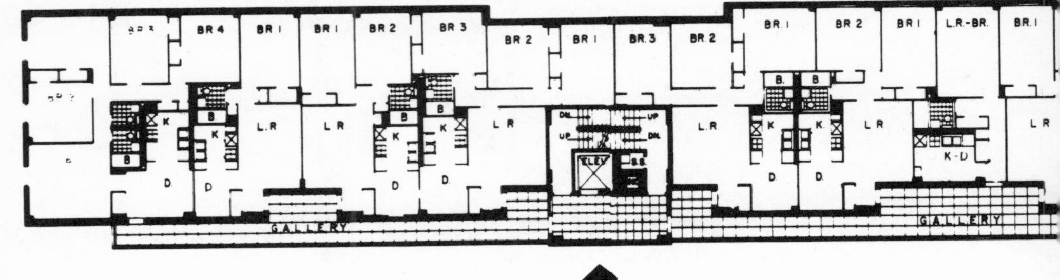

FIG. 72. Typical Floor Plan at Stapleton Houses, Staten Island, New York. Stapleton Houses serves as an example of a single-loaded corridor design. Apartment unit entries are on only one side of the corridor. Living room and kitchen-dining room windows open onto the corridor providing good surveillance opportunities. Note the recessed buffer zone defining the entries to apartment units.

FIG. 73. Aerial View of Stapleton Houses. The juxtaposition of building blocks allows the monitoring of the open corridor in one building by residents in the apartments of the other buildings. (Courtesy of New York City Housing Authority)

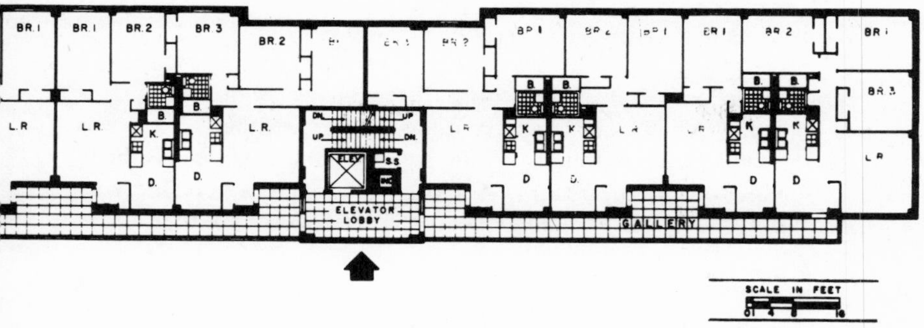

ridors also receive marginal monitoring from the bedroom windows of opposite buildings. The open-corridor window wall also facilities effective police surveillance from the ground level. It is easy to understand, therefore, why the corridors of single-loaded buildings have almost no crime problems, whereas double-loaded corridors are responsible for some 20 percent of all crimes committed in the interiors of buildings.

Typical of the single-loaded corridor building design is a floor plan in which the elevators and fire stairs are located centrally. The open corridor runs from one end of the building to the other, through the central area which is usually enclosed. At least one apartment is located in this enclosed central space, opposite the elevators. These centrally-located apartments have no windows onto the corridors and no visual link to the other apartment entrances because of the two doors closing off the central interior space. Despite the fact that the apartments with windows provide an easy access for criminals, they are the least burglarized. Rather, the central apartments opposite the elevator, with no windows on the corridor, are the most consistently burglarized. In one such middle-income single-loaded corridor building in Manhattan, Columbus Towers, there has been a recent rash of burglaries—averaging four per month. All the apartments burglarized were those located within this central elevator area of the corridor, that is, those immediately opposite the elevators.

At Stapleton Houses, continual surveillance of the gallery corridors is provided through apartment windows: threats such as loitering strangers are detected quickly and reported to the Housing Authority police. By contrast, the entry lobbies of Stapleton Houses are not related to apartment units and suffer from poor visibility. These are the most littered areas of the buildings, suffer the most vandalism, and are where most of the crime occurs.

The typical floor plan at Stapleton also incorporates another design asset not common to single-loaded corridor layouts: the entry area to each of the apartments has been set back an additional four feet to create a small transitional zone separating the entry from the corridor proper. This semiprivate areas, coupled with the facility for continual surveillance activity, has resulted in residents' adoption of this corridor space as their own. Visible assertion of their territorial prerogatives is seen by their placement of lounge chairs outside their doors in hot weather. What was officially designated by the Housing Authority as public space has been claimed as semiprivate by the tenants. Children play in these outside corridor spaces continually, and many leave their tricycles and other toys there overnight.

Housing Authority management is concerned that the pattern of corridor use at Stapleton Houses constitutes a breach of the rules of occupancy. The Authority quite painstakingly informs tenants that there is to be no loitering or other activity in the public areas of the building. Management is further troubled by tenants bickering over their conflicting claims to territory and boundaries in the outside gallery. Settling those arguments is apparently very time consuming. As a result, management continues to issue directives to prevent this occupation of the public corridor, emphasizing the fire hazard and nuisance of it all.

For all its nuisance value, however, territorial bickering has an important function in framing tenants' attitudes toward this space and its violation by intruders. Arguments over the minutiae of territorial boundaries are insignificant when weighted against the benefits accrued: tenants have assumed responsibility for the corridor's maintenance and policing and thereby insure its freedom from crime and vandalism.

Admittedly, the single-loaded corridor is more costly than the typical double-loaded layout, and this is a strong inhibiting factor to its general adoption in low-income housing. However, as we shall see in Chapter 6, in the discussion of Riverbend Houses, the problem is not without solution.

The reduction in ambiguity of public and private areas and paths in projects so as to provide focus and meaning to surveillance

The interior layout and organization of many housing projects is often very difficult to comprehend, particularly when long blocks of buildings are grouped together: interior corridors flow into one another through fire doors; fire stairs are positioned in leftover corners; exits and entrances to long, slab buildings are numerous and difficult to locate. Descending a scissors-type fire stair, positioned identically to its twin, is as likely to deposit one at the rear of the building as at the front. City and Housing Authority police, responding to calls in housing projects with which they are unfamiliar, find it difficult to distinguish one building from another, let alone find their way through the building to the right apartment. The locational simplicity provided by the address system in the grid layout of streets is, by comparison, a much desired attribute.

CIRCULATION CONFUSION: FIRE STAIRS

As was discussed previously, many large high-rise buildings are required by law to have fire stairs no further than a hundred feet from any apartment. This regulation is commonly satisfied by the provision of a scissors stairs in a central location behind the elevator. Separate exits at the ground floor are also required, and it is quite common to have the second exit at the rear of the building, opposite the lobby entry. This practice results in an ambiguity of building layout, with tenants using front and rear entries interchangeably. Criminals evade pursuit simply by alternating fire stairs as they flee the building. There is only a 50 percent chance that a single pursuing officer will exit at the same side of the building as the criminal he is chasing.

A similar scissors-stair arrangement, with separate exits at the ground floor, is provided at Edenwald Houses. It was through an accident of design, however, that the architect was able to exit both the first and second fire stairs adjacent to the main entry. This modification enabled him to achieve three things.

> Any person attempting to evade pursuit by using either fire stair would, regardless of which route he chose, exit at approximately the same point in front of the main building entrance.
>
> Residents and visitors alike, regardless of which entry they choose, must use the same circulation paths and pass within view of the sitting area adjacent to the front door, thus becoming subject to the surveillance provided by this facility.
>
> Much of the reason for using the fire stair as a more convenient route disappears when access doors to the fire stair and the main lobby are positioned adjacently.

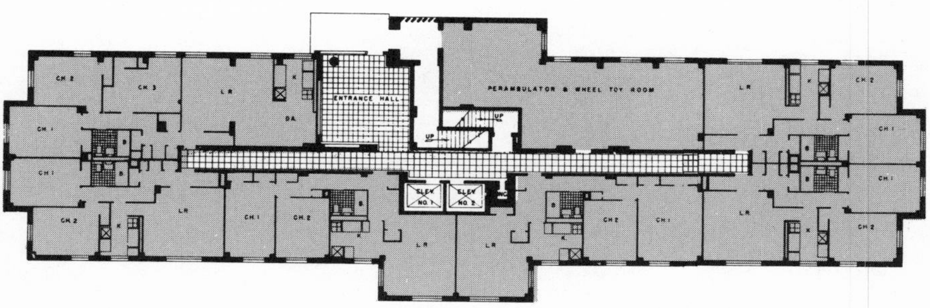

FIG. 74. Ground-floor plan at Edenwald Houses

As a result of this design, the fire exit remains predominantly unused as a secondary means of circulation at the ground level. Edenwald is consequently one of the few projects under the aegis of the New York City Housing Authority in which the security hardware on the emergency exit doors has not been destroyed.

Interviews with Edenwald residents indicate that the securing of the stairwell entrance at the ground level has greatly increased the security of the stairwell at upper levels of the building. The stairs, avoided as unsafe in other projects, are readily used for secondary vertical circulation and for visiting between floors.

Where the fire exit of a building is positioned on the side of the building opposite the main entrance, as in Highbridge, the opportunity it affords to leave a building and move directly toward one's destination becomes a convenience too useful to be resisted. Tenants have often resorted to jamming the latches, on these doors to provide easy access for themselves. However, this practice has had a detrimental side effect: the superintendents have fixed the doors to remain open rather than be continually repairing the latches. The permanently open fire door now provides an easy entrance point for criminals. The stairwell eventually comes to be recognized as a danger zone and falls into disuse by all, save intruders.

Buildings that are longer than the standard 100 to 150 feet (or come under other fire codes), such as those at Columbus Homes in

FIG. 75. Entry to Building at Highbridge Houses, New York. The large window wall at the building entry provides an excellent surveillance opportunity. Residents can see the lobby interior and elevator waiting area from the path outside the building. (Photo by author)

FIG. 76. Fire Exits at Highbridge Houses. The secondary exit at Highbridge is located at the opposite side of the building and is often jammed to stay open. Although at times this makes access to the building easier, it also creates an opportunity for vandals and criminals to enter and leave unobserved. Children rarely realize the potential danger of playing in such an unsupervised and unsafe area. (Photo by author)

Newark and Pruitt-Igoe in St. Louis, have additional sets of stairs which exit to the ground and are connected at every floor through the common double-loaded corridor. Ambiguity of building plan is even more rampant in such designs. The labyrinthine access routes and corridors make recognition of neighbors difficult to impossible; there are simply too many people coming and going. Consequently, residents express fear in using the interior corridors. The many access doors to fire stairs provide almost endless opportunities for intruders to make their way through the building and to surprise tenants at any point along the way. There is no way to tell where someone will appear or where he will exit.

LEGIBILITY OF THE PROJECT AS A WHOLE

Perhaps even more critical than functional ambiguities of building design are those ambiguities which are a consequence of the superblock concept common to large-scale government-supported low- and middle-income housing design.

The problems of orientation in large high-rise projects may be as much the result of uniformity in their design as of their internal labyrinthine arrangements. All buildings are designed and positioned alike so that it is difficult to discern any differences. There is also no orderly, or ritualized, means of progression from street to home. The project looks the same from all angles; all facets of buildings echo the same form. Nothing that tenants do to their apartments or windows can modify the appearance of their buildings so as to impart identity and individuality. Project residents almost universally refer to buildings by the number given them by the Housing Authority on the original site plan. Few know the numbers of buildings beyond their own or even of those immediately adjacent to theirs. When tenants have to describe a building or location to an outsider or to a policeman who does not know the building number system, they are forced to revert to primitive terms—"down that way," "at the other side of the project." Use of city street names or street addresses as a means of locating buildings in a superblock is usually impossible.

In conclusion we find that there are many aspects and facets to surveillance which contribute to the improvement of security. Stated simply, if there is any modicum of morality and accompanying social pressures in a community, opening up all activity in public spaces to natural supervision proves a very powerful deterrent to criminal acts. An existing proof of this principle may be found in New Orleans, by a comparison of Fisher Homes and Guste Homes with St. Bernard Homes and Desire Houses. Fisher Homes and Guste Homes were built in 1965 and 1963, respectively, and follow the open court and corridor design. St. Bernard Homes and Desire Houses were built in 1942 and 1956, respectively, and follow the old double-loaded corridor designs. In New Orleans, after years of building public housing with interior stairs and corridors, the Housing Authority began to build two- and three-story walk-ups with single-loaded corridors around open courts, accessible by open stairwells. The net result: the virtual elimination of all robberies in the public areas of the project, and the elimination of much of the burglarizing of apartments.

The subdivision of housing projects into small, recognizable and comprehensible-at-a-glance enclaves is a further contributant to improving the visual surveillance mechanism. Simultaneously, this subdivision serves to provide identity and territorial definition; gives focus, involvement, and commitment to the act of surveillance. In some housing developments, where the surveillance of the activity of one's neighbors, outside their apartments, was possible, residents were found to be very familiar indeed with everyone's comings and goings—and, occasionally, somewhat critical. The overall effect, however, was to cement collective identity and responsibility—through these social pressures.

For those, however, who intentionally choose the anonymity and unsupervised life of large apartment towers to pursue a life style distant from the social norms, the supervised environment is one to be shunned. For these, however, a secure environment may be quite a secondary concern. There is a probable correlation between those who seek anonymity and dissociation from physical neighbor and the young. Equally, family life and middle age probably correlates highly with expectations of neighbor obedience to a moral code—of whatever definition—as it also does with expectations of a secure existence.

With a little bit of searching everyone in this day and age should be able to find a living environment where one's neighbors share one's moral values, however antagonistic they may be to middle-class norms, but still share a common desire for ensuring a safe residential environment.

5

IMAGE AND MILIEU

- *The Capacity of Design to Influence the Perception of a Project's Uniqueness, Isolation, and Stigma*

The introduction of a large grouping of new buildings of distinctive height and texture into an existing urban fabric singles out these buildings for particular attention. If this distinctive image is also negative, the project will be stigmatized and its residents castigated and victimized.

Government-sponsored housing developments in America, for a variety of reasons seldom articulated, are designed so that they stand out and are recognized as distinctively different residential complexes. It is our contention that this differentiation serves in a negative way to single out the project and its inhabitants as "easy hits." The idiosyncratic image of publicly-assisted housing, coupled with other design features and the social characteristics of the resident population, makes such housing a peculiarly vulnerable target of criminal activity.

The following is a discussion of those many formal ingredients which are felt to negatively differentiate a housing project from a surrounding residential area. Ironically, many of these physical features may have been intentionally provided by the architects as what they felt were positive contributions to the living environment of intended residents.

THE DISTINCTIVENESS RESULTING FROM INTERRUPTIONS OF THE URBAN CIRCULATION PATTERN

One ingredient, mentioned in chapter 2, that contributes to the stigma and isolation of a project is the practice of closing off city streets for the purpose of gaining open space for the interior project grounds. The rectangular grid which is the texture of most American cities has been criticized by planners as an incredibly naive and simplistic approach to urban form and development. Nevertheless, this street pattern, with its constant flow of vehicular and pedestrian traffic, does provide an element of safety for every dwelling unit.

The design of a huge project which closes off internal streets and provides vehicular access only at the periphery, originally heralded as an important new design tool for the redevelopment of cities, has served to single out these areas and make them vulnerable. This, coupled with the obvious disadvantages that come from closing streets which were considered safe areas, serves to further handicap low-income housing design.

THE DISTINCTIVENESS OF BUILDING HEIGHT, PROJECT SIZE, MATERIALS, AND AMENITIES

Publicly supported housing is usually designed to replace high-density slums. Although it is densely designed (to reduce land cost per unit), it is seldom that a housing project is able to achieve the density of the slum it is replacing, since most slum-dwelling units have double or even triple family occupancy. Most architects, faced with the problem of designing a high-density project, opt for high-rise elevator buildings, in order to free ground areas sufficiently large for green and recreation facilities.

High-rise projects stand out very clearly and identifiably from their surrounding community, whether an old tenement area or new, middle-income residential complex.

There are, however, many instances of upper-middle-income, high-rise housing that are in sharp contrast with adjacent, older low-density developments, but which present a more positive image than their surroundings. Therefore, it is important to understand and articulate what it is, exactly, in the form of housing project buildings that makes these differences evident.

High-density, upper-middle-income, high-rise buildings are seldom grouped in projects of more than two or three buildings. In contrast, many public housing estates are designed to include from ten to thirty towers, and because of this scale of development, become predominant visual elements in the urban fabric. An effort is usually made in upper-middle-income housing to treat the facades with high-quality materials—an expensive brick, precast concrete, or stone facing—a luxury not usually possible in public housing. Similarly, a percentage of the units in upper-middle-income housing are provided with outdoor balconies, a feature normally economically prohibitive in public housing.

One should not conclude that public housing is built cheaply, even

FIG. 77. Elevator waiting area in the high-rise buildings of Schuylkyll Falls Housing Project, Philadelphia. (Photo by author)

though for certain reasons—and many have been suggested—frills are strictly forbidden. In fact, the cost per square foot of public housing at times equals the cost per square foot of luxury high-rise housing. Public housing, built by a housing authority, is usually built extremely carefully, with good attention to detail and meticulously supervised construction. The exception to this rule is the current "Turnkey" practice. The turnkey program is a relatively new device whereby housing is built by private developers expressly to be sold to housing authorities for use as public housing.

One of the reasons for intentionally maintaining the visual stigma of public housing was suggested by Adam Walinsky in his article, "Keeping the Poor in their Place."[1] He reasons that in this country, unlike our Western European counterparts, the middle- and working-class population do not look favorably on those members of our society who require government assistance to pay their rent. While we have come a long way from our laissez-faire attitudes of the 1920s in developing a more enlightened approach toward less able members of our society, we are still apparently incapable of providing housing for them which looks better than the worst we provide for ourselves.

The distinctiveness of interior finishes and furnishings

It has long been the policy of housing authorities to design and equip buildings with furnishings which are vandal-proof and wear-resistant. Glazed tiles of the kind employed in hospitals and prisons are standard in the corridors of public housing projects. They are convenient to wash down, graffiti erases from them, and they wear appreciably longer than plaster walls. Corridor lights are now being enclosed in unbreakable plastic, and it is hoped these new fixtures will survive forever. Exterior lighting, with its own unbreakable housing, is usually of the mercury-vapor type, which casts a strong, purplish light.

This attitude toward interior finishes and furnishings creates an institutional atmosphere, not unlike that achieved in our worst hospitals and prisons. Even though the materials are in fact stronger and more resistant to wear, tenants seem to go out of their way to test their resistance capacities. Instead of being provided with an environment in which they can take pride and might desire to keep up, they are provided with one that begs them to test their ability in tearing it down. In the long run, even the institutional wall tiles and vandal-resistant radiators at Pruitt-Igoe met their match.

Design and life style symbolization

Our interviews with tenants have led us to the unmistakable conclusion that living units are assessed by tenants not only on the basis of size and available amenities but on the basis of the life style they symbolize and purport to offer. Building prototypes, from row housing to high-rise, symbolize various forms of class status. The small, two-story row-house unit totaling 1,200 square feet, with a couple hundred feet taken away by an interior staircase, is universally held by tenants to be more desirable than the 1,000-square-foot apartment in an elevator building, equipped with more modern conveniences. As with most of American society, low-income groups, aspire to the life style symbolized by this housing prototype and by the suburban bungalow. They view the row house as more closely resembling the individual family house than the apartment within a communal building. A piece of ground adjacent to a unit, provided for the exclusive use of a family, is cherished and defended, regardless of how small.

By gentlemen's agreement, public housing must never approach the luxurious in appearance, even though it may cost more per square foot. It must retain an institutional image. Unfortunately, this practice not only

FIG. 78. Elevator and Mailbox Area at Pruitt-Igoe, St. Louis. Typically vandalized breezeway entry to the high-rise at Pruitt-Igoe. (Photo by author)

"puts the poor in their place" but brings their vulnerability to the attention of others. Parallel to this, and much more devastating, is the effect of the institutional image as perceived by the project residents themselves. Unable to camouflage their identities and adopt the attitudes of private apartment dwellers, they sometimes overreact and treat their dwellings as prisoners treat the penal institutions in which they are housed. They show no concern for assisting in the care, upkeep, and maintenance of the buildings, no inclination toward the decoration of their apartment units with paint or curtains. Lee Rainwater, in his discussion of Pruitt-Igoe, observes that

> finally, the consequences for conceptions of the moral order of one's world, of one's self, and of others, are very great. Although lower class

FIG. 79. View of the High-Rise at Schuylkyll Falls Housing Project, Philadelphia. Note the pervading graffiti, smashed windows, and other vandalism. (Photo by author)

> people may not adhere in action to many middle class values about neatness, cleanliness, order and proper decorum, it is apparent that they are often aware of their deviance, wishing that their world could be a nicer place, physically and socially. The presence of non-human threats conveys in devastating terms a sense that they live in an immoral and uncontrolled world. The physical evidence of trash, poor plumbing and the stink that goes with it, rats and other vermin, deepens their feeling of being moral outcasts. Their physical world is telling them that they are inferior and bad just as effectively perhaps as do their human interactions.[2]

We are not advocating aesthetic treatment of halls and apartments for the sake of beautification alone, although even the President's Commission on Law Enforcement and Criminal Justice recognized the debilitating effect on the spirit of a deteriorated living environment.[3] In our discussion, aesthetic considerations assume importance for the ways in which they can contribute to the definition and subdivision of the environment as well, as to the psychological state of the inhabitants. Halls and lobbies with uniform fixtures and materials are at times more the result of an aesthetic ideal of uniformity than a commitment to lowering costs. Uniformity and durability represent an attempt to achieve the maximum of neatness, order, and maintenance ease for the project as a whole. This universal denominator eliminates the environmental highs and lows that characterize the private housing market where individuals are responsible for property upkeep. Everyone is aware of how the individual efforts of homeowners—curtains on windows, treatment and disposal of garbage—can grace or disgrace a street. Their most important attribute may be their individual differences: a public display of individualism indicates as much in its precious concern as occasional examples of indifferent neglect. A resident who has resigned himself to not caring about the condition of his immediate surroundings—who has come to accept his ineffectualness in modifying his condition—is not about to intercede, even in his own behalf, when he becomes the victim of a criminal.

URBAN LOCALE

If particular urban areas, streets, or paths are recognized as being safe, adjoining areas benefit from this safety in a real sense and also by association.

It is possible to increase the safety of residential areas by positioning their public zones and entries so that they face on areas which, for a variety of reasons, are considered safe. Certain sections and arteries of a city have come to be recognized as being safe—by the nature of the activities located there; by the quality of formal patrolling; by the number of users and extent of their felt responsibility; and by the responsibility assumed by employees of bordering institutions and establishments. The areas most usually identified as safe are heavily trafficked public streets and arteries combining both intense vehicular and pedestrian movement; commerical retailing areas during shopping hours; institutional areas; and government offices.

These areas have a reputation of safety which is occasionally reflected in low precinct crime rates. There are contradictory statistics available, however. A commercial street which may have been identified by surrounding inhabitants and users as safe will, occasionally, be found to have a higher crime rate than adjoining areas which were rated unsafe. This may be explained by a difference in the type of crime occurring and by the lower chance of its occurrence per area user. Where a purse snatching which occurs on an identified safe street will usually be of the grab and run sort, in an area identified as less safe, it may further involve an assault on the victim. One concludes that both victim and criminal assume that aggravated assault would not be tolerated by witnesses (shopkeepers and/or other shoppers) on a well-trafficked commercial street, or that escape time is critical to a criminal in what is considered a more formally patrolled area. Some commercial street corners, identified as safe, have records, showing up to three times more crimes than any other place in the immediately surrounding residential area. However, the number of pedestrians passing any point on the commercial street is over twenty times the average of surrounding streets and areas. The rate of occurrence may be higher, but the chance of occurrence per user may be lower. However, this explanation is, for the moment, hypothetical. It may also be that where shoppers have come to understand that there is potential risk in using a shopping street, they will not tolerate this same condition on their own streets.

Juxtaposition of residential areas with other "safe" functional facilities: commercial, institutional, industrial, and entertainment

Some institutional and commercial areas have come to be recognized as safe areas during their periods of intensive use; others have a decidedly opposite image. The reason identified for their being safe involves the presence of many people engaged in like activities; thus providing a number of possible witnesses who might choose to come to the aid of a victim. Most importantly, the presence of many people is seen as a possible force in deterring criminals. Many of those interviewed identified staff in charge of commercial and institutional facilities, storekeepers, librarians, or security guards as highly concerned about the safety of adjoining areas. Shoppers feel that neighborhood employees have a more significant stake in ensuring safety than do uninvolved passersby or fellow shoppers. The juxtaposition of the entries to residential units with safe institutional areas was considered of positive benefit by many of those interviewed, although apprehension was expressed about the days and hours when these facilities are closed and radiate no security whatsoever. The juxtaposition preferred was one which created a transitional buffer between apartment building entry and the street and establishments.

The provision of parks and playgrounds within and around housing projects has been a program considered highly desirable by communities, planners, and housing authority officials alike. It therefore comes as a particular disappointment to learn of instances where their provision has been a cause of crime and vandalism.

At Edenwald, the park on the west corner of the project was beneficently designed and positioned to serve both the project residents and the surrounding community. In addition, it is located near a commercial strip which contains a bar and liquor store. Housing Authority police and residents claim the park attracts all the bums and addicts from the neighborhood. Because the relationship between park and adjacent project buildings is not clearly identified, the park has become a no-man's-land—an open congregation area controlled by no particular group. The buildings at Edenwald which suffer the most crime and vandalism are those immediately adjacent to this park. Residents and management feel that the park would have been much safer if its relationship to the project had been more clearly defined. The park, they say, should have been designed so that only one side remained accessible from the street, while the other three sides were enclosed by housing units and their entry areas. The adoption of this design would have facilitated natural surveillance of park activities by adjacent residents.

A similar problem exists at the Woodhill Homes project in Cleveland. The recreation area at Woodhill is isolated from all other activity areas by a rise of ground which segregates it from project buildings and public streets. Use of the recreation facilities by teen-agers has been found to degenerate quickly into fighting over claims to territory. In an effort to prevent such encounters, the project manager has removed the basketball hoops and the baseball field backstop. As a result, the grounds have fallen into disuse, even though they are the only recreation facilities available for blocks around. The disposition of new housing units adjacent to these grounds and the addition of a service road could provide surveillance of the area. Such subdivision would serve to define the grounds as a territorial extension of adjacent housing, while hopefully not restricting its use to residents only. If the recreation area could be further

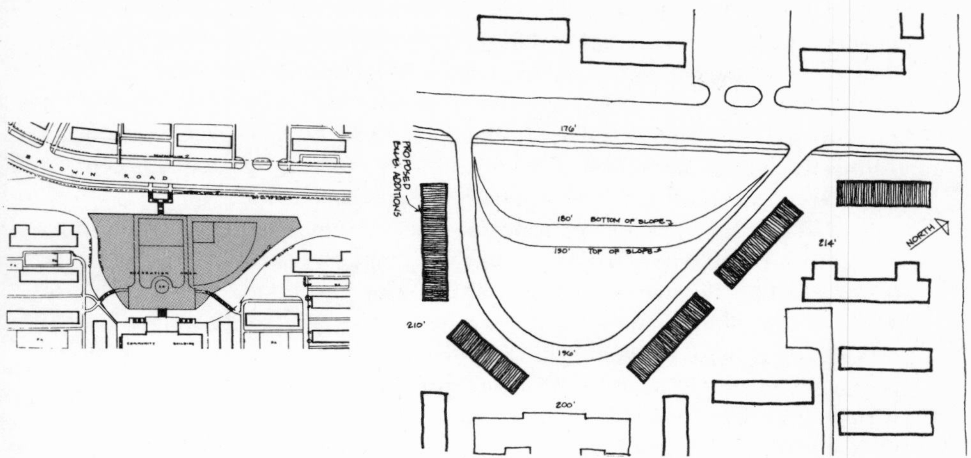

FIG. 80. Site Plan of Woodhill Estates, Cleveland. The existing recreation area is located in an isolated area of high ground and lacks any visual association or relationship to project buildings or surrounding public streets. The plan for modification of the grounds shows the positioning of additional dwellings to improve safety, and earth-moving to bring the play area in closer association with the street.

landscaped so that part of it were lowered to the level of the street below, this portion would receive additional surveillance from the street and from facing buildings.

It should be mentioned, however, that there are examples where the proximity of certain types of institutions act to impair the safety of a neighborhood. A recurring problem of juxtaposition results from the close proximity of housing projects with high schools and junior colleges. The Outhwaite project in Cleveland is a particularly notorious case-in-point since one area of the project actually borders on three different schools. The buildings suffering most frequent burglaries are those juxtaposed with these institutional facilities. Residents and project staff claim that teen-agers hang out on the public grounds and in the interior stairways and lobbies of adjacent units. They harass and are occasionally involved in the muggings of residents. In New York, Philadelphia, and Cleveland high-rise projects with buildings bordering high schools, the enclosed fire stairs are often used by teen-age addicts for selling and using drugs. Where it may not always be possible, or even desirable to intentionally avoid this sort of juxtaposition, it is certainly feasible, to design the site plan of the project so that access to apartment buildings is not from those streets directly opposite schools.

In much the same way, where an area of a project faces on a teen-age hamburger joint or game room hangout, the buildings immediately opposite have higher crime rates. The statistics on location and frequency of crime in Bronxdale reinforce the claims of police and residents. The two hamburger joints on the west side of the project, and the teenage play areas on the east, together generate high crime and vandalism rates in the immediately adjacent buildings. The New York City Housing Authority police has found that those of its projects located adjacent to commercial streets suffer proportionally higher crime rates.

This would lead us to conclude that commercial and institutional generators of activity do not, in and of themselves, necessarily enhance the safety of adjoining streets and areas. The unsupported hypotheses of Jane Jacobs, Shlomo Angel, and Elizabeth Wood must be examined more closely for a better understanding of the nature of their operating mechanisms. The simple decision to locate commercial or institutional facilities within a project in order to increase activity and so provide the safety which comes with numbers must be critically evaluated in terms of the nature of the business, the intended users, their identification with area residents, their periods of activity, the nature and frequency of the presence of concerned authorities, and so on.

The policy of HUD and housing authorities across the country of discouraging commercial facilities on project grounds, while initially directed at preventing unfair competitive situations with neighborhood merchants, may have a rationale of another order to it.

FIG. 81. Site Plan of Outhwaite Houses, Cleveland. The Outhwaite Houses project borders on three different schools. The buildings and grounds of the project which suffer most from vandalism and loitering are those located directly across the street from the schools.

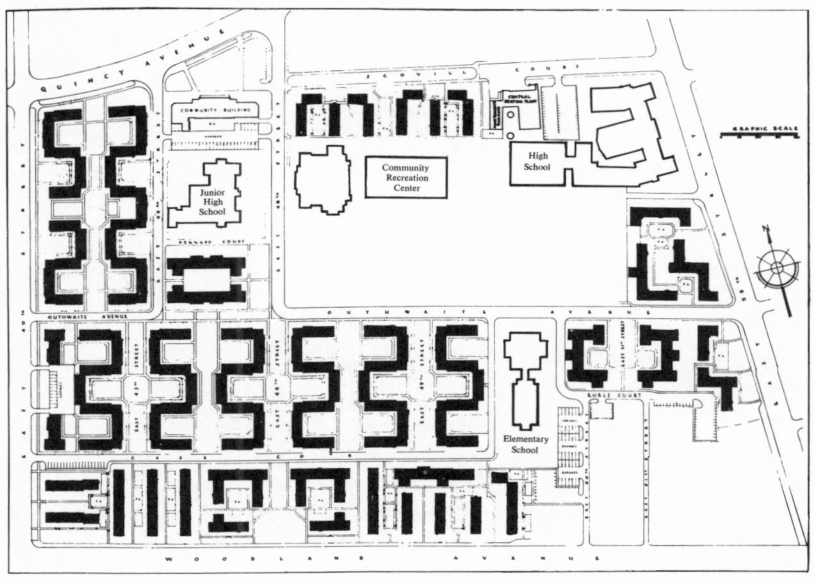

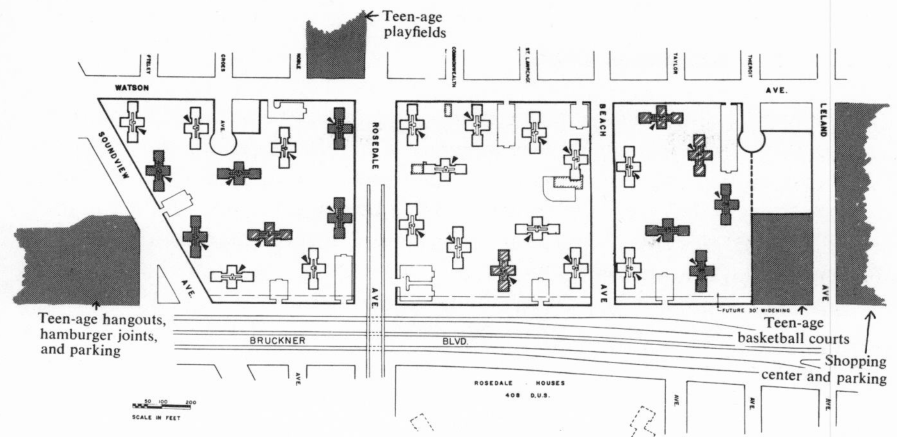

FIG. 82. Site Plan of Bronxdale Housing Project, The Bronx, New York. Bronxdale has 1,497 units at 48.6 dwelling units per acre. The shaded areas bordering the project grounds are either commercial or recreational areas. The shaded buildings are the ones experiencing the highest crime and vandalism rates.

FIG. 83. View of Bronxdale from teen-age hangouts on southwest corner of the project. (Photo by author)

Juxtaposition with safe public streets

Regardless of variations in the physical configuration of project sites, hundreds of tenants interviewed have consistently identified the public streets bordering their projects as being safer than paths which bisect the interiors of the projects. This view conflicts with the opinion held by the New York City Housing Authority police, who feel that the interior grounds are safer and are perceived as safer. Nevertheless, the buildings and areas of projects which tenants have identified as being most *unsafe* are located in the interior of the project and do not front on any through streets. Consistently, tenants have scale-rated their buildings as safer when the entry, entry grounds, and lobby of the buildings face directly onto city streets. Large superblocks, at various densities, have been found to exhibit systematically higher crime rates than projects of comparable size and density that have city streets continuing through them.

The dimensions of juxtaposed areas

From our discussion of the relative merits of juxtaposing housing with other functional facilities, it is evident that a wise evaluation of the problem hinges on an understanding of the thoroughly reciprocal nature of the relationship that exists between the project and the juxtaposed facility.

The success or failure of a particular configuration depends as much on the degree to which residents can identify with and survey activity in the related facility as it does on the nature of the users of that facility and the activities they engage in. This would suggest that the dimensions and nature of the juxtaposition can be significant.

There is little, in this regard, that one can do about the design and location of hamburger joints. But, the size, proportions, and positioning of parks is open to ready manipulation. From experience, the Police Department of the City of St. Louis believes that city parks should be proportioned to facilitate natural surveillance from bordering streets and by adjacent residents. Long thin parks of the same area are therefore preferable to square ones, as they have a longer periphery that can be patrolled. The proportions of a park need not severely limit the facili-

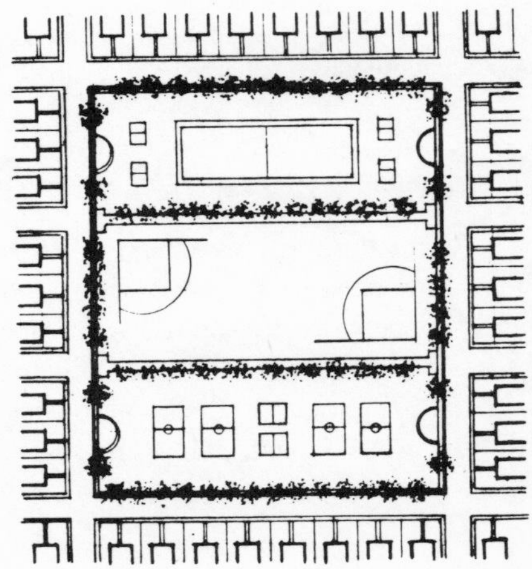

FIG. 84. Site Plan of a Park Which Proves Dangerous. The proportions and dimensions of a large square park limit the ability of surrounding residents, vehicles, and patrols from observing activity within.

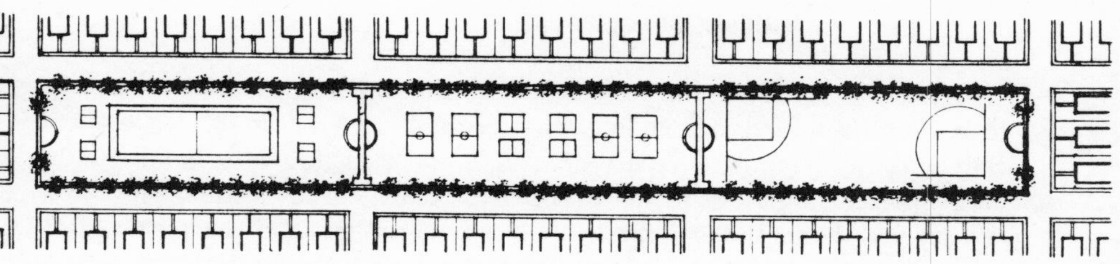

FIG. 85. Site Plan of a Park Which Proves Safe. A long, thin park can provide the same recreation potential while affording ready observation of all internal activity from surrounding buildings and streets.

ties placed within it, or the total area provided. The dimensions of a park are equally as important as the proportions. The narrow dimension of the oblong park shown in figure 85 should not be so wide as to prevent someone on one side from seeing through to the other side. In residential areas suffering high crime rates, the interiors of large parks which cannot be easily surveyed will go unused. Douglas and Garfield Parks, large internal parks on the West Side of Chicago, are cases in point.

Possibly of all defensible space mechanisms recommended, these last two: the design of the image of the residential environment and its juxtaposition with other activities in the urban setting, will prove most offensive to architects and planners.

FIG. 86. Douglas Park in the Lawndale Area of Chicago. Because of the large size of the park, in its present social setting, the interior areas are proving too dangerous to be used.

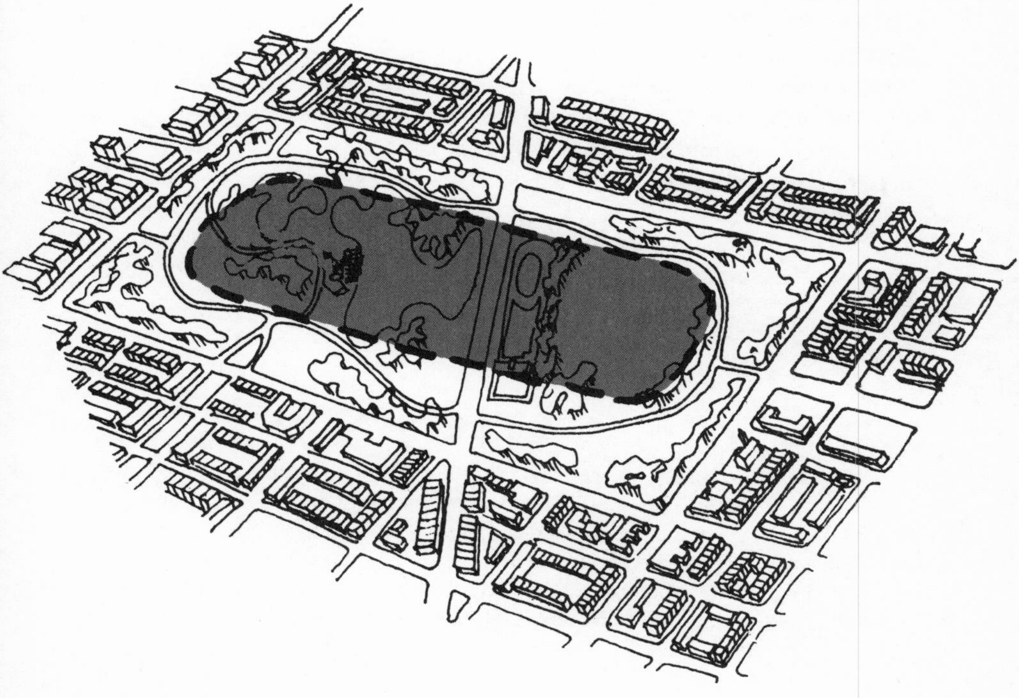

There is probably much to the truism that architects are ego-maniacs. It is a difficult and demanding profession. From the initial encounters with a client to the final supervision of the construction of a building is a long and, at times, arduous experience. Only those with strong egos can survive it and still be able to look with some pride at the results. But in the process of molding this ego and developing the necessary calluses, architects tend to forget that their clients' experience and judgment of their needs in a building may be vastly superior to that of the architect's. In the process of trying to produce a successfully designed residential building, the architect will be endeavoring to satisfy the aesthetic tastes of his peers—rather than those of his client. If his client is rich and well educated, his tastes may be similar to those of the architect. But if the client comes from a low- or middle-income background, it is most likely that he will aspire to the tastes of the class immediately above him, and probably those in vogue ten and twenty years ago. Architects are chagrined and sometimes express moral indignation when they find their low-income clients rejecting a housing project designed in the most current professional idiom, asking instead for something that looks quaintly middle-class. But this middle-class look is the client's image of arrival—his symbol of status. The well-meaning architect who worked hard at designing buildings, which he knows will please his peers and receive recognition in the professional journals, for some incomprehensible reason, finds himself accused of giving the poor "funny houses."

In a similar way, for decades after the original utopian physical planners first set down rules for segregating different activities and functions in the design of new cities, urban designers have been fighting for the reintegration of shopping and institutional facilities with housing. Now with this fight almost won, it appears that someone else is again advocating their segregation. The facts however cannot be easily dismissed. The matter is one of scale: at which level is the segregation to occur? It is possible within the frames of our guidelines to juxtapose schools and shops with housing so as to create the desired walking distance milieu, while at the same time providing for the territorially intact residential enclave.

NOTES

1. Adam Walinsky, "Keeping the Poor in Their Place: Notes on the Importance of Being One-Up," *The New Republic* 151 (July 4, 1964):15.

2. Lee Rainwater, "Fear and the House-as-Haven in the Lower Class," *AIP Journal* 32 (January 1966):29.

3. "Society has not devised ways for ensuring that all its members have the ability to assume responsibility. It has let too many of them grow up

untaught, unmotivated, unwanted. The criminal justice system has a great potential for dealing with individual instances of crime, but it was not designed to eliminate the conditions in which most crime breeds. It needs help. Warring on poverty, inadequate housing and unemployment is warring on crime. A civil rights law is a law against crime. . . . More broadly and most importantly every effort to improve life in America's inner cities is an effort against crime. A community's most enduring protection against crime is to right the wrongs and cure the illnesses that tempt men to harm their neighbors" (*The Challenge of Crime in a Free Society,* The President's Commission on Law Enforcement and Administration of Justice [New York: E. P. Dutton, 1968], p. 69).

6

CURRENT PRACTITIONERS OF DEFENSIBLE SPACE

This chapter discusses examples of recently completed housing projects which employ a variety of physical features to provide natural security for their inhabitants. They are different from the examples cited in the development of our defensible space hypotheses in that they (1) are all current; and (2) represent *conscious* decisions on the part of contemporary architects to build environments which have an inherent capacity for assuring the residents of security. A project's being *current* has additional significance beyond either its possible fashionableness or the likelihood of its being a response to the magnitude of the current crime problem. Contemporary building codes and fire regulations are different from those of a few years ago. Codes have a way of changing every ten to fifteen years and of markedly affecting both the internal design of buildings and their relative disposition on project sites.

The architects who, in 1948, produced the Brownsville Houses discussed in chapter 2, worked within existing fire and building codes, and succeeded in providing many security features. The same architects, attempting to produce a 1300-unit project eight years later, would have found the codes drastically changed and might have discovered themselves unwittingly producing a project not unlike the unsafe Van Dyke Houses, simply by conforming to the new fire regulations and building codes. The superior security properties that were an integral part of their earlier designs would have been forfeited to the new by-laws. In past chapters, physical features of projects were cited with the prime purpose of formulating the defensible space hypotheses. We were not particularly concerned with whether or not they met present-day codes; our purpose was to examine and identify working solutions, past and present. We realized that the problems involved in adapting these designs to meet current codes and regulations would have to be faced later. Contemporary projects with defensible space attributes do meet current regulations.

Building economics are another reason for looking at current examples. Present interest rates and spiraling construction costs make the incorporation of many building features which were standard ten years ago an impossibility today. Unfortunately, even some of the features illustrated in this chapter—features of buildings built as little as five years ago—are priced out of today's market. They are included with the knowledge that today's circumstances are unusual, and that the current economic situation facing residential development will have to be altered if the nation is to begin to answer any of its pressing housing needs.

The projects that follow have been categorized by density, income-level of inhabitants, and urban location. They range from high-density, inner-city solutions to relatively low-density, suburban solutions. It was decided to adopt this structuring system so that projects could be discussed on an integrated basis. It would also have been possible to categorize individual design features and then to survey different projects employing each feature. However, since many of the defensible space components operate only in concert with other components, the manner of their combination in a project must be seen in totality in order for the success or failure of the total system to be properly measured (see table 12).

The projects chosen here for discussion by no means represent an exhaustive list. Rather, they are intended to represent prototypal solutions, ranging from those built in densely urbanized settings—settings with public financial support—to those in suburban areas developed under private ownership. There are many examples of work closely resembling those chosen which were excluded to avoid redundancy. We apologize to those architects and planners whose work, though pertinent, was passed over, and most especially, to those who took time to respond to our questionnaire at length and to assemble illustrative plans and data. No little time was spent agonizing over which projects to include. Those who do not find their work illustrated may find, nevertheless, that their ideas contributed significantly to the formulation of our defensible space hypothesis.

TABLE 12

Categorization of Defensible Space Prototypes

Density	*Project*	*Type*	*Size*	*Location*
High				
170 units/acre (80 units/acre)	Riverbend Houses	inner city, lower-middle-income	624 units 3.7 acres (108 units 1.3 acres)	New York, New York
Medium				
50 units/acre	North Beach Place	inner city, low-income, public	229 units 4.6 acres	San Francisco, California
37 units/acre	St. Francis Square	inner city, lower-middle-income	299 units 8.2 acres	San Francisco, California
30 units/acre	LaClede Town	inner city, middle-income	680 units 22.7 acres	St. Louis, Missouri
Low				
18 units/acre	Hyde Park (Row Housing)	inner city, middle-income	270 units 15 acres	Chicago, Illinois
16 units/acre	The Californian	suburban, upper-middle-income	190 units 12 acres	Tustin, California
12 units/acre	Easter Hill Village	suburban, low-income, public	300 units 25 acres	Richmond, California
7 units/acre	Tower Hill	suburban, middle-income	44 units 6.3 acres	St. Louis County, Missouri

Another criterion used in the selection of projects was to choose the simple rather than complex. Projects were intended to read primarily as direct statements of prototypal defensible space designs. Many other solutions, incorporating identical security features, were encumbered by other features of a compositional or amenable nature. We have reluctantly excluded them in favor of predominantly security-oriented examples, because we felt their other qualities detracted from the thesis we wish to present. Finally, it should be kept in mind that the extent of the success of the illustrated projects in inhibiting crime and improving security has not yet been fully measured. They are discussed here because they embody many self-evident features and have a general history of low crime rates in comparison with other projects of similar density, occupancy, and location. A full-scale, scientific measurement of their success and failure, and the way in which the different components of their design contribute to the defensibility of the overall project, will have to wait for the completion of our studies over the next few years.

RIVERBEND HOUSES, NEW YORK

Riverbend Houses in Manhattan is a State and federally financed, low-middle-income housing project, totaling 624 units, built at a density of 170 units to the acre with parking facilities provided at 0.4 cars per unit. It is located in Harlem, between 138th and 142nd Streets, and is bordered by Fifth Avenue on the west and Harlem River Drive on the east. This section of Harlem, just north of the Puerto Rican ghetto, suffers a felony rate roughly three times the New York City average.

Riverbend residents are 98 percent black and include many civil servants. The rental charges are not sufficient to permit the use of doormen, yet the project has suffered only six burglaries and muggings since its opening in October 1968. A variety of security features have been incorporated in the design of the project which together contribute significantly to its defensibility. Many of these features are common to recently constructed projects and will be discussed at length. However, there are two principal components in the design of Riverbend which are nearly unique to the American architectural vocabulary and which, acting in

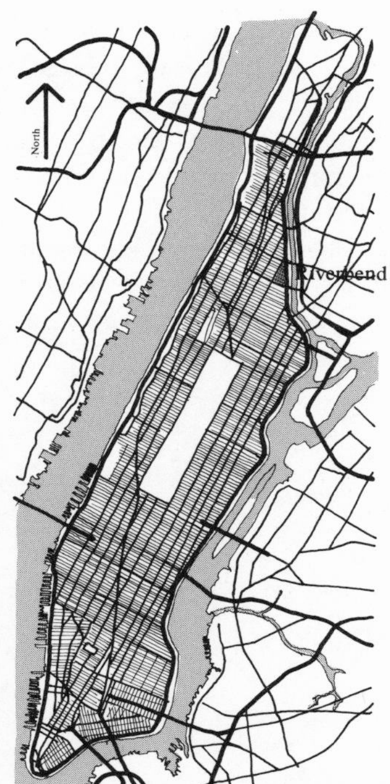

FIG. 87. Location map—Riverbend Houses, New York

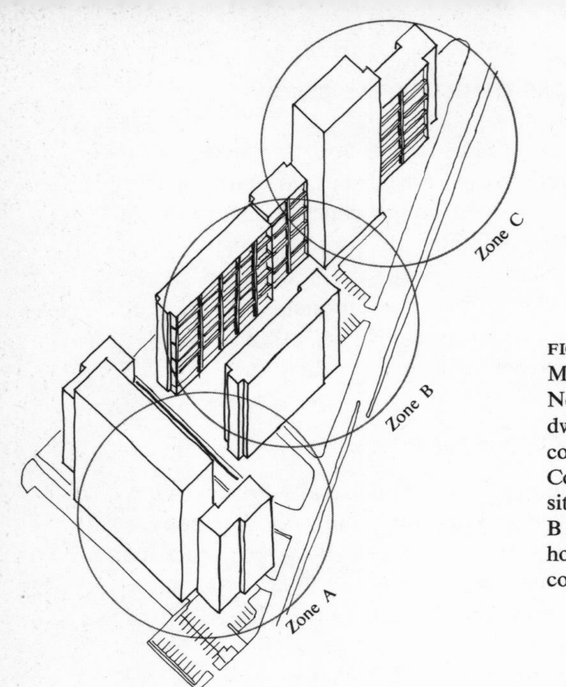

FIG. 88. Site Plan of Riverbend Houses, Manhattan. Architects: Davis and Brody, New York. Prototype of high-density (170 dwelling units per acre), low-middle-income housing in an inner-city locale (East Coast). For purpose of discussion, the site has been divided into three zones. Zone B contains the slabs of "piggy-back" row-house units served by single-loaded open corridors.

concert with the other security devices commonly employed in high-rise, urban apartment buildings, combine to give this project its remarkable safety record. One of these features operates at the scale of the individual dwelling unit and involves the way in which the apartment has been disposed, relative to its access corridor; the second functions at the scale of the project site plan and involves the positioning of the high-rise, single-loaded corridor slabs in relation to each other, the intervening shared grounds, and the surrounding urban fabric.

The Riverbend development contains three different residential prototypes within it: the traditional high-rise double-loaded corridor apartment building; the single-loaded corridor high-rise building; and a building composed of two-story duplex apartments, piled five-high upon each other for a total height of ten stories. The unique security features at Riverbend relate to this latter prototype: the duplex apartment slabs (sometimes called "piggy-back" row houses) and their disposition with respect to each other. For discussion, the Riverbend site plan has been divided into three zones: A, B, and C. Zone B, containing the piggy-back apartments is the most successful of the three, from the point of view of defensible space design.

Access to apartment units in Zone B is from a common lobby at the street level, from these by elevator to a floor lobby, then along an open sidewalk leading to the units. At the entry to each two-story apartment unit, one is required to walk up a few steps and pass through an individual outdoor patio that leads to the door of the apartment itself. A common

FIG. 89. View of two-story apartments at Riverbend. Note steps which separate patios from walkway. (Photo by Norman McGrath, courtesy of Davis, Brody & Associates)

FIG. 90. Ground-floor plan of duplex apartments and view along outside walkways.

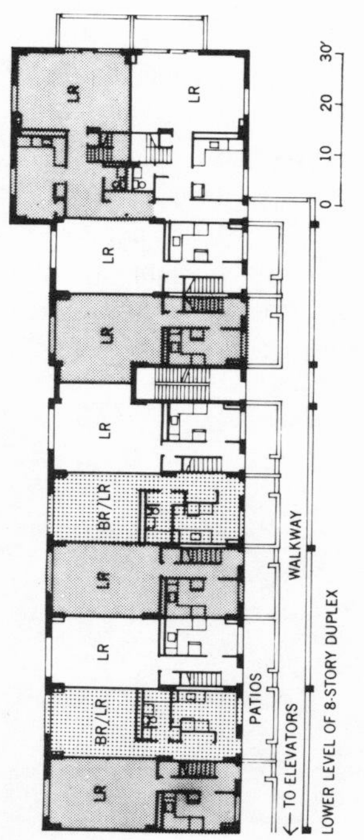

playground and community area is situated between the two slabs of duplex apartments, and is constructed on the roof deck of a two-story garage. This play deck is separated from the surrounding city streets and is accessible only from within the project by elevator from the lobby. Zone B is so designed that the outdoor access corridors to the units of both of the two ten-story slabs face each other across this common recreation deck.

The living room, dining room, and kitchen are on the lower of each unit's two levels. A staircase in the apartment interior leads to the bedrooms and bathrooms on the second level. Both bedroom and living room levels within the unit look onto the outdoor access corridor. Surveillance of public spaces within the building is simple and routine. The corridor and lobbies at each floor are always open to view from the units across the common courtyard, and from the ground below.

Entrance to each apartment patio and unit requires a ceremonial climbing of three steps. These three steps symbolically demarcate the semiprivate terrain of the family patio. The patio itself is screened by a wall which is six-feet high from the corridor side, but only four-feet high from the internal patio side. Anyone ascending the steps and entering the patio space intrudes into the territorial bounds of a particular family; a stranger's presence in this area requires immediate explanation. No loitering is tolerated here, except by the immediate family and its friends. It should also be noted that anyone climbing the steps and entering the patio is easily seen from the interior of the unit.

The access corridor itself serves as many as ten units on each side of the elevator lobby, yet is identified by tenants as a semiprivate space shared by these families. Residents and friends do pass time in the corri-

FIG. 91. The Play Deck at Riverbend. View of play deck above the parking area at Riverbend. Excellent surveillance is provided by the surrounding building both from the outside corridor and from within the units. The area is defined as semiprivate in that it is accessible only from within the buildings. (Photo by author)

dor, but an unrecognized individual who loiters too long, or who hesitates in making his intentions clear, comes under immediate surveillance and into question. If he persists, a direct encounter will occur, either with a resident or with a resident-alerted guard or superintendent.

Where the hierarchy of defined private and semiprivate areas is a key factor in this design, the surveillance potential created is equally significant. The arrangement of the two high-rise slabs (containing the duplex apartments) is such that their outside corridors face each other across the common play area, allowing residents to easily and casually monitor the comings and goings of people on all the floors of the opposite slab. From within a unit, a resident is only able to monitor his patio and a small portion of the corridor serving his own apartment, but, on the other hand, he can take in at a glance all the activity on the corridors of the opposite slab. If he shares a common concern with his neighbor opposite, he is in a good position to do him a service. As it is, a system of mutual assistance has grown up, based primarily on the sharing of a common and centrally located play deck.

Residents state that they recognize by sight but do not necessarily know all members of families in the slabs opposite. It is interesting to note that while they usually know the people on their own floor by name, they can only recognize a few of the families living on the other floors of their own building. Because people are in a better position to carry out monitoring and surveillance from the slabs opposite, it becomes all the more imperative that the two slabs achieve some mutual definition of territory and shared concern. Hence the territorial significance of the commonly shared central play area.

There is one important criticism to be made of the design of the patio and corridor system: surveillance activity inherent in this design would be greatly facilitated if the wall that bounds the individual apartment patios were somewhat lowered or constructed as open screens rather than solid walls. It is doubtful that this would seriously interfere with the privacy potential of the individual patios, and it would markedly improve the light and sun penetration into the patio. More importantly, the lowering of the patio wall would allow tenants in adjacent apartments and in the slab opposite to see a bit more into that area of the patio where a burglar can now hide himself while attempting to force a living room window. It would also allow residents to naturally and easily observe from the interior of their units the comings and goings of people along greater lengths of their own corridors, as well as along the corridors of the opposite slab. It has been suggested that the decision to place bars on the windows of the patio was primarily based on a recognition of the criminal opportunities created by the solid wall defining the patio.

The economics of Riverbend do not allow for doormen at the individual entries. Instead, four security guards patrol the project in two shifts from 4:00 in the afternoon until 8:00 in the morning. It is unpatrolled during the day. Riverbend's success, therefore, depends mostly on its physical design and offers an excellent example of a low-income residential development which cannot support the expense of a doorman.

Other Riverbend features contribute to its success as an example of defensible space design. The number of entrances to the Riverbend complex is limited to four. All are tied to city streets. Three lead directly off of Fifth Avenue, an intensively used vehicular and pedestrian artery. The fourth leads into the project from Harlem River Drive, but is seldom used.

An intercom system functions adequately, though not perfectly, to restrict access to the lobby and elevator area at each of the entries. The system suffers intermittent damage from impatient youngsters who have forgotten their keys. However, repair (or replacement of lock strike plates) usually follows in a day or two. It is interesting to note that no serious security breach has been found to have occurred during intervals when the lobby entry-door lock was broken. This has been credited to the strong security image that the project normally has.

An improvement could have been made to the door design that would have reduced the frequency of broken strike plates. Had the doors been made to swing open into the vestibule rather than into the lobby, the door's frame, rather than the lock's strike plate, would have been what held the door in place. Forcing a door open against its frame is a much more difficult task and would have resisted the occasional kick of an impatient youngster or determined intruder. The intercom itself is quite effective. Residents have been found to check identities carefully before opening the lobby door electrically from their apartments. Similarly, most residents make some effort at closing the entry doors behind them rather than letting strangers in simultaneously with their own entry.

The lobby and elevator waiting areas front on the street behind large plate glass panels. They are well lit and easily visible from both the street and vestibule. Residents and visitors preview these areas before they enter. Once in the lobby and waiting for the elevator, they are confident that they can be easily seen by both passing pedestrians and cruising vehicles on Fifth Avenue. People in the lobby feel that just as they can be seen, so would a mugger, and that this is an important deterrent.

Each elevator contains a closed circuit television camera housed in a corner to provide surveillance. It should be noted that the television screen does not scan the entire internal area of the elevator, and it is possible for as many as two discretely placed people to be standing in the elevator without registering on camera. The television camera can be monitored in the lobby before entering the elevator. If cable television comes into use at Riverbend, empty channels on home TV sets will also be employed to monitor the elevators.

Anyone now entering or leaving an elevator must pass before the

FIG. 92. Bordering Street at Riverbend. View north along Fifth Avenue showing close juxtaposition of building entries with street. Shops, because they are integral with the project, play an important security function during the daylight hours. (Photo by author)

FIG. 93. Vertical Circulation Cores at Riverbend. Elevator waiting areas at each level are well glazed so as to allow surveillance both from different levels in the interior of the project and from the street below. (Photo by author)

FIG. 94. Elevator Waiting Area at Typical Floor at Riverbend. The elevator waiting areas are well glazed so that activity within them is easily visible from the bordering streets and from elsewhere in the project. (Photo by author)

camera. While the cameras may be monitored in the management office or by security guards who happen to be in the lobby, their real effectiveness lies in the opportunities they create for casual observation by tenants. The elevator is no longer a secret space. Interestingly, there have been no instances of attempted camera vandalism since their installation in 1969.

The fire stairs at Riverbend are, for the most part, windowless, making them the one public area which cannot be easily monitored. There are two sets of such stairs in the terraced apartment slabs. One is located within the elevator core, and the other at the end of the corridor. The door at each level in the elevator core stair opens from either side, and this stair is used by residents who have only a floor or two to go up or down. The skip-stop elevator used at Riverbend is notoriously slow. A faster elevator would have provided potentially greater security by reducing stairway use, but was judged too expensive.

The second set of fire stairs is located at the end of the corridor of each slab. These stairs are intended primarily for emergencies. They can be entered at any floor but can only be left at street level. This is an important precautionary device, although we found the latch on some doors jammed. Both sets of fire stairs, as mentioned before, are windowless, except for a long strip of wired glass in each entry door. Fire regula-

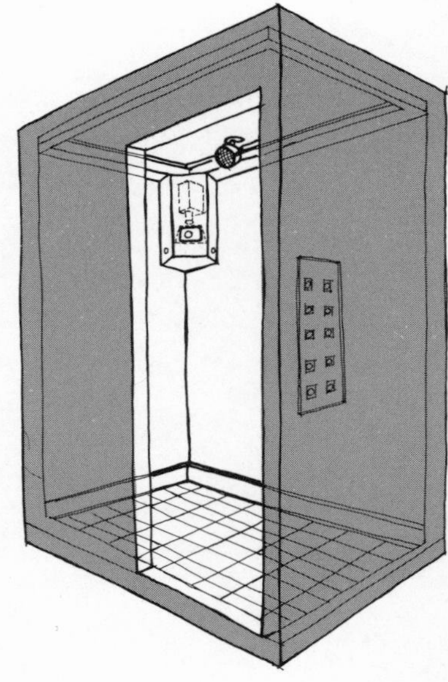

FIG. 95. TV-Monitored Elevators at Riverbend. Illustration of TV camera location and position of additional flood light in the elevators at Riverbend.

FIG. 96. Parking Areas at Riverbend. Half the parking area at Riverbend is covered by the play deck and proves the area most prone to theft and vandalism. (Photo by author)

tions make this a common practice in contemporary housing. Ten years ago, window walls at the mid-landing between floors were quite commonly provided.

Because of a parking requirement of 0.4 cars per unit on this restricted site, the architects at Riverbend located a parking level under the central recreation deck. Although access to the parking area is by key and is carefully restricted, there have been numerous reports of theft and vandalism. This is a common problem in all enclosed residential garages which do not employ attendants. Predictably, cars located in the area of the site where parking is exposed do not experience such problems.

As architects know, slabs composed of duplex apartments with open sidewalks in the air are not a unique design solution. This concept represents what was possibly the most common design for low-income housing used in Western Europe. England and Holland, in particular, have traditionally employed almost no other high-density prototype for family housing. The decision to employ this prototype in a contemporary American elevator-equipped high rise with patios, and achieving it all within the severe economic restraints of low-middle-income state-subsidized housing, is the unique contribution of the Davis and Brody firm. Riverbend was

FIG. 97. Single-Loaded Corridor Housing in Europe. This housing type, common to most Western European cities, is still in use today. (Photo by author)

designed for a upper monthly rent limit of thirty dollars per room, which is low for New York City. The additional cost of the single-loaded exposed corridor is tempered somewhat by the piggyback duplex-upon-duplex solution which requires a corridor only every second floor. This has allowed for the creation of the walkways and the "elevated patios."

Riverbend's other security features are noteworthy, but by no means unique to this complex. Together, however, they do succeed in providing a very secure environment for the tenant, without creating the fortress appearance common to high-rise middle-income developments. In addition, Riverbend enhances the safety of surrounding streets as well as contributing significantly to the safety of its residents.

In summary, Riverbend represents a most inventive solution to the creation of a defensible space environment in a situation where high density is mandatory. It is unfortunate that only Zone B of the entire site plan creates this environment. This zone contains 108 units of a total of 624. Where the entire project is built at 170 units to the acre, Zone B, if considered in isolation, would only provide 80 units to the acre—hardly what might be called extreme density.

It can, of course, be argued that the density could be increased if the terraced, two-story apartment units were stacked up a few more tiers. This suggestion suffers one serious restraint, the higher one goes the less visible are the open access corridors from the play deck below. The access corridors benefit from surveillance from the units in the opposite slab *and* from the play deck, so that the higher the building, the greater the angle made by the line of visual contact with the ground below. Thus, after six stories, one cannot see from the ground what is happening on the corridors above. In addition, added height tends to separate the upper units from important territorial association with the play area, and would possibly result in development of a detached attitude typical of most residents in high-rise buildings over six stories. The net result may very well be disassociation, not only from play grounds, but from neighbors who share these grounds.

Another repercusion of increased height is the anonymity produced by large numbers of tenants sharing a single building. Zone B at Riverbend, probably created more by the accident of peculiar site conditions than by intent, may be optimal just as it now is.

NORTH BEACH PLACE, SAN FRANCISCO

Located in the northeast section of San Francisco, between Coit Tower and Fisherman's Wharf, the 229-unit, 4.6-acre project is in a predominantly low-income residential area which includes some warehouses and industrial buildings. North Beach Place was designed as public housing and completed for occupancy in 1953. It is almost an exact replica of a late 1920s working-class housing prototype built by the more enlightened of city governments in Austria, England, and Holland. But for minor modifications, such as the provision of large parking areas, it is a perfect transplant, down to the decision to expose the form work on the raw concrete structure.

The project is a three-story walk-up, at a density of fifty units to the acre, and consists of slabs of buildings grouped in a horseshoe around common courtyards. The slabs are tied together at the ends by exposed stairs and access balconies at the second and third levels. The intervening courtyards are used alternately for parking and play areas.

The apartments on the second and third levels are reached via single-loaded corridors exposed to the weather. Open stairwells provide access to the upper levels and are located at the opposite ends of each courtyard, in close proximity to the two parallel streets which define the length of the project: Bay Street and Francisco Street.

Most ground-floor units are entered from the common interior

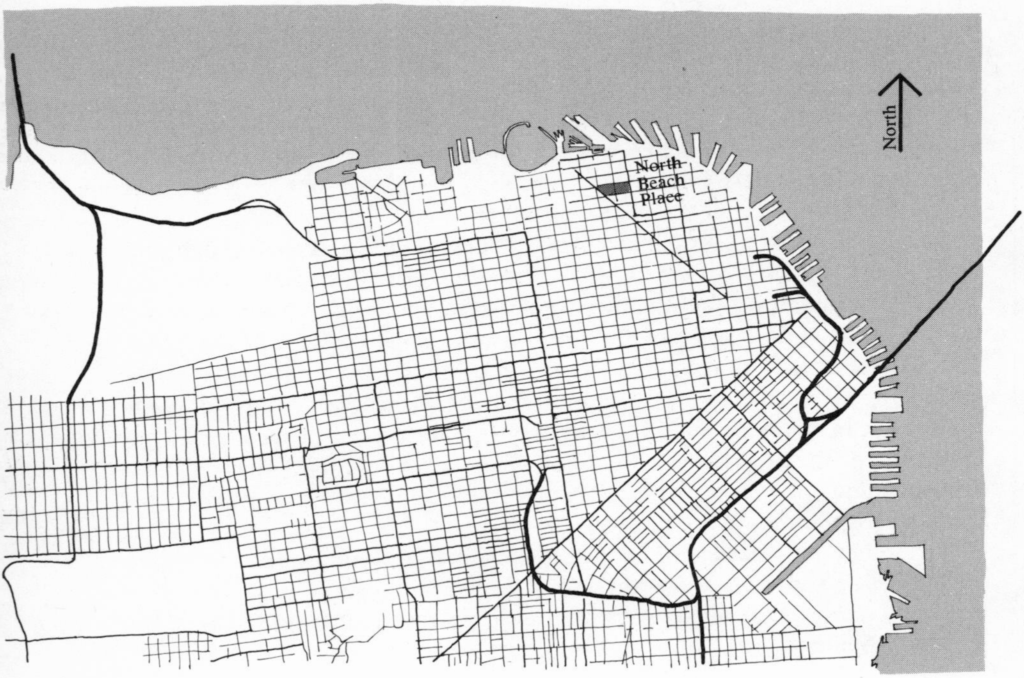

FIG. 98. Location map—North Beach Place, San Francisco

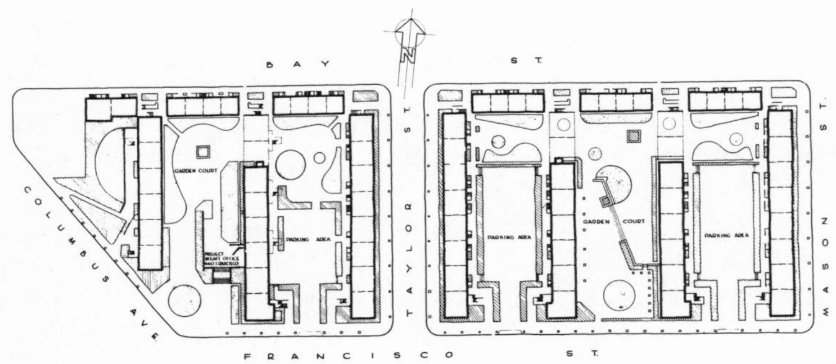

FIG. 99. Site Plan of North Beach Place. Architects: Gutterson and Born, San Francisco. Prototype of medium-density (50 dwelling units per acre), low-income housing in an inner-city locale (West Coast).

FIG. 100. View of North Beach Place looking east along Bay Street. Units face and open onto the sidewalk where the project borders surrounding streets. (Photo by author)

FIG. 101. U-Shaped Court at North Beach Place. The open corridors, serving the second and third floors of the apartment wings, face one another across a commonly shared entry court and parking area. (Photo by author)

FIG. 102. Exposed Vertical Access Stairs at North Beach Place. The vertical stairwells are open to surveillance and serve the additional function of symbolic portals defining the U-shaped courts. (Photo by author)

courtyard, although those ground units facing Bay Street are entered directly off the street.

The open corridors which provide access to the second- and third-story units face each other across a commonly shared entry court and parking area, and so share surveillance. As in Riverbend Houses, surveillance opportunities are reinforced by the fact that units face each other across a territorially defined and collectively used area.

The stair towers at the Francisco Street side of the project also serve to define the gateway to the courts, further symbolizing each court's, and the entire project's, restricted use. Whereas the placement of parking within the shared entry court was a significant decision in enhancing the security of both the units and the vehicles, the isolation of the play areas into a distinctly separate court seems to have worked out poorly. Although these play areas are, for the most part, fenced off from Francisco Street, they are, unfortunately, also isolated from the unit entries. In addition, the windows facing the play court are small, there is no access to the court directly from the units, and almost no passage of adult residents through the area.

A particularly fascinating feature of the project's design is that the ground-floor units along Bay Street enter directly off the sidewalk. This is a somewhat unique occurrence, since the ground-floor units of walk-up buildings have been designed to open to the grounds immediately in front of them, almost independently of what has been placed above. They were designed as if they were single-family houses within a row-house configuration. This feature serves to provide the Bay Street side of the project with surveillance and territorial identity, where the Francisco Street side has neither.

In order to provide a transition and buffer zone for the doors to the ground-floor units on Bay Street, the entry areas have been set back a

FIG. 103. Play Courts at North Beach Place. In contrast to the entry and parking courts, the play courts are poorly defined and are not easily accessible to residents. The only mechanism for surveillance is the apartment windows facing down on the play area. However there is no direct way of entering the play court from the entries to the individual apartment units and no sharing of circulation routes. (Photo by author)

FIG. 104. Street-Oriented Apartments, North Beach Place. Territorially defined through changes in texture and color of paving; raised stoop; glazed door and window; and overhang from balcony above.

few feet from the street, defined by a low wall, a set of steps, and a landing turned at right angles to the street. Textured brick has been used to differentiate the ground surface area immediately adjacent to the building, contrasting sharply with the cement sidewalk of the rest of the block. Combined with the steps and landing, the whole serves to create a semi-private zone adjacent to the entry door which clearly will not tolerate ambiguous use or loitering. As a further surveillance feature, the entry has been constructed with a window that immediately abuts the door, thereby providing residents with an additional device for seeing out onto the street and the entry landing area.

Although the entries off Bay Street have been singled out for special comment, it may not be possible to transpose the ground-floor apartment units as designed in the North Beach area to high-crime areas in other cities. However, by providing a further setback from the street, and with additional symbolic, territory-defining devices to improve the buffer area between the windows and entry and the streets on which they face, the design might be made workable even in Manhattan. A protective grill for ground-floor windows might, however, prove an additional necessity. While the physical layout of the project exhibits excellent defensible space features, the aesthetic treatment of the buildings leaves much to be desired. Tenants complain of the mean quality of the exposed concrete surfacing. While it may be delightful to an architect, to the residents and housing authority it represents a factory or bunker aesthetic.

The most staggering realization to come from our comparison of residential developments is that the ill-fated Pruitt-Igoe housed a population of no greater density than North Beach. Both were built at fifty dwellings per acre, but Pruitt-Igoe at far greater cost per unit.

ST. FRANCIS SQUARE, SAN FRANCISCO

St. Francis Square is a medium-density, low-middle-income housing project built to be occupied by working-class families in cooperative ownership. It is located in what used to be a low-income, relatively high-crime area in the city of San Francisco. The area is undergoing renewal and now finds itself surrounded on two sides by new upper-middle-income residential and commercial developments and on the other two sides by a public housing project and an old, deteriorating residential section. The project is composed entirely of three-story walk-up garden apartments.

Defensible space design operates at St. Francis Square both at the scale of the apartment unit clustering and in the overall site plan. Although the project is built at thirty-seven units to the acre, with .75 parking spaces per unit, the architects have been able to capture the feeling of a spacious but well-scaled single-family row-house development.

The project's site plan consists of three playing squares, defined on all four sides by a block of building, and separated from other squares by parking. Each building block contains two to five double units. A double

FIG. 105. Location map—St. Francis Square, San Francisco

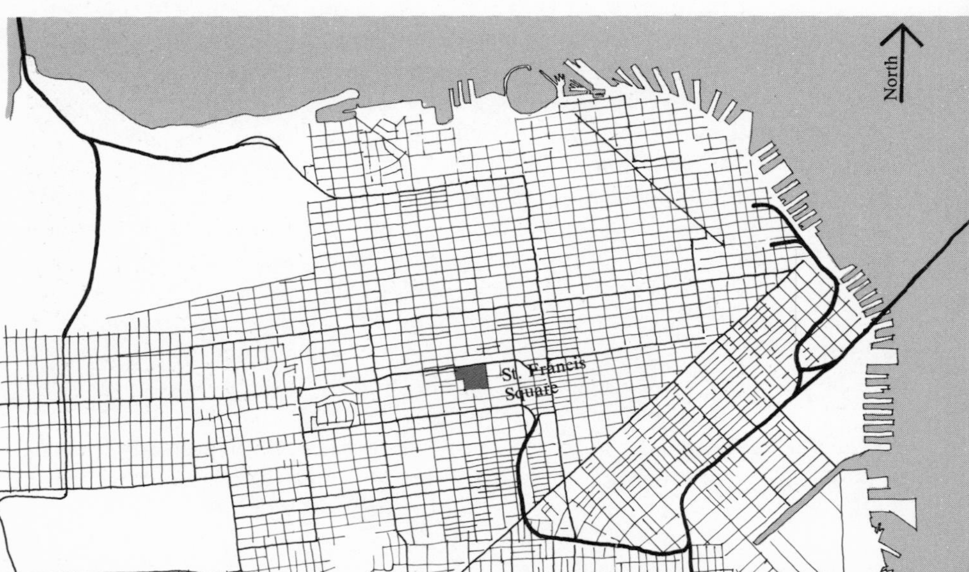

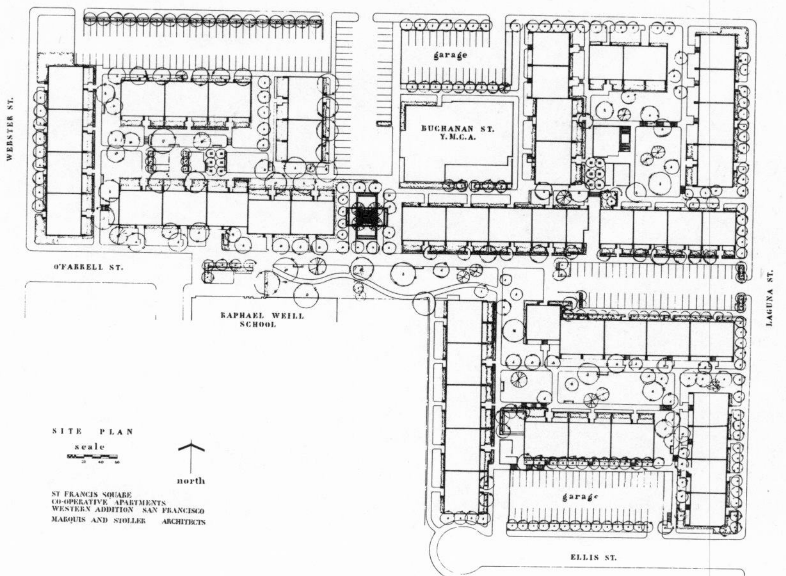

FIG. 106. Site plan of St. Francis Square Apartments, San Francisco. Architects: Marquis and Stoller. Built in 1969; 299 apartments in three-story building blocks. Prototype of medium-density (37 dwelling units per acre), lower-middle-income housing in an inner-city locale (West Coast).

FIG. 107. Aerial View of St. Francis Square. The three-story building blocks consist of a series of attached units in which six apartments share a common entry. The building blocks are grouped to surround play courts. (Photo by author)

FIG. 108. Interior Court at St. Francis Square. The interior play courts are accessible from the street and from the apartment buildings. To provide surveillance, some unit entries open onto these courts, while other entries face the street. (Photo by author)

unit consists of two, three-story tiers of flats, side by side. The two tiers, or six apartments, share a common entrance path, entry door, lobby, and stairway. The second vertical fire-exit stair is provided as a fire escape connecting the third-floor balcony to the second-floor balcony; it is assumed that in an emergency, residents will jump down the remaining distance to the ground.

With only six families sharing an entry, most people speak of the stair and lobby as an extension of their private dwellings. The fact that the architects also chose to further distinguish those six-family units by stepping them back and forth and down the hillside also contributes to unit definition and to the residents' proprietary attitudes. Tenants tend to refer to the six-family unit as "my house."

To meet fire codes, the entry to each unit is separated from the stairwell by a door and vestibule. These serve to provide a distinctive transitional buffer area which separates and defines the entry to each apartment. A second exit from each tier of six apartments leads to the rear of the building and is a weak point in the defensibility of this space and of the project as a whole. This vulnerability is somewhat mitigated in some building blocks by rear gardens, which provide a buffer for the rear exits.

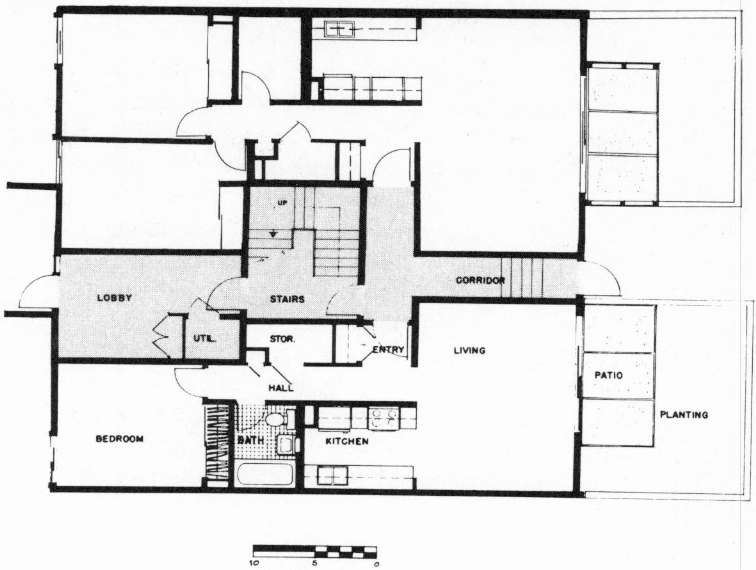

FIG. 109. Ground-Floor Plan of Two Units sharing a Common Entry at St. Francis Square. Three levels of two apartments per floor, together share a common entrance path, entry door, lobby, stairway, and corridor to the rear play courts.

FIG. 110. View of the Individualized Entries at St. Francis Square. The individuality of each six-family unit is further emphasized by the way the architects have stepped them in and out and up and down the hillside. (Photo by author)

Front and rear exits seem positioned in an inconsistent manner. Front lobbies are located interchangeably: off surrounding streets, off parking lots, and off the interior play courts. Rear entries, while never located to face surrounding streets, do lead from both parking lots and play courts. This inconsistency may contribute to the defensible space of St. Francis Square in that the court areas are not fenced off. Clearly, the most important decision was to position as many entries as possible facing surrounding streets. This serves to define the project and ensure the safety of both the streets and apartment units. In this light, however, the positioning of three parking areas on Geary Boulevard was most unfortunate. The decision to allow the interior playing areas to be accessible from the street, rather than from the apartment buildings only, may have required that some unit entries face these courts, if only to provide surveillance. The same reasoning may be applied to the justification of the design of the parking areas.

Yet a more consistent and possibly safer design might have evolved from the adoption of the Anselivicus-Montgomery site-plan rationale employed in the St. Louis Tower Hill project, discussed later in this chapter. Here, parking and play courts are combined into one common area; the front entries to all these units also face onto this area. Application of this design principle would require alteration of the St. Francis Square project only where building blocks face adjoining streets. All entry lobbies would then face the street, rather than the rear parking and play area; the play courts would be fenced off and accessible only from within the building.

St. Francis Square resembles The Californian project in Tustin, an upper-middle-income project (also discussed later in this chapter), in

FIG. 111. Play Court at St. Francis Square. The architects have given careful consideration to means for humanizing and enriching the environment. Concrete paving has been textured in different ways and broken up with brick; trees have been planted to break up the paving areas; earth fill has been used to create a variety of changes in level. (Photo by author)

that the architects endeavored to subdivide the grounds into a hierarchy ranging from public to private spaces. However, St. Francis Square is distinctly different in that most areas are territorially defined for the use of particular inhabitants and are readily surveyable by them, at each level in the hierarchy. This lack, we will see, is a grave failure in the design of The Californian.

At thirty-seven units to the acre, including parking, the St. Francis Square design is an incredibly impressive solution to medium-density low-income housing. Many low-income housing developments built to answer similar densities are conceived as high-rise elevator solutions. St. Francis Square challenges the justification of ever having to do this again. The project answers almost all of the requirements of defensible space design: it defines territorial areas and paths of transition from public to private; it provides for easy and natural surveillance of public areas; communal amenities are located in public areas to create a casual association that defends commonly shared pursuits and focuses surveillance; the number of families sharing an entry is limited to six; and finally, the image of the project is that of a single-family row-house development. Not at all bad for low-income housing.

LACLEDE TOWN, ST. LOUIS

LaClede Town is a low- to middle-income housing project in the Mill Creek urban renewal area of St. Louis's inner core. It was financed under a Federal Housing Assistance Program 221(d)3. LaClede Town contains a mix of row housing and three-story walk-up garden apartments densely grouped at thirty units to the acre. Parking has been provided for 1.25 automobiles per dwelling unit.

All units face immediately onto a pedestrian and vehicular street leading into the existing street grid of St. Louis. Cars are parked near unit entries, at right angles to the curb. Parked cars, front doors, front walks, sidewalks, and street share in the security of joint and mutual surveillance. Residents within the building can easily observe whatever happens on the sidewalk, street, parking area, and areas immediately in front of their houses. Similarly, passing vehicles and pedestrians can observe these areas, and they are easily accessible to formal police patrols.

Semiprivate and community spaces are located at the rear of the dwellings. The building units themselves define these areas by encircling them. These semiprivate spaces are not fenced off from public access, but the limited number of entry portals serve as symbols to indicate that they are the more private zones of the project.

A small, raised, patio deck, bordered by two low walls, further defines the rear entry to the two- and three-story row houses. The patio

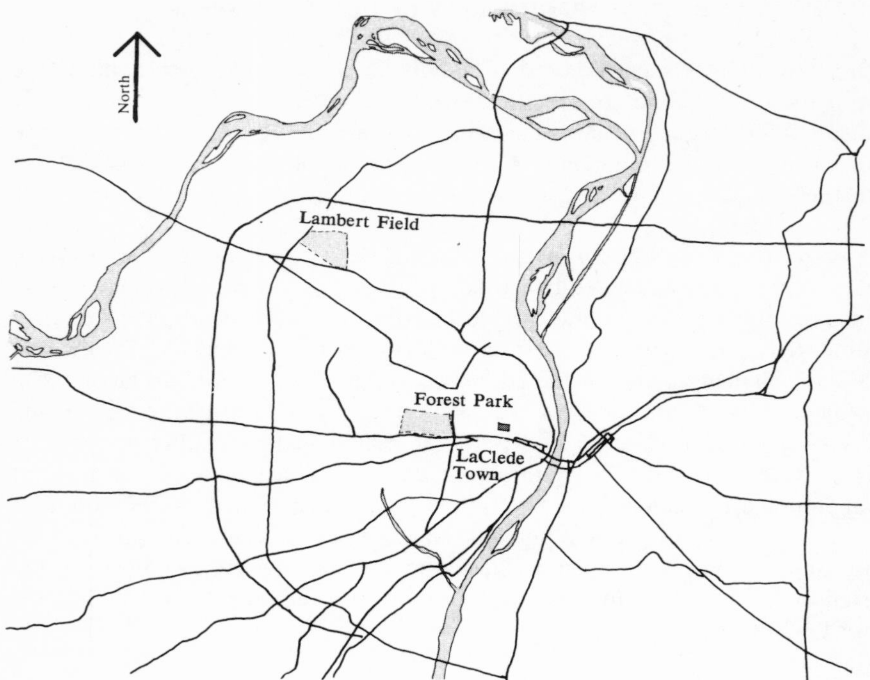

FIG. 112. Location map—LaClede Town, St. Louis, Missouri

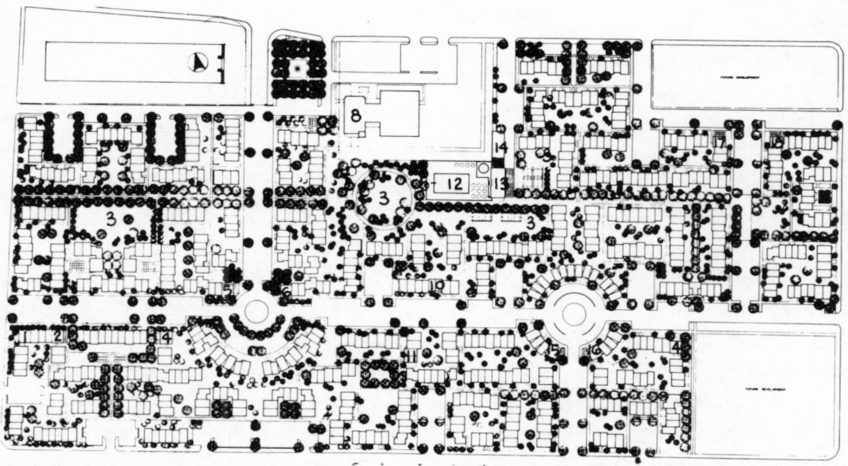

FIG. 113. Site Plan of LaClede Town, St. Louis. Architects: Clothiel Smith and Associates, Washington, D. C. Built in 1965; two- and three-story buildings. Prototype of middle-density (30 dwelling units per acre), low-middle-income housing in an inner-city locale (Midwest). LaClede Town's 680 units of 221d3 housing are primarily in two- and three-bedroom sizes (although there are also units of one and four bedrooms. Among the units are numerous nonresidential uses—an English-style pub (far left), a delicatessen (top left), and an art gallery (bottom left). Guide to LaClede Town's facilities (see map above): 1 office; 2 delicatessen; 3 play areas; 4 laundromats; 5 pub; 6 coffee shop; 7 dry cleaner; 8 church; 9 park; 10 newspaper office; 11 art gallery; 12 wading and swimming pools; 13 bath house; 14 maintenance; 15 radio school; 16 confectionery; 17 hair-dresser; 18 ladies clothing.

FIG. 114. Street at LaClede Town. View down one of the vehicular arteries. Note how streets, parking and lighting are in juxtaposition to front entries, providing mutual security. (Photo by Bob Williams)

serves a variety of private family functions, but operates predominantly to distinguish the private outside space adjacent to the unit from the semi-private, common rear yards.

A similar mechanism defines the territory of the walk-up garden apartments. Entry is from a common court defined by changes in level, texture, and lighting, and by the grouping of a small cluster of units. A semirestrictive semiprivate zone is thus created. The design further facilitates surveillance of the entry court both from the street and from the units themselves.

FIG. 115. Interior Common at LaClede Town. The semiprivate commons are located at the rear of the dwelling units. Individual two- and three-story row-house units also have a concrete patio and low fence which separate the rear entry from the adjoining commons. Access to the commons from the street is restricted to a few portals. The grouping of the units to define the commons further declares this space to be semiprivate. (Photo by Bob Williams)

Variations in surface texture and color articulate each row house and garden apartment in LaClede Town, producing an ambiance of privacy, individuality, and security. The architects have also occasionally stepped back individual units within a long row-house block, or mixed three- and four-story units in with two-story units. Their intention was to give the whole project a spontaneous feeling, as if private row houses had sprung up individually on the site over time. The resulting pattern is not dissimilar to the effect created naturally in the older neighborhoods of our cities, where individual families alter buildings and fronts to suit their own evolving needs and tastes.

HYDE PARK, CHICAGO

The Hyde Park row-housing proposals of Harry Weese and I. M. Pei are interesting examples of defensible space prototypes for small-scale, medium- to low-density redevelopment within an older existing urban fabric. The projects of both architects are designed at approximately

FIG. 116. Location map—Hyde Park, Kenwood Development, Chicago, Illinois

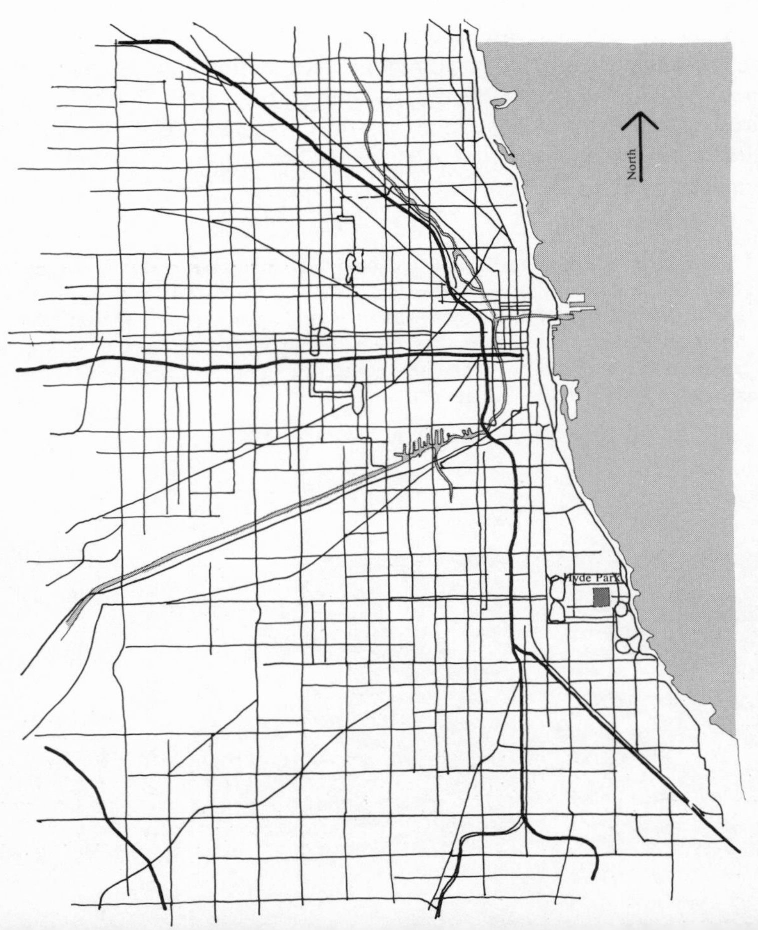

eighteen units to the acre. They consist of row-house developments which follow the existing grid of Chicago streets, except for the provision of off-street parking areas and the removal of the rear alleys to create a common community court. These courts are entered predominantly from the rear of the dwellings and serve the activity of some twenty-five to thirty families.

The units are disposed on their site in a manner similar to the patterns of an older neighboring single-family residential development. They have been provided with a formal entry area, immediately off the sidewalk, defined by low walls, a paved walk, and a set of stairs which leads a half flight up to the ground-floor level. These devices serve to designate very clearly the ten feet in front of the dwelling, and to put this area under the zone of influence of its occupants. Activities on the street

FIG 117. Site Plan of Hyde Park, Kenwood Development, Chicago, Illinois. Architects: I. M. Pei and Associates, New York; Harry Weese and Associates, Chicago. The project consists of a mix of high-rise and two-story row-house buildings. (Our concern is with the low units only.) Prototype of small-scale, middle-density (row-house units are built at 18 dwelling units per acre), middle-income urban renewal housing in an inner-city locale (Midwest). (Courtesy of the architect)

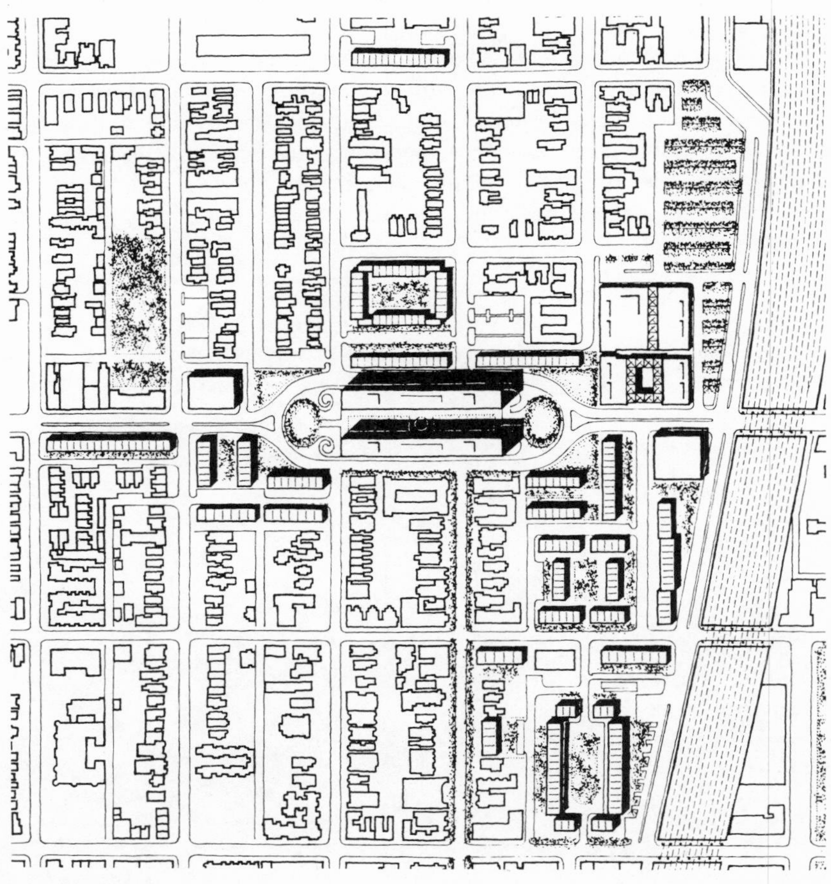

FIG. 118. Row-House Street at Hyde Park, Kenwood (Harry Weese designed cluster). Individual units have been given a ceremonial entrance marked by a small grass front lawn, fences, stairs, and a vestibule. (Photo by author)

are easily monitored from the dwelling units proper and from passing vehicles.

The dwellings group around a common interior play area and community court which, in the case of the Weese design, is also accessible from the public street through a one-story opening in what is otherwise a perfectly enclosed square. The I. M. Pei design, which does not use buildings to totally encircle the square, employs an eight-foot wrought iron fence to complete the encirclement. In both cases, the interior courts are open to public use. Where neighboring children and adults do avail themselves of the recreation facilities in these courts, they clearly come under the surveillance and zone of influence of the immediately surrounding residents.

FIG. 119. Rear Court at Hyde Park, Kenwood (Harry Weese designed cluster). View of enclosed common court used for play and seating. Access is from all individual units and from a few portals which lead to the street. (Photo by author)

FIG. 120. Access Portal to Interior Court at Hyde Park, Kenwood (Harry Weese designed cluster). The gates are kept open during the day to allow neighboring children entry and are closed at night to limit accessibility. (Photo by author)

FIG. 121. Rear Court of Alternate Scheme, Hyde Park, Kenwood (I. M. Pei designed cluster). Attractive fencing demarcates interior court area in the Pei plan. (Photo by author)

The rear of each unit is separated from the common rear play areas by a patio defined by six-foot-high wooden and brick fencing, sometimes totally enclosing the rear space, and at other times allowing the one side facing the common patio to remain open.

The off-street parking area is provided with resident surveillance by the positioning of units so that the front doors face this area. Unfortunately, unlike the LaClede Town proposal, the off-street parking area is removed from, rather than directly on, a through street and so does not benefit from this additional form of potential surveillance.

THE CALIFORNIAN, TUSTIN, CALIFORNIA

The Californian is a newly completed twelve-acre residential community in southern Los Angeles. It is a privately developed low-medium-density project, built at sixteen units to the acre—a higher rate than surrounding development which varies from four to ten units per acre.

The project is located at the outskirts of Tustin, a small town near Santa Ana, with a relatively low crime rate, even for Los Angeles. The design of the project—the individual units, their grouping and site plan—closely follows the directives and schematic prototypes developed by Chermayeff and Alexander in their book, *Community and Privacy*.

The scheme is included here for discussion, not so much for its defensible space attributes (they are very much wanting), but because it appears to be accomplishing something similar. To the uninitiated, the differences may not be immediately apparent. All the more reason, therefore, that they be discerned.

In essence, this is a design for an internalized pedestrian community, surrounded on three sides by its own parking, and sealed off from adjacent city streets. Chermayeff and Alexander, in their treatise, strove to create a community subdivided into a hierarchy of increasingly more private zones. At the most private level, the single-family unit was de-

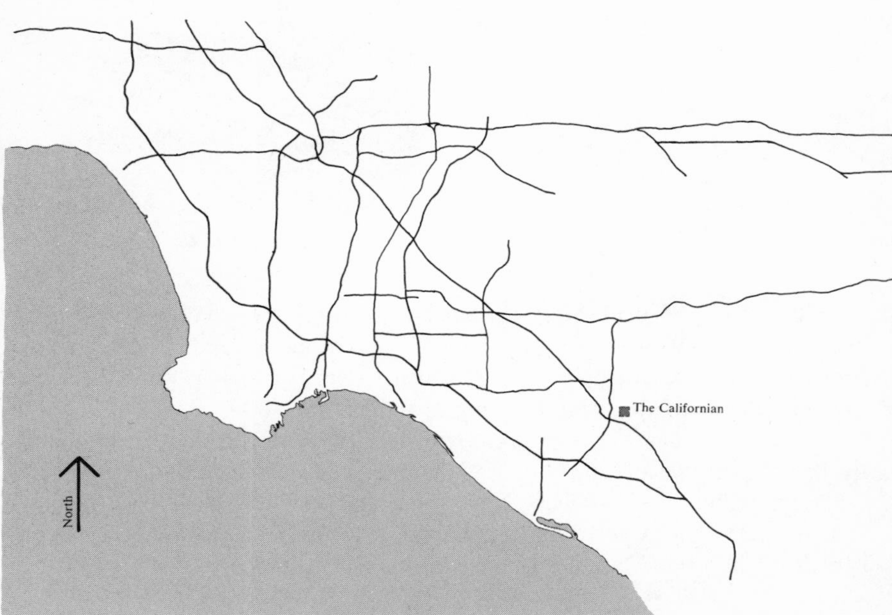

FIG. 122. Location map—The Californian, Tustin, California (Los Angeles)

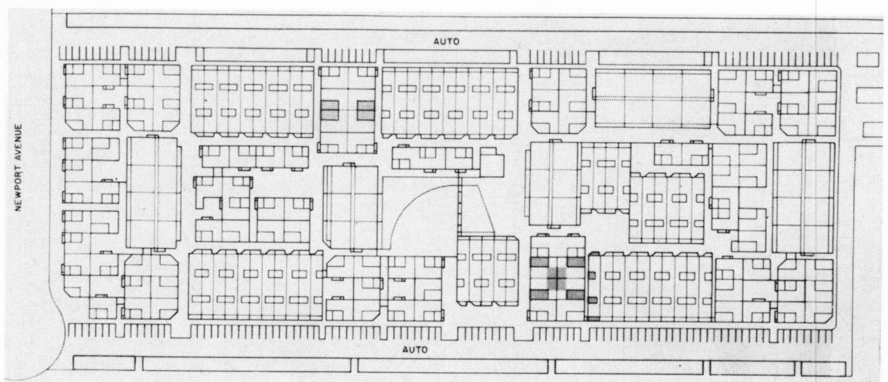

FIG. 123. Site Plan of The Californian, Los Angeles. Architects: Bachen, Arrigoni and Ross, San Francisco. Prototype of low-density (16 dwelling units per acre), upper-middle-income housing in a suburban locale (West Coast). (Courtesy of *Progressive Architecture*)

FIG. 124. Interior View of The Californian. Aerial view of The Californian clustering showing one- and two-story units around access paths and courts. (Photo by author)

FIG. 125. Street View of The Californian. View of The Californian from the only side of the project which faces any public streets. (Photo by author)

signed around its own enclosed courtyard. As a result, few windows, except those in the second-story apartments, look out onto the adjacent walks or courts. The intermediary subdivisions of the hierarchy share collective walks and courts in a variety of combinations. Major recreation and community facilities for the entire project—a pool, adult play area, community center, and rental office—are centrally located.

The intentional separation of vehicular from pedestrian traffic has resulted in isolated parking areas and pedestrian paths, both devoid of surveillance opportunities. This configuration, coupled with the windowless internal pedestrian streets, requires residents to walk from parking area to home through an almost totally unsurveyed no-man's-land.

The architects, like Alexander and Chermayeff, were primarily concerned with defining and enhancing the privacy of the individual dwelling unit. The designation of a hierarchy of semipublic and semiprivate spaces remains little more than designation, since the subdivisions are unsupported by physical or social opportunity to enforce their hierarchy, except at the level of the individual unit. The semipublic and semiprivate spaces may have been designed for the use of certain geographical subgroups, but there are few windows, restrictive portals, or formally designated agents to act as the natural or authoritative surveying bodies. Proximity is the only mechanism which even begins to suggest a definition of the intended users of these collective and semiprivate spaces. The decision to make the private dwelling inward-looking has removed much of the opportunity for natural surveillance and for other associated claims to area influence.

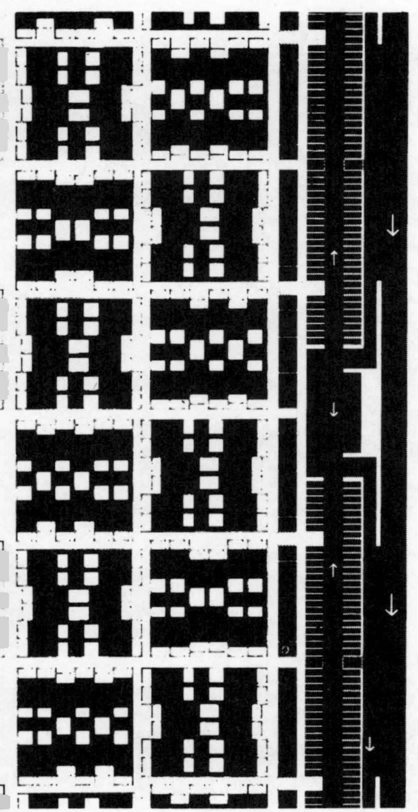

FIG. 126. Site Plan from *Community and Privacy*. The site plan of The Californian closely follows the principles and schematic designs developed by Chermayeff and Alexander in their book, *Community and Privacy*. (Reprinted, by permission, from *Community and Privacy* by Serge Chermayeff and Christopher Alexander. Copyright 1963 by Serge Chermayeff. Reproduced by permission of Doubleday & Company, Inc.)

FIG. 127. View of Project Parking Area, The Californian. In order to create a total pedestrian environment within the project, the parking has been limited to the periphery of grounds. Parking is totally dissociated from units. (Photo by author)

FIG. 128. Pool and main communal area at The Californian. (Photo by author)

FIG. 129. View of Interior Courts and Entry to One-Story Units at The Californian. The separation of vehicular from pedestrian paths, coupled with windowless internal pedestrian streets requires residents to walk from parking area to home along almost totally unsurveyed paths. (Photo by author)

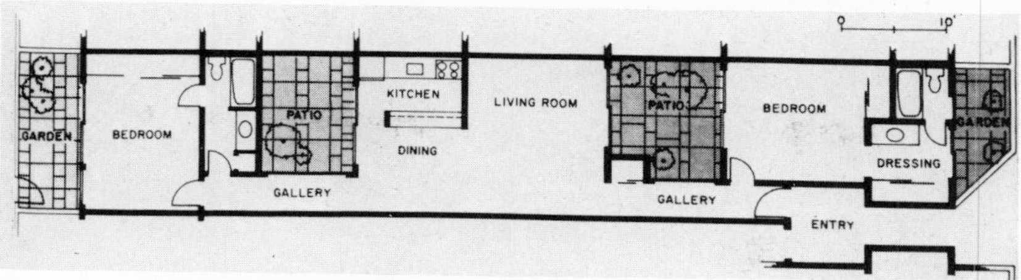

FIG. 130. Plan of ground-floor unit, The Californian

FIG. 131. Access Paths and Individual Court Entry at The Californian. Walkways are under little if any surveillance from within the dwelling units and are in no contact with surrounding public streets. An occasional second-story window will look down on a walk below. The courtyard, shown through the open door, is inward facing and serves most of a dwelling unit's windows. (Photo by author)

FIG. 132. View of Typical Street and Dwellings Bordering The Californian in Tustin, California. The standard dwellings which make up most residential development in Tustin may actually provide more security to both units and street. The positioning of entries and walks directly on the street provides a superior opportunity for surveillance and territorial definition. (Photos by author)

By comparison, the typical suburban development bordering the project, shown in figure 132, benefits from street surveillance; it, in turn, benefits the street by providing surveillance from within. The positioning of entries and walks directly on the street extends territorial concern from dwelling unit to street. But for a few areas—an occasionally well-defined entry to paired apartment units and a stretch of two-story apartments looking out along a street—the project's space is totally undefined and "defenseless."

The authors have, in effect, strangely succeeded in giving the total project the look and feel of a warehouse district on a Sunday. Everything is walled in, and there is no activity anywhere. The pursuit of privacy has produced large, outdoor public zones rivaling the interior corridors of high-rise, double-loaded apartment buildings. The design of public and semiprivate paths through the project is especially poor. No windows face the walks; surveillance is not routine. The self-contained image projected by these solid walls may imply to a casual stranger that it would be difficult to effect entry. In practice, however, this is not true. The walls of the unit courtyards are easy to scale. Once within the courtyard or vestibule serving two units, a criminal is hidden from outside view and can enter either unit at his leisure. In a high crime area, this project, with its unsurveyed parking areas, walks, and courtyards, would prove to be dangerously insecure.

In their concern for providing private realms, the authors of this scheme have ironically succeeded in creating low-density equivalents of the fortress-style high-rise, upper-income apartment buildings common to Eastern cities. Things may be safe within the walled confines of the individual unit, but once beyond these walls, one is clearly on his own; there is no attempt at extending territorial responsibility. Interestingly, the equivalent of the dangerous, anonymous public streets surrounding high-rise developments in New York are found in the internal pedestrian walls of this California project. One walks there, cut off from all contact with life—a situation not unlike the experience of the internal corridors of high-rise public housing developments.

The Californian is perhaps the best testament to the necessity of linking territorial definition with surveillance capacity. Neither operates to create defensible space without the other.

EASTER HILL VILLAGE, RICHMOND, CALIFORNIA

Easter Hill Village is a 300-unit, low-density, two-story row-house public housing project in Richmond, California. It is unique not so much for its overall site planning, which is weak in defensible space, but rather for the concern that the architects and site planners showed for the areas immediately bordering the units. Certain features have been employed which are virtually unknown to public housing, though not uncommon in private developments. The rear of each unit has been provided with a low fence to define the rear yard; and the front of each unit has been provided with a small individual front porch with an unfenced front yard.

In the summer of 1964, ten years after its completion, a survey and interview was undertaken by Clare C. Cooper of the Center for Planning

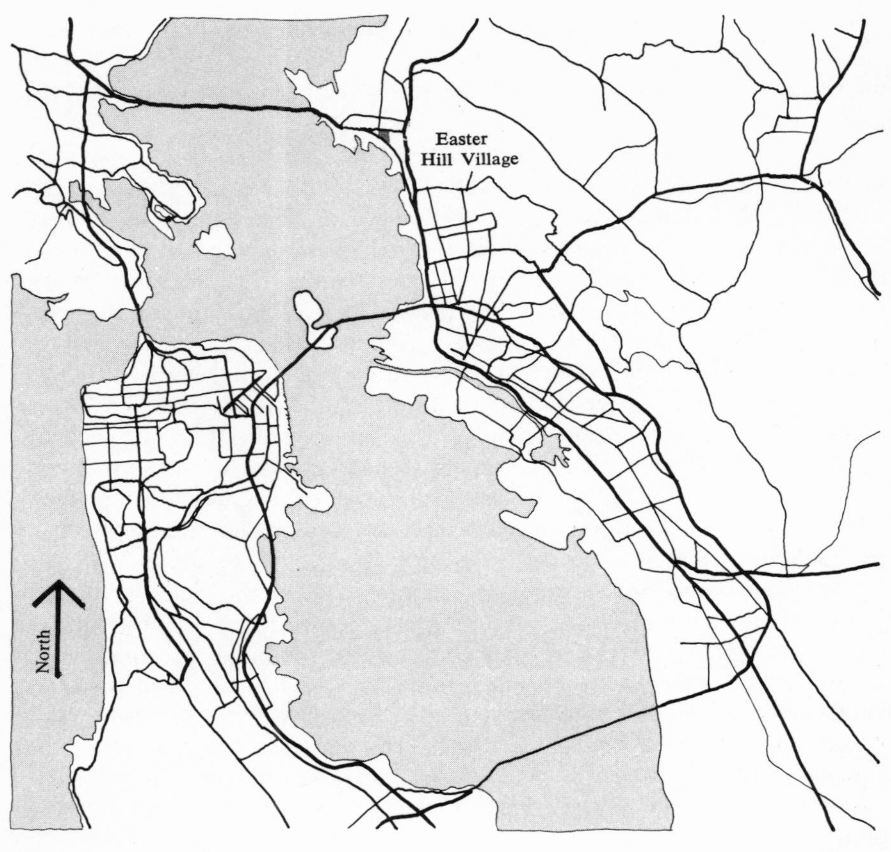

FIG. 133. Location map—Easter Hill Village, Richmond, California

and Development Research, Berkeley, to determine the extent of success of the design proposals. Almost universally, residents spoke about the attributes of the privately defined rear yard and the significance of the front porch. Most residents would have preferred the rear fences to be six or more feet high, and thus more visually defined and screened. The family could then utilize this area as private outdoor space. In discussing these areas, Clare Cooper observes that

> whereas the backyard at Easter Hill Village appeared to be a space into which family activities overflowed from inside the house, the space at the front of the house had more social connotations, forming both a

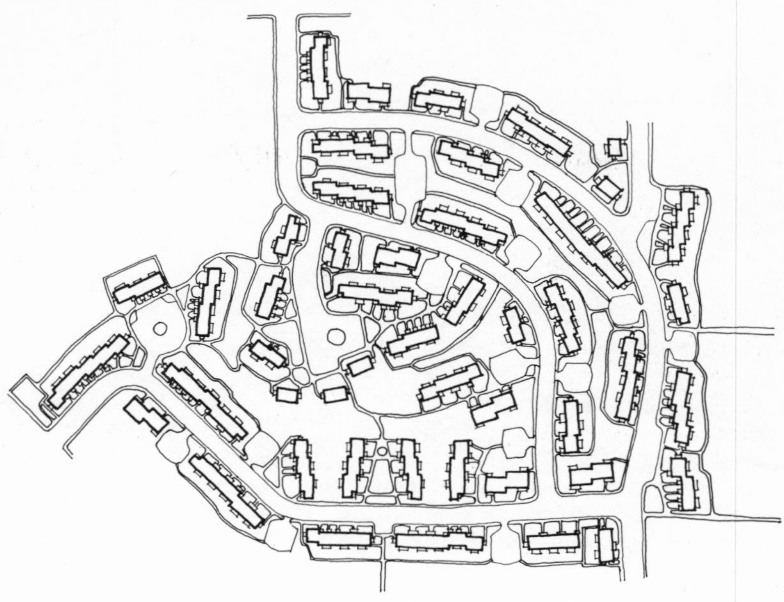

FIG. 134. Site Plan of Easter Hill Village, Richmond, California. Architects: Hardison and DeMars, San Francisco. Landscape Architect: Lawrence Halprin, San Francisco. Built in 1954; contains 300 apartments. Prototype of low-density (12 dwelling units per acre), low-income housing in a suburban locale (West Coast).

FIG. 135. Public Walks and Front Entries at Easter Hill. The front porch to each unit serves to define a semiprivate zone, in front of the dwelling, in effect declaring the front lawn an extension of the family domain. (Photo by author)

FIG. 136. Rear Walks and Yards at Easter Hill. The rear yard of each unit at Easter Hill Village is defined by a frame fence. The rear walk, however, is open to the street. Residents admit that their own rear yards are lacking in privacy. (Photo by author)

> barrier between the privacy of the house and the completely public nature of the surrounding neighborhood, as well as a link between the small social group of the family and the larger social group of the community. . . . The front porch and the front yard were important as locales where tenants could add individuality to their homes and maintain status in their own and their neighbor's eyes. As such, then, they performed just as important a psychological and social function as do the carefully tended front lawns of suburbia.[1]

Having come this far in their conceptualizing of private and public spaces, it is surprising that in their site plans the architects did not also choose to restrict entry to the rear access paths to groups of ten to fifteen families by fencing them off into a collective rear yard.

TOWER HILL, ST. LOUIS COUNTY, MISSOURI

Tower Hill is a middle-income forty-one-unit project not atypical in its size of a small suburban development package. It makes two significant contributions to a defensible space vocabulary: (1) the use of earth-moving techniques to complement the natural topographical features of the site and to achieve a multi-level separation between the public front and private rear of the dwellings; and (2) the grouping of units and their front entries around a central public square and parking area which is also the main entry to the project.

FIG. 138. Site Plan of Tower Hill, St. Louis County, Missouri. Architects: Anselivicus and Montgomery, St. Louis. Contains 44 apartments. Prototype of low-density (7.0 dwelling units per acre), middle-income housing in a suburban locale (Midwest).

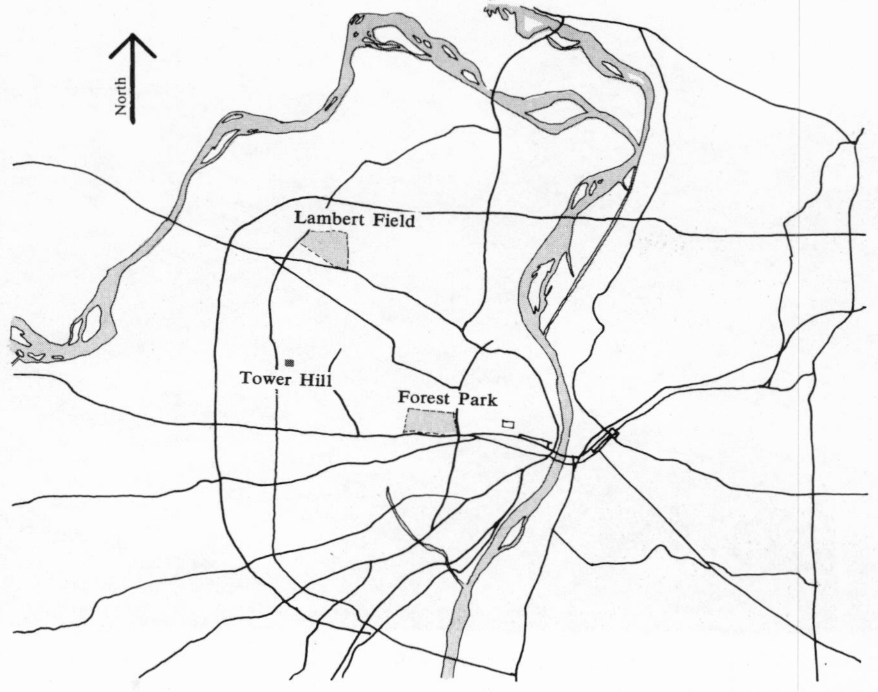

FIG. 137. Location map—Tower Hill, St. Louis County, Missouri

FIG. 139. Central Parking and Play Area, Tower Hill, St. Louis. Entrance to each row-house unit is off the central area devoted to parking and play. There is a sharing of surveillance between unit entry and central area. (Photo by author)

FIG. 140. Front Door at Tower Hill, St. Louis. Individualized green areas near the stoop of each front door provides semiprivate sitting areas with high visibility around the entrances. (Photo by author)

FIG. 141. Rear Patio at Tower Hill, St. Louis. The rear areas at Tower Hill are collectively used for recreation, except for the patio area which is defined for individual family use. (Photo by author)

The architects have reasoned that the entry to the house immediately opposite the parking area in a suburban family dwelling inevitably becomes the main entry to the building, whether front or rear, whether designated or not. They have also reasoned that the most public zone of the project is the space occupied by the road and public vehicles. Consequently, in what must appear to many architects as blatant pandering to the automobile, and a questionable expression of an automobile-oriented life style, the architects have intentionally chosen to make the focus of the project its large central parking lot.

The architects have been accurate in their predictions. The parking lot, the sidewalks bordering and defining it, and the entries to the units immediately facing these walks, have become the development's recognized public zone. Since a good percentage of the vehicles are in use during the working day, the emptied parking area daily becomes a significant play space for the children living in Tower Hill.

The private areas of the project are located behind the dwelling units, a level or two below the grade of the parking and entry area. They are screened from this public area by the dwelling units themselves, coupled with the steep grade differential. The grounds area in the rear, immediately adjacent to the dwelling unit, is developed as a private patio, usually facing off the playroom space one or two levels below the entry.

The project has proven to be a very successful defensible space design. Vehicles enter Tower Hill only through the common parking space and public area; the front doors all face this area (and each other).

Entry by foot is quite difficult, except along the designated routes and public paths. The project is ringed with artificial berms; anyone entering another way would appear odd indeed and become subject to surveillance and question.

Whereas all the projects discussed in this chapter, ranging from Riverbend at eighty units per acre to Tower Hill at seven, are significant contributors to the evolution of a defensible space vocabulary, each suffers its imperfections. But then, these projects were not conceived primarily with a "defensible space" purpose in mind. In our pursuit of problems we have identified, we have found solutions in each project that probably surprise its authors. It must be disconcerting, therefore, for them to find their work given either praise or faint damnation. The significance of these current examples lies in their contribution to defining a new realm of architectural concern. We ask the indulgence of these architects with regard to the criticism directed at their work. It is, after all, a very unfair game, for we are holding them up for measurement against a scale of our own creation.

NOTES

1. Clare C. Cooper, "Fenced Back Yard—Unfenced Front Yard—Enclosed Front Porch," *The Journal of Housing*, 1967, no. 5, pp. 268–274.

7

MODIFYING EXISTING ENVIRONMENTS

This chapter is a presentation of two ways of creating defensible space after the fact: through modification of two existing housing projects. Although they represent diverse problems and require different solutions, each is typical of a large number of public and private housing developments throughout the country. The first proposal, *Clason Point Gardens*, is prototypal of security design for walk-up projects of moderate residential density. The second proposal, *Bronxdale Houses*, is more pertinent to the design of high-rise housing in urban areas. The Bronxdale recommendations may also be seen as a model for achieving security through use of a combination of physical modifications and electronic technology.

• *Clason Point Gardens*

Clason Point, a two-story public housing row-house development in the Bronx, New York City, consists of 400 duplex apartments located in forty-six row-house buildings. The grounds consist of seventeen acres, with approximately 21 percent of the grounds covered by buildings.

FIG. 142. View of Clason Point Gardens from bordering street, before modifications. (Photo by author)

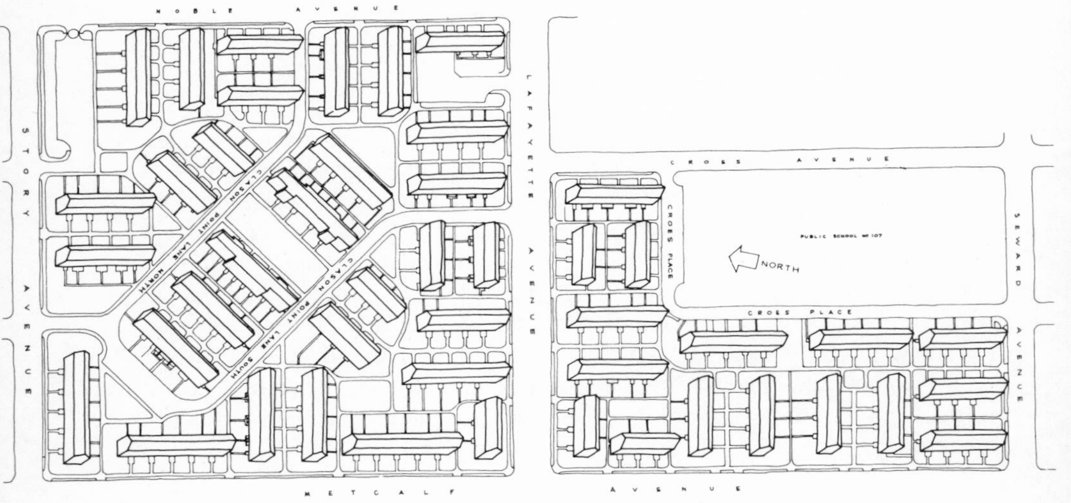

FIG. 143. Site Plan of Clason Point Gardens. A mix of two-story row houses and walk-up flats, located in The Bronx, New York: Built in 1941; 400 units, at a density of 24 units per acre.

FIG. 144. View Down Front Walks at Clason Point, Before Modifications. Front and rear yards are undifferentiated as are the main access paths from the service paths. There is no definition of private zones; every area of the project is completely accessible from neighboring public streets. The paths into the interior of the project are poorly lighted, making evening use dangerous. (Photo by author)

Clason Point Gardens is a rather lackluster project occupied by three major tenant groups: (1) elderly white families (32 percent), (2) Puerto Rican families (24 percent), and (3) Negro families (29 percent). Despite the provision of front and rear yards and separate duplex apartments, this project bears the strong stigma of public housing. Prior to modifications, the public character of the project was easily recognizable from afar. The unfinished faded gray cinder block buildings gave the project the appearance of army barracks, and it stood out in marked contrast to surrounding streets lined with individually owned red-brick row houses.

Wide gaps between buildings along the street edges of the project revealed a vaguely defined system of internal paths and yards within. The project conveyed the impression that entry by strangers would not be resisted, even though all paths and grounds areas are adjoined by (and in clear view of) residential buildings.

Our hypotheses focused on the impact these design features had on the ability and willingness of residents to maintain and control the security and use of areas near their homes. Preliminary interviews revealed that tenants were extremely fearful of being victimized by criminals, both during the day and in the evening; they had severely changed or curtailed their patterns of activity as a result of the atmosphere of heightened danger; they felt they had no right to question, and were afraid to question, the presence of strangers as a means of anticipating and preventing crimes before they occurred. Adolescents from neighboring projects used the grounds as a congregation area, instilling fear and anger in many Clason Point residents. Because of the public character of the project, residents felt they had little recourse but to accept the omnipresence of strangers. In public housing projects, strangers are only informally accountable to local residents. Since residents do not have legal proprietary rights, individual tenants feel they cannot legitimately question intruders unless they are violating a public law or some housing project rule.

Proposed modifications

A variety of architectural modifications to buildings and grounds were undertaken in an effort to expand the domain in which individual tenants felt they had the right to expect accountability from strangers and other residents. Even though this manner of accounting remains largely social and informal, it was hypothesized that design modifications could lead individual tenants to watch strangers more diligently and clarify the range of behavior which could be defined as reasonable, in contrast to that which would require their personal response or, ultimately, police attention. We hypothesized that through spatial reorganization we could set up a dependent relationship between spatial organization and social expectations; that informal expectations would become more exacting and differentiated if the organization of the physical setting provided clear, well-marked distinctions between public and private zones, and eliminated the functionless, "no-man's-land" for which no individual or group of tenants could be considered accountable.

Crime and fear of crime could, we suggested, be significantly reduced in a situation where increased clarity concerning behavioral guidelines was established. Tenants would then feel they had the right to impose social pressures on strangers and neighbors. Interviews and observations were conducted prior to the construction of a variety of architectural modifications. These modifications were undertaken to achieve the overall objective of increasing the intensity and extent of the territorial prerogatives that tenants felt toward project areas. On completion of these modifications, the changes in tenants' conception of the socio-spatial order of the project were to be assessed, and an extensive examination made concerning positive behavior and attitudes released as a by-product of the redesign. A comparison of project crime and vandalism rates as recorded by the New York City Housing Authority Police and superintendents was to be made before and after modifications.

The selection of Clason Point as a prototypal low-density project was undertaken with full recognition that while this project was typical of much public housing across the country, (1) it was not typical of New York projects; (2) its primary problem was fear of crime, rather than an *extraordinarily* high incidence of crime; and (3) the project already embodied many of the characteristics of physical design we would advocate as a means of controlling crime through physical design.

Design directives to increase security were focused primarily on modifications of the grounds. These directives had six goals.

To intensify tenant surveillance of the grounds.

To reduce the public areas of the project by unambiguous differentiation between grounds and paths; thus creating a hierarchy of public, semipublic, and private areas and paths.

To increase the sense of propriety felt by residents.

To reduce the stigma of public housing and allow residents to relate better to the surrounding community.

To reduce intergenerational conflict among residents within the project.

To intensify the use of the more semipublic grounds of the project in predictable and socially beneficial ways, and so encourage and extend the areas of felt, tenant responsibility.

A comprehensive design recommendation was made to differentiate grounds according to a hierarchy of public-to-private zones of use. These changes were intended to limit the amount of available space over which surveillance must be maintained; increase opportunities for natural surveillance of public areas by locating them in plain view of apartment units; eliminate any ambiguity concerning the use of the grounds; and increase the confidence of the residents in supervising the behavior of residents and nonresidents.

The proposal called for the public areas of the project to be restricted to and aligned along a central pedestrian path entending the full length of the project, from Story Avenue to Seward Avenue. This public walk was to be augmented by a series of secondary public paths leading into it from the surrounding streets. In all instances, the new public paths were located to face building fronts so as to maximize natural surveillance of the passage of people by residents.

To highlight the public quality of the major pedestrian walk, the

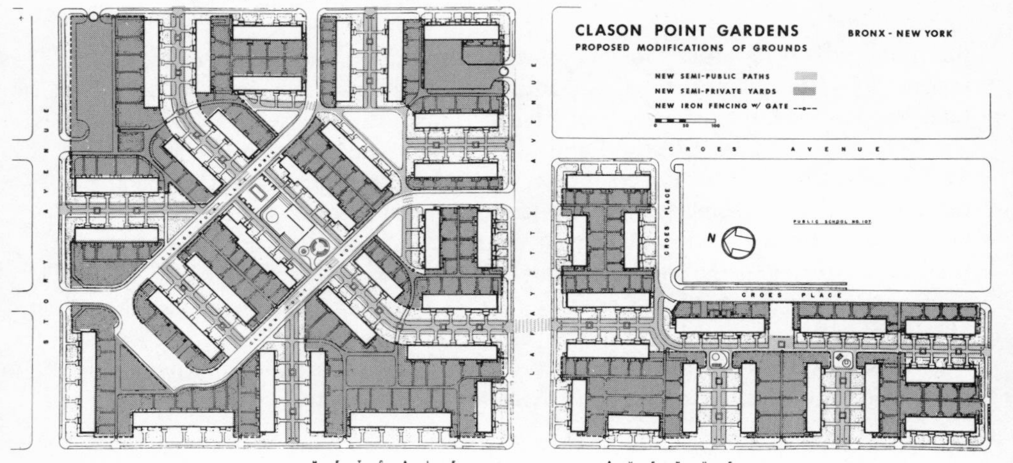

FIG. 145. Revised Site Plan of Clason Point Gardens. Proposed reassignment of grounds into public, semipublic, and semiprivate areas.

FIG. 146. Partial view of an area of Clason Point Gardens, showing existing buildings, grounds, and path systems.

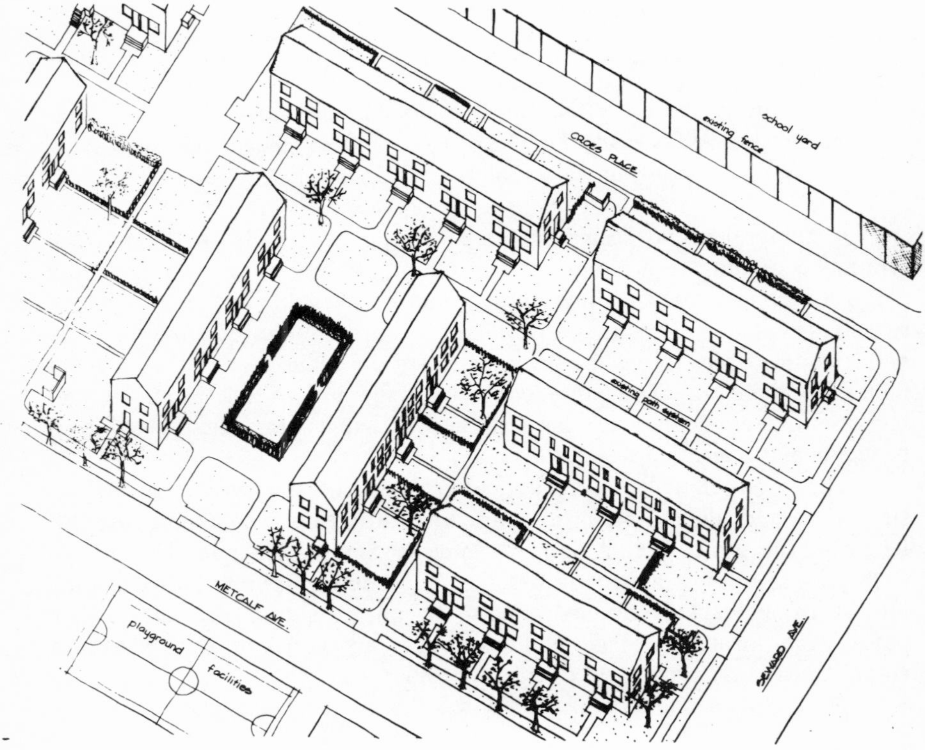

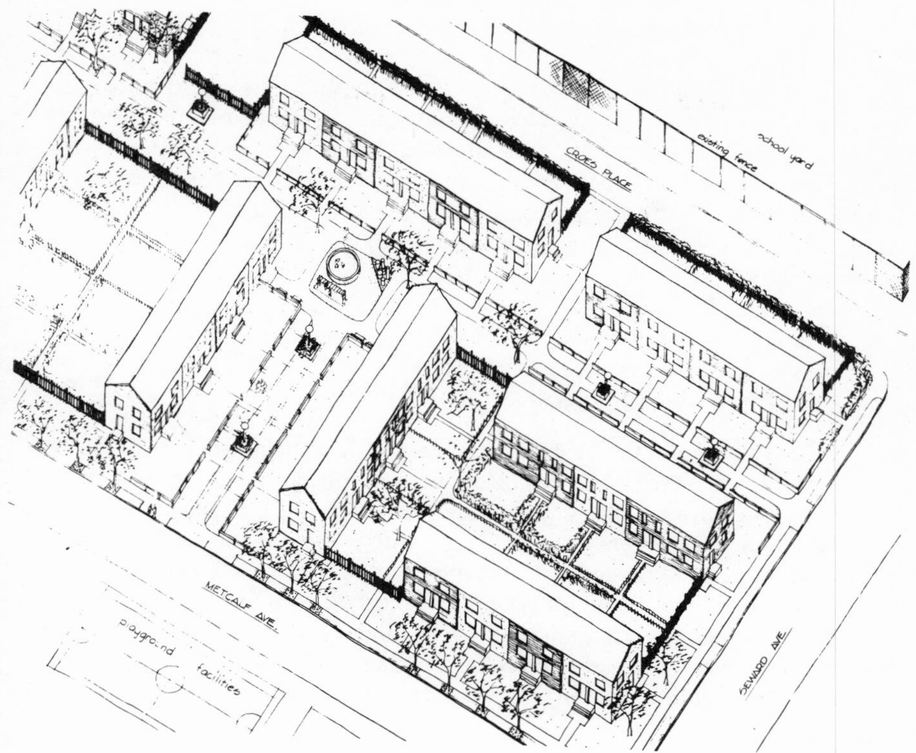

FIG. 147. Partial view of an area of Clason Point Gardens, showing proposed modification to buildings, grounds, and path systems.

design called for (1) widening of the path, using colored and decoratively-scored paving; (2) differentiating small private areas (front lawns) outside each dwelling from the public path with low, symbolic walls; and (3) the addition of public seating in the center of the public path, located at a distance from private dwellings sufficient to eliminate conflicts over use, but close enough to be under constant surveillance by residents.

At selected intersections of the primary and secondary paths, "play-nodes" were to be created for young children—with seating nearby to allow for supervision.

New and decorative lighting was to be employed to highlight the new public paths and recreation areas at night, so as to extend the residents' surveillance potential and feelings of security.

Backyard areas shared by clusters of eight to twelve families were to be differentiated from the public paths and play areas by tubular steel gates and fences. Entrance to the rear areas would be accessible to residents of the cluster only through their own homes. Because the rear yards were to be closed off, the back doors to the units could no longer be used as an alternate entry; visitors and tenants would now have to use the front doors of apartments and approach them from the lighted public paths only. It was hypothesized that the newly enclosed rear areas, composing some 60 percent of the project grounds, would now be maintained by the residents of each cluster, working in associaton with one another.

Refacing of buildings

As part of the effort of removing the public housing image of Clason Point, buildings were to be surfaced with a stucco finish indistinguishable from brickwork. This finish was to be applied in a range of colors selected by the tenants themselves. Units within the row-house block were given individual expression by alternating the colors of brickwork. It was hoped that this would provide residents with an increased sense of individuality and proprietorship, thereby inducing greater maintenance and care of lawns and paths, increased potency in dealing with intruders, and increased watchfulness over areas adjacent to their dwellings.

Redevelopment of the central area

In the pretesting interviews conducted at Clason Point, tenants were asked to identify the areas of the project they thought had the most crime, as well as those they were the most fearful of. Almost uniformly, tenants identified the areas immediately adjacent to their homes as being the safest, and those that were distant, unknown, and unused as most unsafe. However, one particular area, the central green space, was identified by most tenants, regardless of where they lived, as the most dangerous part of the project. This, they claimed, was where "pushers" hung out, where neighborhood addicts came to meet connections, and where one was sure to be mugged at night.

On further interview and observation, it was found that the area was also used by teen-agers, of both sexes, who congregated in one corner of the square after school. Younger children would occasionally throw a ball around, but since the ground was uneven, intensive ball playing was difficult. As Clason Point is otherwise mostly devoid of play areas and equipment, it was decided to transform this no-man's-land into an intensive community recreation area for all age groups. By making it well peopled by young children, teen-agers, parents, and elderly, it was felt that it would be possible to bring social pressures to bear which

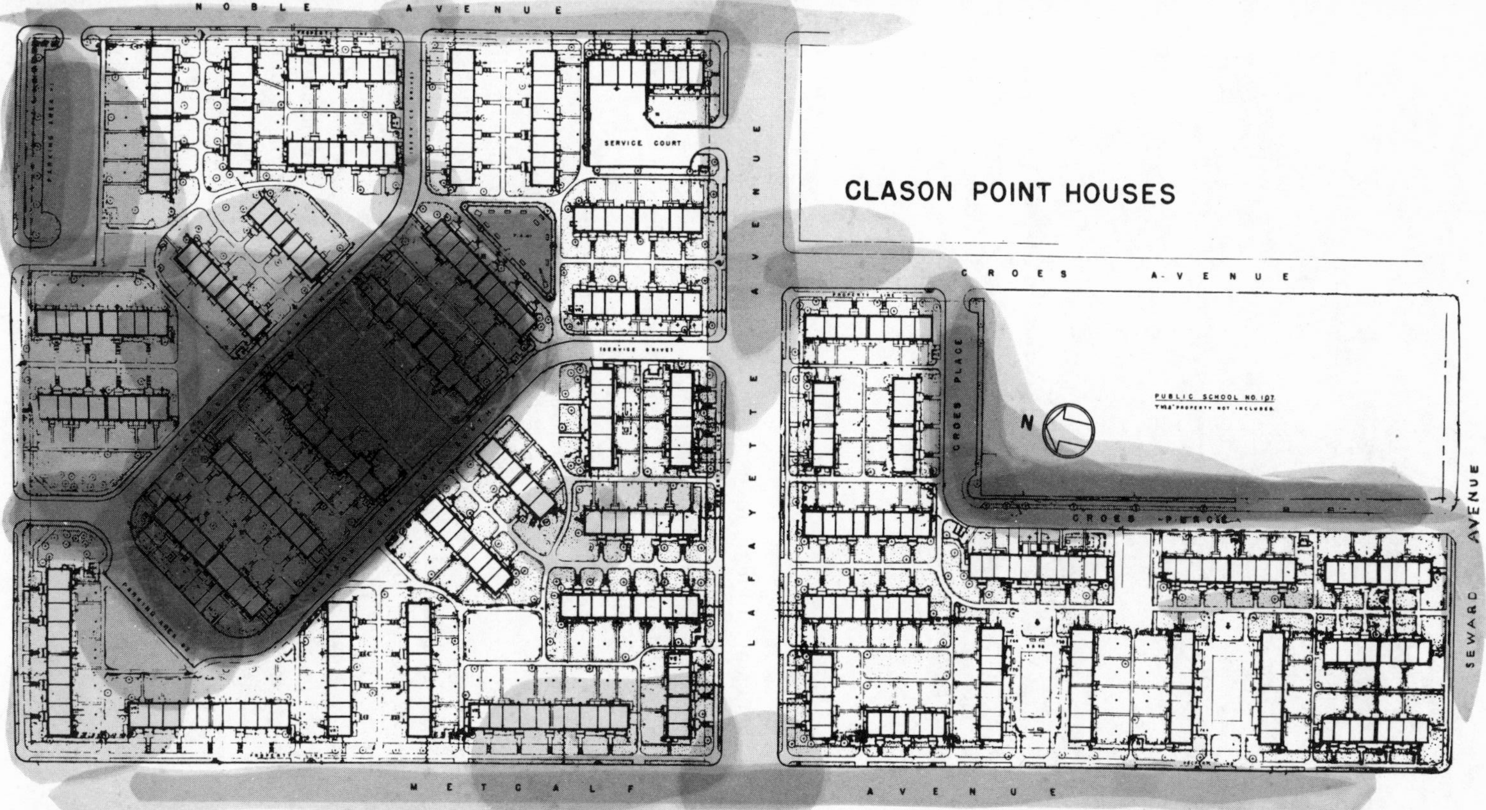

FIG. 148. Clason Point Fear Map. Dark areas on the site plan are a composite of the zones residents have designated as being dangerous (dark areas are those reported dangerous by at least six respondents).

FIG. 149. View of Central Square Before Modifications. The most dangerous area in Clason Point Gardens was identified both through tenant interviews and police reports as being the central square. This photo shows the square as it was, including a few benches and one pair of centrally located lights. (Photo by author)

would be of sufficient strength to expunge the addicts. As this central green area was also located at the intersection of a few of the newly created main paths, it was felt that it should be designed as a natural extension of the pedestrian system and be treated in a similar way with lighting, paving, and seating.

As the area was to serve decidedly different age groups, it was felt that an effort should be made to define, through aesthetic treatment, the zones intended for the different users. The design of the adult area was therefore treated in a conservative, orderly, almost restrained manner. In contrast, the teen-age area was designed using curvalinear patterns, intense colors, and large odd-shaped rocks. These two areas, representing the prime contenders at any housing project, were separated by a large, walled-off central play area for younger children.

The adult area was designed for sitting, spontaneous gathering, and tabletop games. The straight, geometric quality of the individual features is expected to invite use primarily by adults, without the need of explicit signs defining or restricting such use.

The adolescent and teen-age area was to be constructed out of rough-hewn wood, and arranged in a circular fashion especially suited to group use. It was to be surrounded by exposed rock to accentuate its rugged, partly-formed character, and was to be separated from the rest

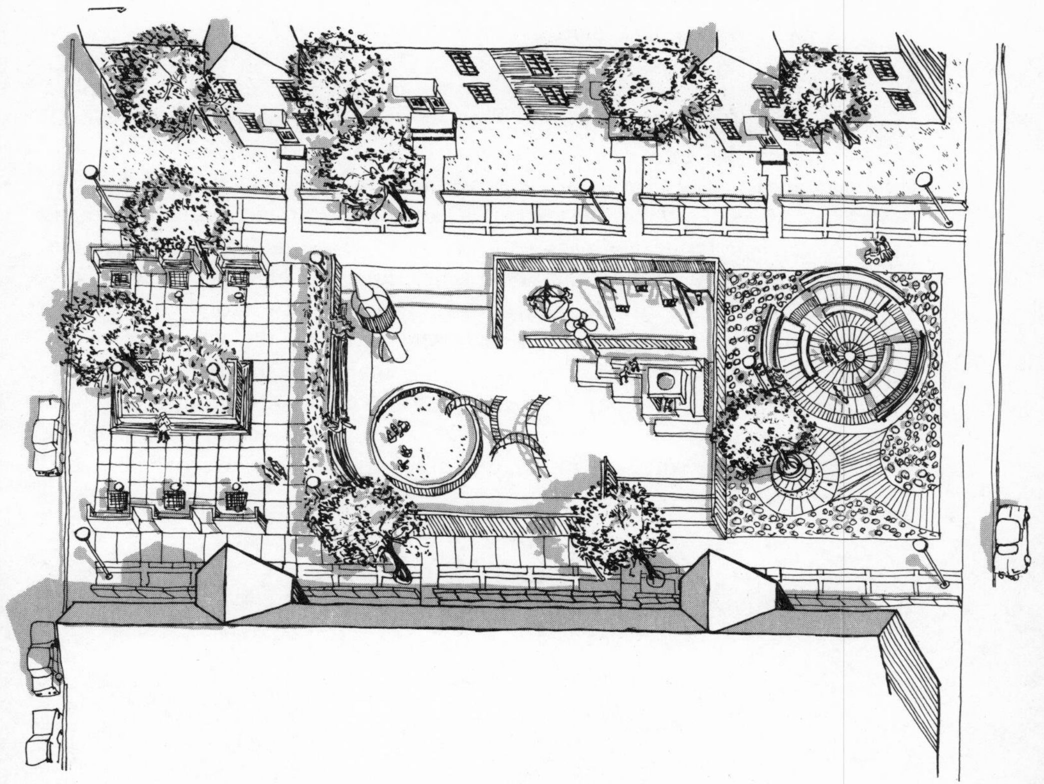

FIG. 150. Proposal for the Modification of the Central Square. The central square was designed for the intensive use of three age groups: (from the left) the elderly, the three- to ten-year-olds, and the teen-agers.

of the recreation area by a low wall. The design was expected to draw adolescents because of its primitive properties, without need of additional designations. Surveillance of these areas will be maintained by neighboring apartments, and from the adjacent vehicular street.

The middle play area was designed for use by young children and preteens, and includes various built-in play equipment and additional seating for parents supervising play. It was also intended that this area operate as a buffer between adolescents and adults.

It was hoped that all this activity would transform this most dormant and frightening area of the project into the most alive and safe area: the new focus at Clason Point.

At this writing the rehabilitation of the project has been complete for over twelve months. During this test period, felonies were down to one-third of the previous year's level. Measures of tenant satisfaction showed statistically significant improvement in the reduction of fear, in increased surveillance on the part of tenants, and in their evaluation of the quality of their living environment. The newly modified central play area is very intensively used by the community, and this has succeeded in discouraging its use by drunks and addicts. Tenants now maintain some 80 percent of the project grounds, appreciably reducing the workload of the maintenance staff. The most successful of the newly defined semiprivate rear yards are those shared by the smallest number of families. Those shared by twenty-five families or over are creating controversy in the development of a rule system for determining collective use of space and for gate closing.

FIG. 151. View of Modified Central Area. The area has been transformed into a community recreation facility. It has been extensively lighted for night use. (Photo by author)

FIG. 152. View Down Main Access Path as Modified. View of the same area as figure 144, on completion of the modifications. The main access paths have been widened, using colorful concrete paving, and have been extensively lit. Lights are housed in combination with planter boxes and benches. Front lawns have been defined by curbing units. Note that the concrete-block buildings have been re-surfaced in brick, and colors have been applied so as to give all units individual identity. Rear yards which comprise 60 percent of the project grounds have been fenced off with six-foot-high cast iron fences and are now accessible only from the housing units themselves. (Photo by author)

FIG. 153. View of Project from Surrounding Streets, After Modifications. The fencing closing off the rear yards limits access to the project to the front walks. (Photo by author)

• *Bronxdale Houses*

Our work up to the present time indicates that of all public housing, high-rise, double-loaded corridor, multiple-family projects are those with the most difficult crime problems. In addition to the problem areas articulated earlier, tenant populations are heterogeneous, with some families viewing public housing as their housing of choice, and others as the housing of last resort. Housing policy specifically prohibits the use of doormen to maintain surveillance over individual buildings; law and tradition have resulted in building interiors being understood as open to the public. Buildings are restricted to the use of residents, only when they agree to finance the installation of intercoms through additional rental charges. By comparison, private residential complexes can afford far more comprehensive systems of patrols and surveillance.

The redesign of existing high-rise projects to enhance public safety is especially problematical, because there is little opportunity to make effective physical modifications to existing building interiors (such as increasing the visibility of public lobbies, corridors, and elevators). Also, building and fire code requirements governing high-rise housing are stringent, so that otherwise feasible design solutions for enhancing security are found to be in conflict with fire codes.

FIG. 154. Aerial view of Bronxdale Houses. (Photo by author)

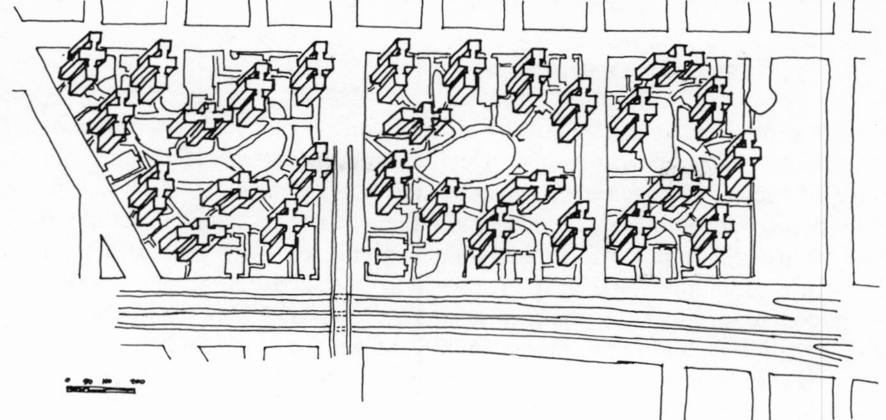

FIG. 155. Site Plan of Bronxdale Houses. The interior grounds are open to adjacent street and are not differentiated so as to be associated with any groupings of buildings.

NATURAL SURVEILLANCE THROUGH ELECTRONIC DEVICES

The use of modern electronic equipment at Bronxdale was undertaken in an effort to resolve a problem of uniquely modern creation: the high-rise apartment tower. Because of their size and organization, high-rise buildings do not usually allow tenants to maintain surveillance over areas in and around buildings. Elevators and stairs are completely sealed from sight and sound; floors are separated by unused fire stairs and soundproof fire doors. These designs eliminate the natural surveillance provided by vertically organized walk-up buildings with exposed stairs which allow tenants to hear and respond to activities in the entire building.

A large number of tenants sharing the use of a single entrance makes it impossible for an individual to distinguish his neighbors from strangers, or to determine whether adolescents who linger near the entrance reside in the building. The social rules governing behavior in walk-up tenements are less ambiguous: the presence of any stranger inside the entrance lobbies can be questioned.

Finally, walk-up buildings have many windows facing the street, or near building entrances. The windows of ground-floor apartments in high-rise public housing buildings are designed to be at least a half a story above the ground. Although this design feature has helped to reduce the incidence of ground-floor burglaries, it has eroded an important surveillance function of first-floor apartments.

Electronic devices will be tested at Bronxdale Houses to develop methods for restoring to high-rise buildings the opportunities for surveillance and contact that are present in walk-up structures, both inside the building and on the grounds.

A major function of these experiments is to develop methods of using electronic equipment which maximize their meaning to residents as a natural addition to the repertoire of mechanical and electronic systems: locks, intercoms, television, and telephones. Resident-monitored TV pictures of their building lobby, elevator, and nearby grounds, if successful, should provide additional windows on their world. Residents should be able to use these pictures to maintain surveillance over the arrival and departure of children and visitors; to watch over children at play; and, as an added by-product, to come to recognize their neighbors and the tenants in adjacent buildings. Sound equipment will be employed to compare the relative benefits that can be achieved through enhancing auditory communication among apartments and between elevators and halls.

Our proposals for the use of electronic devices are part of a coherent framework of design directives developed for multiple-occupancy dwellings. In each instance, the electronic addition is oriented toward restoring the quality and quantity of information about the areas outside apartments naturally available to residents of walk-up buildings.

A second priority is to increase the ease with which residents can contact police and other authorities and to allow police more effective use of limited manpower by providing electronic assistance to their patrol of the public areas of projects.

The purpose of the proposed test program is to examine the feasibility of electronically assisted surveillance and its potential for greater application throughout all housing projects. Experimental work on a limited scale is necessary:

To experiment with electronic systems and to determine their most effective and prudent use.

To examine the effectiveness of electronic systems as a security measure and determine patterns and intensity of use by residents.

To obtain detailed information concerning resident attitudes to electronic equipment before and after installation, especially as it relates to questions of violation of privacy and individual rights.

To eliminate technical deficiencies, and to create an operating procedure for dealing with breakdowns, vandalism, and unanticipated shortcomings of the systems.

To examine the relative benefits and failings of surveillance systems as operated by tenants, versus systems operated directly by Housing Authority Police.

Physical design proposals to improve security at Bronxdale Houses

Experimentation with electronic equipment will be integrated into a wide range of physical modifications to the Bronxdale complex, designed to improve security on project grounds and building approaches. A detailed explanation of the functioning of the electronic system follows a description of these physical modifications.

Bronxdale is made up of twenty-eight seven-story buildings sited on twenty-seven acres divided into large blocks. The central areas of each of these blocks are, for the most part, grassed over and underutilized. Buildings have an entrance arrangement with front and rear doors to each lobby. These entries are virtually indistinguishable from one another. The physical modifications we have proposed in the interest of security fall into three categories.

> Grouping of buildings into clusters around parking and play areas, taking advantage of natural opportunities which presently exist.
>
> Modifications to building entrances to create a breezeway into building courts and to accommodate a telephone intercom for opening the entry door to the lobby.
>
> Development of the central area of the grounds for more intense use as a public path and as facility for play activities for teen-agers and adults.

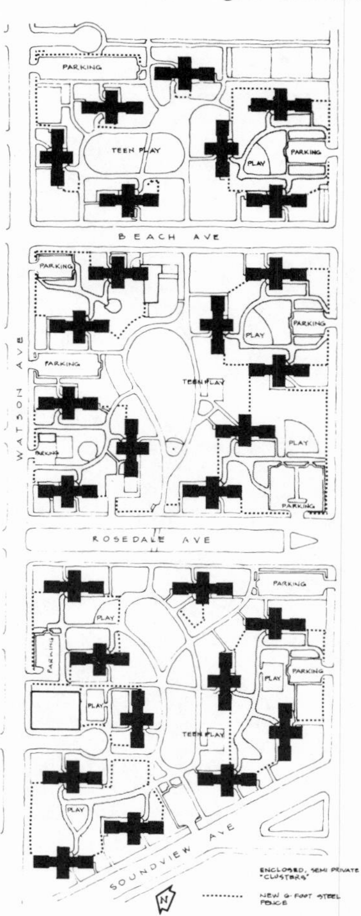

FIG. 156. Site Plan of Bronxdale Showing Proposed Ground Modifications. The grounds have been reorganized so as to group buildings into clusters containing play areas for young children, sitting areas, and parking areas.

Grouping of buildings

A second modification involves redefining grounds areas adjacent to buildings and intensifying the use of these areas.

> Subdivision of grounds of the project into clusters containing three to four buildings is to be accomplished through the use of six-foot-high iron fences which allow for visual contact outside the cluster but channel access to the entrance breezeways.
>
> Further intensification of activity within the subdivided grounds will be encouraged by locating new play equipment and seating areas in these zones. Mothers watching their children on TV from their apartments will also serve to screen strangers and any unusual activity taking place within these clusters.

FIG. 157. A typical cluster at Bronxdale

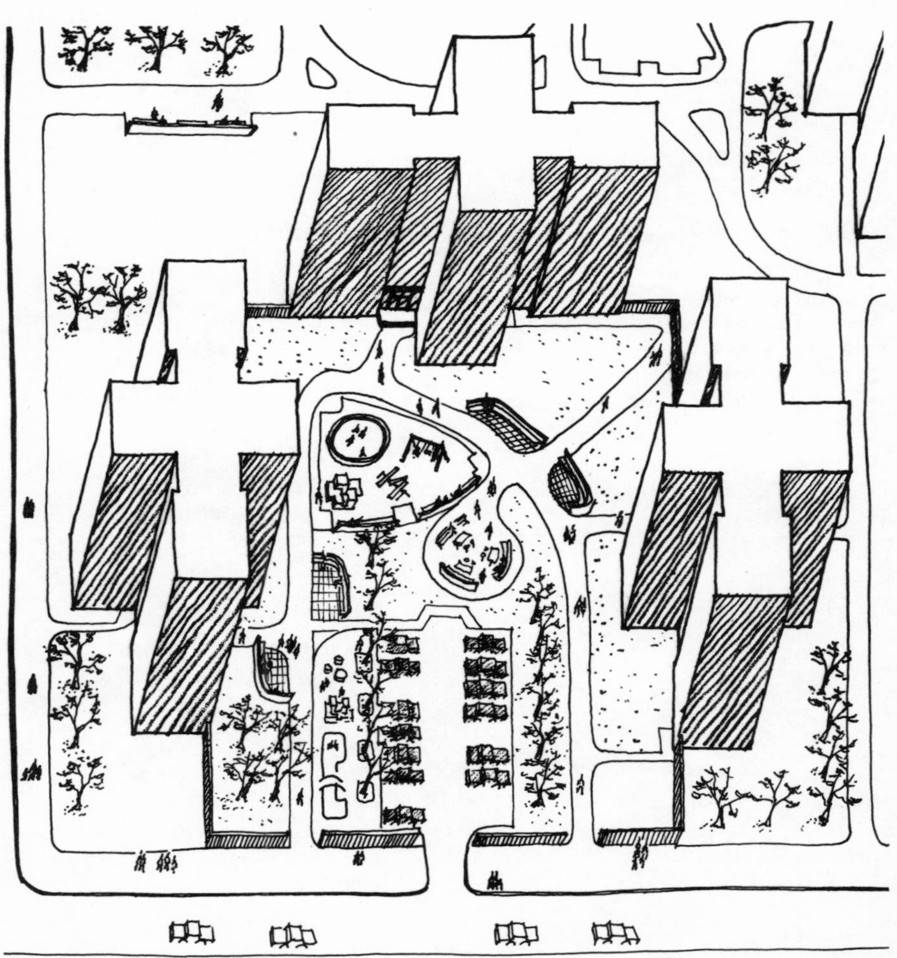

Building entrance modifications

Entry redesign will serve to make the installation of telephone intercoms operationally effective, and to create a breezeway through buildings grouped around a central court. Figure 163A shows the existing lobby entrance and the two-door entry, with the elevator waiting area around the bend, out of sight. Were the buzzer-reply system installed within the existing physical plan, as shown in alternate two, its effectiveness would suffer from the ambiguity inherent in the double-door system.

The solution proposed, alternate one, involves creation of a breezeway corridor between the front and rear doors, and the placement of the

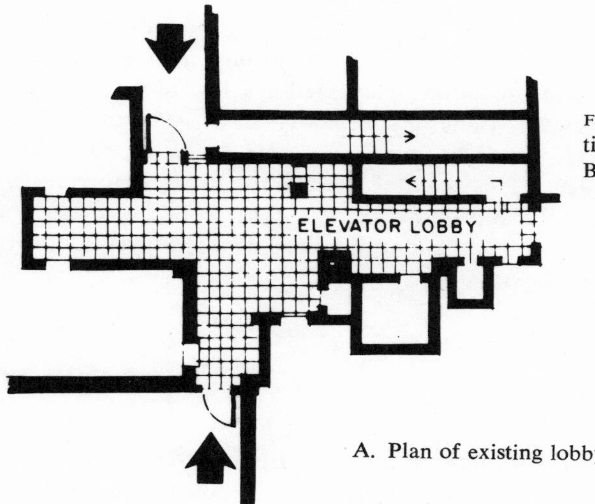

A. Plan of existing lobby

FIG. 158. Plans showing modifications to the lobbies and entries of Bronxdale apartment buildings.

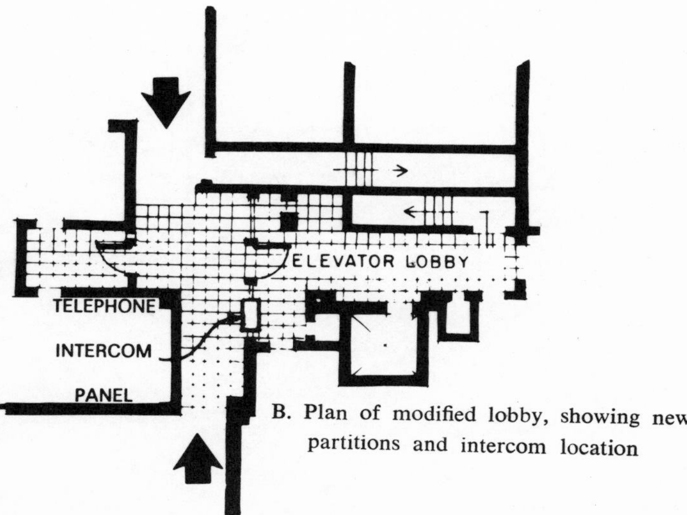

B. Plan of modified lobby, showing new partitions and intercom location

buzzer-reply system between the breezeway and the elevator waiting area. This permits residents to use the breezeway as a public passage and provides them with the ability to survey the elevator area before making a decision to enter the building door and lobby.

Development of the central area of grounds

The existing public path system through the project grounds is redundant and fails to channel pedestrians along predictable, well-lit, or patrolled routes. The extent and persistence of crimes can be attributed in part to the ambiguity of the central grounds areas. Interviews with tenants reveal that these areas are minimally used and are experienced as foreboding. Our physical design proposals call for modifications to the path system to create a strong public route through the project.

Finally, although there are public play facilities for adolescents and preadolescents nearby, project youngsters were found not to be using them if they were not perceived as their "turf." Further physical design proposals call for development of the central grounds to be used for recreation by project children. This proposal serves the twofold purpose of reducing intergenerational conflict and providing separate play facilities for older children living in the project.

Electronic surveillance proposals

Proposals for use of electronic equipment are intended to augment physical design solutions to the special security problems of high-rise housing. In this project, unlike Clason Point, goals that can be achieved by physical redesign alone are more modest. Elevators cannot be glazed, and corridors inside high-rise buildings cannot be opened to external view or eliminated. Where extensive physical redesign is not possible, use of electronic equipment is the only recourse open. The systems used for the experimental program at Bronxdale Houses include:

Video surveillance of the lobbies, elevators, and adjacent play and parking areas on individual home TV monitors (unused channels of their TV sets).

Video surveillance of public grounds and central paths by tenant patrol monitors.

Audio surveillance of elevators by residents.

FIG. 159. View of Modified Lobby at Bronxdale. Modifications to the lobby involve the installation of a new wall with accompanying telephone intercom system. Closed circuit TV cameras have been installed to allow monitoring of the lobby by each tenant on his home TV set. Tenants will also be able to monitor the elevator in their building. The interior areas chosen for closed circuit TV coverage are exactly those which have been identified as suffering the highest incidence of crime.

FIG. 160. Tenant at Bronxdale watching her children at play on her TV set (Photo by author)

FIG. 161. Tenant Patrol Monitoring the Public Paths of the Project. The public walks at Bronxdale, different from the lobbies, elevators, and semiprivate play areas of each building, will be monitored by tenant patrols.

Audio surveillance of corridors by residents through individual apartment doors.

Direct communication system from tenants to police, including installation of broadcast system from the telephone in the local police room to a walkie-talkie carried by patrolman.

Initial experimental work is expected to incur higher costs than later extension of electronic systems to other projects. Consequently, not all systems were proposed for project-wide trials at Bronxdale. Most systems will be tested on clusters of buildings, and some require testing on only one or two floors of a single building. This conservative testing strategy is in harmony with our belief that electronic technology should be assessed in detail on a small scale to determine its effectiveness and its psychological and sociological consequences prior to large-scale tests on a single project, or universal extension of some components to all public housing projects. With the advent of cable TV, these systems can be installed almost without cost.

The following is a schema for the individual proposals for use of electronic equipment at Bronxdale Houses.

VIDEO SURVEILLANCE BY TENANTS

Clusters of buildings were selected for experimental installation of tenant-monitored video surveillance. Installation of this equipment is planned to coincide with physical modifications to grounds (installation of six-foot fences and redesign of the building entrances (installation of the intercoms). The system requires a TV camera in the lobby, a camera in the elevator, and a roof-top camera looking down on a cluster's internal play and parking areas.

VIDEO SURVEILLANCE BY TENANT PATROL MONITORS

A major use of video equipment at Bronxdale will be to allow designated tenant monitors to maintain surveillance over the public paths through the project and large central area playgrounds. Hopefully, this will help to encourage use of central grounds as a public street and will, in turn, further ensure the security and use of these areas. Monitoring of these TV cameras by selected tenant patrols, and restricting the areas under surveillance to public zones, were both deemed desirable to avoid the possibility of invasion of privacy, or the use of TV equipment for unanticipated functions.

For maximum effectiveness during peak crime hours, the system was designed with cameras that can pan, zoom, and change focus based on input from a monitoring console. These cameras will be able to operate during the day and at night, without the need of vastly improved lighting.

AUDIO SURVEILLANCE OF ELEVATORS BY RESIDENTS

Limited experiments were proposed for the design and use of less expensive audio surveillance devices. This was necessary to determine whether the high degree of refined information provided by TV surveillance is actually necessary to achieve a substantial reduction in crime and fear of crime. If providing audio information yields similar effects, it can be implemented far more rapidly and at a vastly reduced cost.

The system involves two-way transmission of sound from inside the elevator to each corridor in the building, and from the corridor nearest the immediate location of the elevator into the elevator. This self-contained electronic system is mounted on the elevator cab in a vandal-proof container, with microphone pick-ups and speakers on each floor.

AUDIO INTERCOM INTERVIEWER FOR APARTMENT DOORS

A primary security design problem of double-loaded corridor buildings results from the sound buffer between hallways and apartment interiors. This sound insulation is partly intentional and partly a result of fire wall and door construction. While audio privacy may be desired by tenants, it may be operating as a contributant to undetected crimes, where it provides excessive insulation of tenants from the corridors outside their doors. It was hypothesized that if more sound from halls was audible to tenants in their apartments, they might be inclined to respond more readily to the early signs of crime. Similarly, neighboring tenants might be more aware of one another's arrivals and departures, and come to discriminate strange from normal sounds.

The system recommended for experimental installation at Bronxdale involves fitting doors of individual apartments with an audio interviewer with the following features:

> Microphone and speaker in each door, operated on long-life battery cells, designed for two-way communication, including "listen" and "speak" buttons, with volume controls.
>
> Design of the unit to remain "on" at all times, at low volume, where its lowest level of amplification is equivalent to sounds produced when listening through a window. At the highest adjustment, it allows tenants to monitor sounds the full length of the corridor with a high degree of resolution.

This system can also be adapted for use as an inter-apartment intercom among adjacent residents on a floor.

DIRECT TELEPHONE COMMUNICATIONS FROM TENANTS TO HOUSING AUTHORITY POLICE AT BRONXDALE

One of the primary factors influencing tenant attitudes about calling police involves the current system of dialing a central city-wide number and then speaking with a dispatcher who notifies the local patrolmen to answer the call. We proposed a trial system at Bronxdale in which tenants could speak directly with the local patrolman by dialing a separate telephone number in his booth. As the local patrolman may be out on call, this required additional equipment to convert the telephone call to a broadcast band on his walkie-talkie. After the phone in the police room has rung twice and remains unanswered, it is switched automatically to a recording and broadcasting device which informs the caller that the police are on patrol, that they have twenty seconds in which to leave a message, and that this message will be broadcast to police on patrol via walkie-talkie. The patrolman receives the telephone call on his walkie-talkie and checks with central command for a disposition on the case. He then proceeds directly to the caller's apartment.

8

SUMMARY AND RECOMMENDATIONS

Over the past twenty-five years, the population of the United States has been shifting from rural areas and small towns to the larger metropolitan concentrations; from the central areas of the country to the peripheral coastal and Great Lakes cities. To accommodate these new concentrations, two phenomena have occurred: the middle- and upper-income populations have, for the most part, moved their residences out of the older central areas to create and occupy a new suburbia, distinguished by its large scale and low density; while the rural migrants, poor, and disadvantaged, have moved in to occupy the remnants of older central city.

This is, of course, an over-simplification. Many urban areas still house large concentrations of middle- and upper-income families. The overall trend, however, is unmistakable. The Federal Government has participated in assisting the nation in accommodating these shifts. Guaranteed low-interest mortgages, in combination with highway programs, made suburbia realizable. The problem of inner-city needs has been partially answered through various low-income housing programs, low-interest mortgage programs for rental and cooperative purchase, and public housing for the very poor.

The increase in land costs stemming from these concentrations has made building in the inner city, or in the core areas of suburbia, costly. The obvious response has been to increase building density so as to spread the high land costs among as many apartment units as possible. This, in turn, has produced a new housing prototype: the large high-rise project containing half-a-dozen apartment towers and housing a thousand or more families with children. High-rise residential buildings are, of course, not an entirely new or foreign concept to America. Almost every city has examples of luxury high-rises which have been housing wealthy families comfortably in center-city since the turn of the century. But as mass housing for low- and middle-income families with children, they are a new phenomenon, and one which has brought many unanticipated problems.

Our survey of urban housing reveals that high-rise elevator buildings as family housing is, at best, a minimal solution, regardless of income group. However, for poor and broken families, for immigrant, rural families new to urban life, the effect of living in a high-rise building is proving catastrophic. Housing officials in St. Louis, Philadelphia, Newark—to name only a few—are finding that the cost of placing welfare families with children in large high-rise housing developments may, in the short period of five years, be the destruction of the physical plant of the project itself. (No means has yet been devised for measuring the extent of destruction to family and personal lives.)

When in 1965 the Federal Government decided to change the rules for admission to public housing, many welfare families, previously excluded, were allowed entry. In the intervening seven years, the high-rise buildings to which they were admitted have been undergoing systematic decimation. Some have been gutted and others totally abandoned: witness the wreck of Pruitt-Igoe in St. Louis, Rosen Apartments in Philadelphia, Columbus Homes in Newark. Almost every major city has its own example.

With all this going on, it is no surprise that housing policy is undergoing re-examination and revision, but the old failures continue to be built. The explanation is disheartening: the men and the bureaucratic sections of housing agencies involved in managing projects are currently separated from those concerned with new construction. This is true on the national level at HUD Washington, as it is true in many regional HUD offices and local housing agencies. Success for the department responsible for building new housing is measured by *how many new* units are built each year and not by what kind of units, how much they will cost to maintain, how long they will last, or how satisfactory a living environment they will provide. The daily experience of the management and maintenance departments, if ever transmitted back to the development departments, is seldom seriously considered.

One of the more alarming aspects of high-rise developments is the danger of raising children in them. The argument that middle- and upper-income families have lived in high-rise elevator buildings for years without trauma cannot be used convincingly as justification for providing this type of housing for low-income families. There are attending circumstances in one living environment and life style which do not exist in the other. Middle-income families with children living in urban high-rises seldom form more than half the occupancy of a building. (Where they do indeed form the majority, as in university and graduate student housing, there is evidence of problems similar to those experienced in public housing.) In addition, middle-income apartment buildings housing over a hundred families commonly have one or two resident superintendents and possibly a doorman to restrict access. This is not always the case in low-middle-income developments and *never* the case in public housing.

Most importantly, however, middle-income families can learn to make a success of high-rise buildings because there are usually two adult heads of household and the mother assumes the role of caretaker of the children. Children in middle-income families are usually watched over carefully, are given opportunity for recreation away from home, and effort is expended in teaching them behavior rules necessary to the creation of a conflict-free, dense multi-family existence. By contrast, children of low-income families are generally unattended. The rule system for expected behavior is often minimal and sporadically enforced. Inclement weather means their play is restricted to building interiors. It should not be surprising to find that much of the vandalism and resulting maintenance costs in housing projects is laid to the mischief of children. Most recently the elevators of high-rise, low-income apartment buildings have become the new frontier of exploratory recreation for young teen-agers. The result has been nothing less than calamitous: children have died from falls and decapitations and have suffered broken limbs and dismemberment.[1] The damage to elevator equipment has been equally devastating. Youngsters not only commonly remove elevator doors entirely, but have found ways to anchor cables so that the elevator motors and pulleys tear the cabs from their railings—ripping apart an entire elevator shaft for the full height of the building. We can conclude, therefore, that the many differences in family structure and life styles, the difference in funds for staffing and accoutrements that make high-rise housing workable for middle-income families make it unworkable for low-income families.

But there are still other factors operating, and these stem from the largely rural backgrounds of low-income residents. It is difficult even for a family born and raised in an urban environment to adjust to high-rise apartment life if they have not lived this way before. For a rural family, the problems of adjustment are greatly aggravated. Urban life is

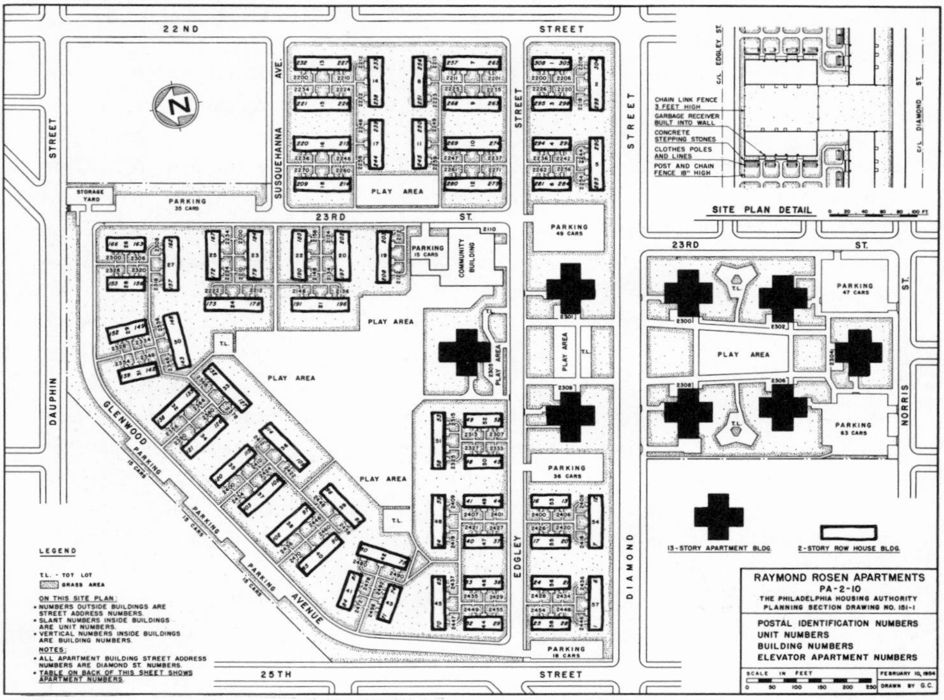

FIG. 162. Site Plan of Rosen Apartments, Philadelphia. Plan shows mix of thirteen-story high-rise and two-story row-house buildings. (Courtesy of Philadelphia Housing Authority)

FIG. 163. View of row houses and high-rises at Rosen Apartments, Philadelphia. (Photo by author)

FIG. 164. View of Front Yards of the Row Houses at Rosen Apartments. The condition of grounds and entries of row-house units at Rosen Apartments shows that they are cared for by tenants. (Photo by author)

much more confined and restrictive to people accustomed to the freedom and abundant space of rural or small-town life. Children find the difference even more stiking and show resentment and difficulty in adapting; balanced adjustment for them may actually never occur.

Where, in the process of adaptation, a middle-class family will not perform too differently in one building type versus another, the performance of a welfare family proves to be greatly influenced by the physical environment. In a 1022-unit public housing project in Philadelphia, Rosen Apartments, composed of a mixture of high and low buildings, about one-third of the apartment units are in two-story row houses and two-thirds in thirteen-story apartment buildings. The social profile of families in both building types is almost identical in terms of ethnicity, ages of children, and family income. The row-house units, however, are larger and house families with more children. On a percentage basis, there are as many broken families living in one building type as the other. But statistics reveal that the high-rise buildings, with similar but smaller families, suffer seven and a half times as much vandalism, robberies, and arrests of loitering drug addicts. Although the row-house buildings are more susceptible to burglary, the rate is the same in both building types.

FIG. 165. Typical entry area of thirteen-story high-rise buildings at Rosen Apartments. (Photo by author)

FIG. 166. Typical condition of access stairs in thirteen-story high-rise buildings at Rosen Apartments. (Photo by author)

The project, since its inception, was always occupied solely by black families. Twenty years ago, when the project was just completed, and there was a restrictive admission policy, the families allowed into these projects were more in the mold of the recognizable working class—only 28 percent of the families were on welfare. They were also of urban origin, rather than rural immigrants. In those days, the crime and vandalism rates in the towers were about 10 percent higher than in the walk-ups. In 1965, when the guidelines for admission were altered, many welfare and broken families were admitted. The percentage of welfare families in both building types is now 62 percent. In 1961, there were approximately 22 percent broken families in each building type, and now, there are 80 percent. The problem has become so severe that new tenants are extremely reluctant to accept an apartment above the sixth floor. The reason given is that they will not consider living where they cannot reach the ground or their apartment by their own power, or be able to call down for assistance. As one tenant explained it, "There is just so far you can be expected to go into a cave." The Philadelphia Authority has found the vacancy rate in the high-rise increasing alarmingly and is now seriously considering adopting an official policy of not leasing new apartments above the sixth floor.

Although it has been shown that upper-middle-income families with children can make a better success of high-rise apartment living, other factors make this life style difficult even for these families. In considering the vulnerability of high-rise apartment buildings to criminal assault, there is little variation between low- and middle-income groups. Middle-income families living in a high-rise 221(d)3 cooperative, for which Federal guidelines prohibit the use of doormen, find themselves as victimized as public housing tenants—particularly if these buildings are located in high-crime areas. The anonymity that comes with increased numbers does not appear to vary with income group. For all their internal controls on children—and good intentions—a building which is open to entry by anyone, and in which it is very difficult to distinguish resident from intruder, is one which is criminally vulnerable.

The following general guidelines seem to emerge: for low-income families with children—particularly those on welfare or suffering pathological disorder—the high-rise apartment building is to be strictly avoided. Instead, these families should be housed in walk-up buildings no higher than three stories. Entries and vertical and horizontal circulation corridors should be designed so that as few families as possible share a common lobby. This puts a density limit of about fifty units per acre on a housing project composed solely of this housing type. Although this density may be too low for New York City, it will satisfy density requirements of most other cities. It should be remembered that with all their appearance of high density, Pruitt-Igoe was built at only forty-eight units to the acre, and Van Dyke Houses in Brooklyn at eighty units per acre. The density restriction of fifty units to the acre is therefore not really that difficult to suffer.

For high-income families, another set of guidelines is possible. Apartment residents who can afford to pay for doormen and superintendents are able to relegate responsibility for control of their living environment to formally designated authorities and so can afford to live at almost any densities they chose. Restricted only by the limit to which one can tolerate sharing a common entry with large numbers of people, the greater the numbers, the more economical is the use of doormen. However, there is a point (at about 200 families), where doormen themselves have difficulty keeping track of who belongs and who doesn't. At this point, the embarassment of challenging a possible new tenant makes the system break down.

Interestingly, for low-income elderly, the high-rise apartment building seems to work very well indeed. Their success has been demonstrated in many different cities, including instances where they have been located in high-crime areas. Examples of this are Van Dyke II in the Brownsville section of Brooklyn and Washington Park in Lower Roxbury, Boston. The governing condition, however, is that the building be exclusively for their use: no families with children should be permitted to share the same building. Contrary to many planners' idealistic formulations, housing authority managers find that most elderly prefer to live among themselves, away from noisy children, and from physically active teen-agers in particular. A good many elderly, it appears, would prefer not to be even remotely adjacent to a housing project containing children.

Because the elderly are, for the most part, retired and as a result have much free time on their hands, they tend to socialize a lot. It is quite common for a group to spontaneously set up a table at the entry to their building so as to control access. In this way, they effectively come to serve as their own doormen. As they usually are all in bed by midnight, there are seldom difficulties resulting from comings and goings after the volunteer doormen have gone off duty.

To facilitate the operation of tenant doormen in a high-rise building for the elderly, entry should be limited to one portal which is easily controlled visually. The provision of an alarm which will call the police automatically is a good back-up device to place at the tenant volunteers' disposal in case someone has pushed his way past them and into the building.

A reasonable way to increase the density of a housing development which must be built at greater than fifty units to the acre is to mix in a few high-rise buildings for the elderly with the three-story walk-ups built for families with children. It is important, however, to keep buildings housing the elderly to themselves. They should be located at the periphery of the project, immediately adjacent to surrounding streets, and if possible, physically separated from the buildings housing children and play areas. By this method, a public housing project on, say, five acres of land, housing 220 families with children on four of its acres at fifty-five units per acre, and 230 elderly families in a single high-rise located on the remaining acre, could achieve a combined density of seventy units to the acre—a density that begins to be reasonable even for New York (at least for its peripheral boroughs). It should be noted, too, that the elderly normally prefer high-rise buildings to having to put up with the inconvenience of walk-ups of any sort.

Throughout our discussion in this and preceding chapters, there have been recurring references to density and the need to meet the rules of building economics. It has been suggested that the very advent of the high-rise apartment building was created by increasing concentrations and the corresponding increase in land costs.

There is, however, a danger in labeling density, per se, as the culprit, because many different building types and configurations can be built at the same densities—witness the Brownsville–Van Dyke comparison in chapter 2 and the figures mentioned previously in this chapter. But, in the pursuit of ever increasing density, there is a break point beyond which available building-type alternatives diminish. The workable couple of high-rise slabs composed of piggy-back apartments isolated in our discussion of the Riverbend Apartments was built at eighty units to the acre, and this may be the reasonable upper limit of defensible space housing.

Most housing projects in New York City, built at a density of over fifty units an acre, are built as high-rise, elevator, double-loaded corridor buildings. At fifty units per acre and below, there are prototypes to choose from, other than high-rise. Not surprisingly, a correlation between density and crime rate for all New York City projects reveals that there is no evident pattern until one reaches a density of fifty units per acre. After that, however, crime rate increases proportionately with density. The explanation, of course, has already been given: above fifty units per acre, the NYCHA has confined its projects exclusively to high-rise, double-loaded corridor buildings. Crime rate may not correlate specifically with density, but it *does* correlate with building height and type. Unfortunately, above eighty units per acre, there appears to be only one building prototype available—the high-rise, double-loaded corridor, elevator tower—and that option does correlate strongly with crime rate.

Nationally, we are witnessing an ever increasing demand by housing officials to build at increasing densities, including those well above the critical mark. What then can be done with the problem of density, and why does it control design so rigidly? Density is usually expressed in persons, or dwelling units per acre. A particular density can also denote a residential building prototype. For example, individual detached housing in an urban setting usually sits on one-sixth acre and has a corresponding density of six dwelling units to the acre. Row housing (sometimes called town housing) has a density of from twelve to eighteen dwelling units per acre. Walk-up buildings have a density as high as fifty units per acre, depending upon the number of floors. Elevator buildings place no theoretical limit on density and normally range from fifty units per acre to as high as 400 units per acre. The former is common; the latter rare. Unfortunately, density is seldom a question of choice but is usually determined by building economics. Competitive demand for residential space in desirable urban settings drives up the cost of land in a free-market economy. A correspondingly larger number of units must, therefore, be placed on a more expensive piece of land in order to keep the land and development cost per unit down.

High-density solutions, however, may not always be the result simply of the dictates of real estate economics. They may also stem from the need to rehouse a large low-income population from a high-density slum in a city where the relocation opportunities are few. High density, in this instance, may be the result of a very well-intentioned commitment on the part of housing and renewal officials, but this in no way excludes their having to cope with the range of problems brought about by high-rise living. The pressure on a housing authority to increase the density of housing projects is sometimes caused by the very bureaucratic processes set up by the Federal, state, and municipal agencies committed to the construction of low-income housing.

Although real estate speculators and the government have now brought us all to the point where we accept, as inevitable, increasing land costs and increasing densities, they are, in fact, much of our own creation. So long as land-use zoning restrictions are so easily manipulated—zoning amendments so readily pushed through planning boards—land speculators will continue to hold out land for higher costs, knowing that the density can always rise to meet them. It is an ever increasing, self-perpetuating spiral, and until we develop a rationale for restricting density, based on more than competitive land costs or the capacity of support facilities, we will be parties to our own demise. Western European countries—Holland, Sweden, and England—who strictly control allowable residential densities suffer few of these problems.

There are, of course, other contributing agents to high land costs and the resultant high density, and these need different remedies. For example, it is often necessary for housing developers to purchase land with existing buildings on it in order to create land for new housing. The cost of these old buildings, which are only to be torn down, must be included in calculating the land costs. Since this procedure is essential to any strategy for revitalizing existing cities, the Federal program for land cost write-down must become more than the marginal effort it is now.

A uniformly low-density environment should not, however, be seen as the single panacea to crime problems. Instead, an endeavor must be made to isolate those factors that operate in making walk-up environments (garden apartments as dense as fifty-five units to the acre) crime inhibitors and some high-rise environments (ranging from densities of 45 to 200 units per acre) magnets and breeders of crime. In chapter 2, evidence produced from a comparison of two neighboring housing projects of identical density but of radically different building prototypes—one high-rise slabs (Van Dyke Houses), the other densely grouped walk-ups (Brownsville Houses)—demonstrated that density in itself is not the controlling factor. Other physical variables affecting crime exist as the hidden culprits of high-density structures, and these must be isolated and identified. Theoretically, it should be possible to develop designs for relatively high-density structures (100 to 150 units to the acre) which incorporate all of the defensible space directives. But it is clear from some of the preliminary work we have done in this direction that there will also be an increase in the cost (per apartment unit) of the building. The question, then, will be to determine which solution provides the most benefits: more costly high-density buildings, or less expensive, lower-density buildings.

In chapter 1 we mentioned the current phenomenon of middle-class communities fleeing to the suburbs, or safer urban communities, to escape ghetto crime. The Forest Hills controversy is typical of still another form of reaction: the unified resistance of a white middle-income community to the location of a new public housing project within its midst.

Forest Hills is a middle-income, predominantly white community, located in an area of the Borough of Queens, most distant from Manhattan. Neighborhood housing is mixed multi- and single-family, the streets are clean, the schools well maintained and staffed. In 1966, the New York City Housing Authority announced that following its new policy of building scattered-site housing, an 828-unit project would be built on an 8.5-acre site in the Forest Hills area. The community objected, following what has now become a typical pattern across the country. Its complaints were listened to but not acted on, as the city administration felt that its program was sound and had positive, far-reaching implications. However, as work on the project continued, the number of units to be placed on the site grew from 828 to 840. The design which was previously proposed as a mix of three ten-story buildings, three twelve-story buildings and one twenty-two-story building, was now limited to three twenty-four-story towers, each containing 280 units. As construction got underway in fall of 1971, the community began actively demonstrating against the project. Being an election year, much press and media coverage was given to the controversy.

There are various and separate issues that must be addressed in the discussion of Forest Hills. In most public discussion they are commonly lumped together, becoming confused and indistinguishable. It is all the more important, therefore, that each of the issues be examined on its own merit.

Central to their position is the belief held by the Forest Hills community that residential locations adjacent to low-income areas or housing projects result in an increase in neighborhood crime. These are opinions which were formulated from personal experiences of various sorts and have, with time, hardened into a communal lore. Many middle-income whites are new residents to their neighborhoods; the communities they lived in in the past were undergoing rapid change and came quickly to be occupied by low-income families. The old inhabitants claim that they found themselves confronted with more and more crime, burglaries, muggings, and vandalism; their children were threatened in schools, and the streets were no longer safe for evening strolls or pursuit of recreation activity.

Some statistical evidence tends to reinforce these claims. Certain precincts in Greater New York have developed decidedly higher crime rates than others. For residential districts, the highest crime rates occur in areas occupied by the families with the lowest income. This finding parallels the national pattern. While it is true that the poor have been found to make up the largest percentage among apprehended and convicted criminals, it is also true that they have been found to be the most victimized population in the nation. Public housing projects surrounded by other public housing have more crime in them than those surrounded by middle-income communities.

Crimes engaged in by the poor are very much like the jobs they engage in: they require minimal skills and are pursued when need dictates. The low-income criminal, unlike the professional or white-collar criminal, does not have a developed specialty. He preys on his immediate neighbors and depends on brute force and opportunity as it arises. This criminal activity, however, can be the most directly oppresive form of crime, as it is the most immediately threatening to person and property. The low-income criminal also has few connections with lawyers or police to deal for him when he is apprehended. He and his crimes are the most obnoxious to society, and his arrest makes for good crime fighters' statistics. For all the impressive statistics and jails crowded with ghetto residents, there is little impact being made on serious national crime. Unfortunately, there is no solace to be had in this understanding. Street crimes and burglaries are the most threatening, because they are crimes of personal confrontation and, hence, the most destructive of the feelings of well-being, security, and stability.

Housing projects located in precincts with high crime rates have been found, statistically, to suffer higher crime. It must follow, therefore, that communities adjacent to high-crime areas will suffer in a similar way. It does not, however, necessarily follow that a small public housing project located within a middle-class community will radically increase

FIG. 167. Precinct Felony Rate × Project Crime Rate. (Sources: New York City Housing Authority Police data for 1970 and New York City Police data for 1970)

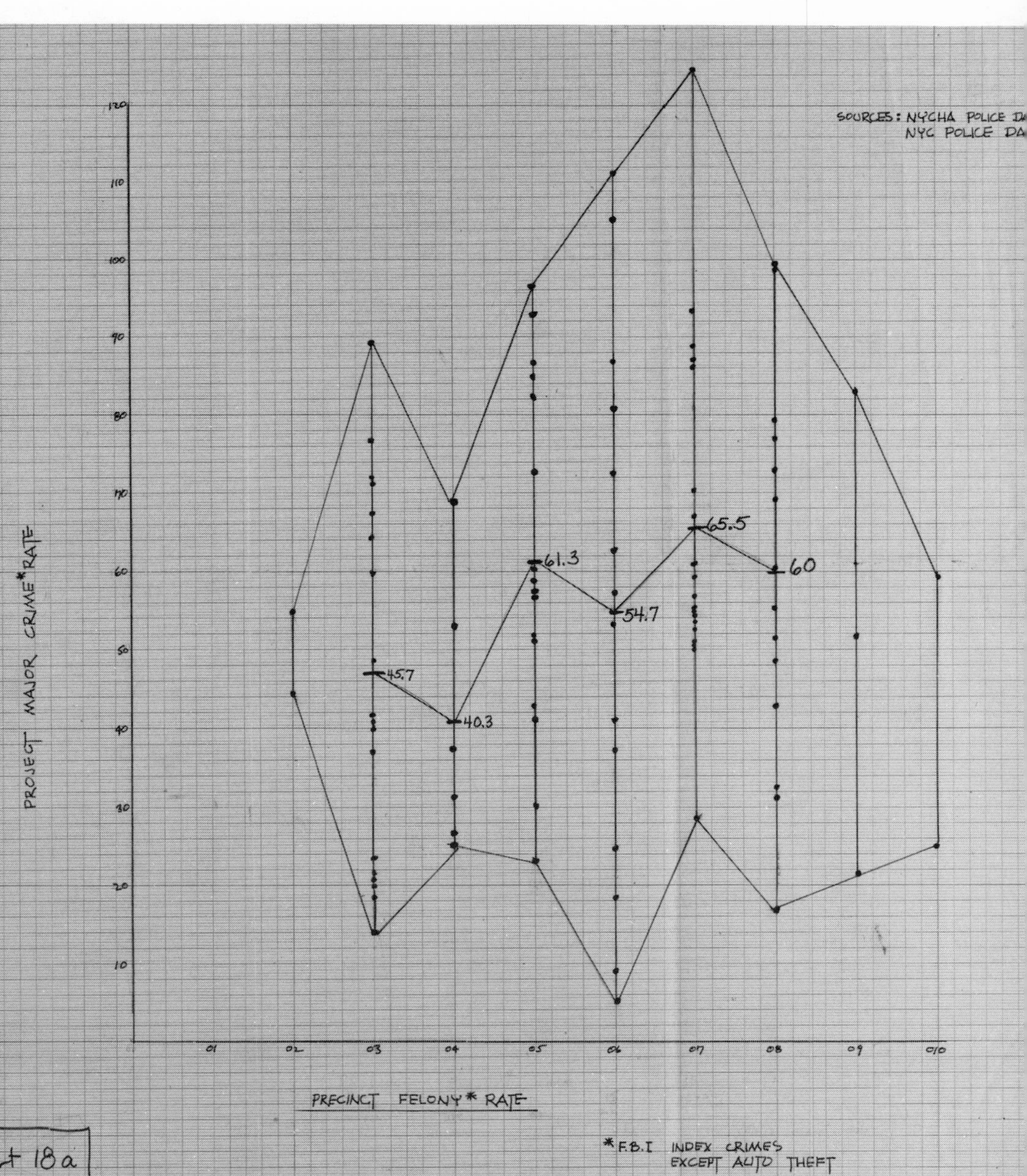

that community's crime rate. It should be pointed out, however, that we have been unable, as yet, to find a source of data which will allow us to measure the truth of this hypothesis. In most housing projects, the resident criminals form a very small percentage of the population, whereas the victims usually include everyone. All that we can predict with reasonable assurance is that the location of a housing project within a low-crime community will benefit the housing project residents appreciably.

A second issue can now be introduced for consideration: a housing project composed of high-rise double-loaded corridor buildings is much more vulnerable to criminal activity than its walk-up counterpart. By making the project small and locating the high-rise buildings in a "nice" neighborhood, one can go a long way toward creating a workable solution. However, if the project is large (750 units or over) it will have serious internal problems, even if located in a good community. Approximately 50 percent of the apprehendees in housing projects live in the project they are victimizing. Few criminals, however, will operate within the actual building they live in, if the buildings are small (fifty units or less), as they are too easily recognized. Large housing projects composed only of high-rise buildings and located in a high-crime area are the worst possible alternate and will produce crime rates four to five times that of small projects of low density located in relatively low-crime areas.

In conclusion, it would appear that the residents of Forest Hills may have some reasonable grievances, but their concerns are greatly inflated. Dispersal of low-income population within middle-class communities may bring some difficulties to the native inhabitants, but the problems they solve for the poor are immense by comparison.

A far stronger case can be made for the grievances of the future inhabitants of the housing project, were they in fact able to voice a collective opinion. The size of the project and the buildings in which they will be placed are highly conducive to their eventual victimization. Reducing the 840-unit project, built at 100 units to the acre, to a more reasonable size would help both project residents and the surrounding community and, not so incidentally, may go a long way towards salvaging the concept of the vest-pocket housing program.

Living in contemporary cities is living in a very shared environment, of rich and poor, of black and white, of old residents and new. In cities where a strongly defined societal structure exists, in which common goals and values are shared, and where the class lines are clearly defined and accepted, the close living proximity of rich and poor is possible and even convenient. Witness the structure of southern cities in the U.S. of as little as thirty years ago, or of Western European cities of the prewar era. But in contemporary Western urban society, social lines and boundaries are not well defined, understood, or respected. There is also little in the

FIG. 168. View of Vest-Pocket Project in Setting of Surrounding Community, Queen Lane, Philadelphia. Vest-pocket public housing project of 139 units in a single building. The project suffers a marginal crime and vandalism rate. (Photo by author)

physical structure of our cities that reflects social stratification. In these circumstances, the close physical proximity of different income or ethnic groups may become intolerable. The flight of the middle class to the suburbs for the purpose of creating both economically and socially exclusive enclaves bears witness to this phenomenon. City planners, for idealistic motives not always fully thought through or formulated, advocate economic mixes in their housing developments. But their values and notions are little more than utopian and may not be shared by either their rich or poor clients.

Paradoxically, at a time when we are all just learning to open up—to question the value of the individual pursuit of wealth at the expense of society—the idea of a defensible space environment may be interpreted by some as a methodology for restriction and closing down. At a time when the Western world seems to have approached acceptance of the notion of an open society with accompanying open institutions, it is strange to find many of its proponents advocating what may appear as a retrenchment tactic. It is sad to have to conclude that the free and fertile soil of the liberalized imagination may also have nurtured the seeds of its own restriction. The challenge to the establishment's rights, methods, and motives may be being used by some in our society who, unlike the question-

FIG. 169. Entry Buffer Area at Queen Lane, Philadelphia. The lobby and entry area face directly on the street. The project grounds are differentiated by a change in level, use of low walls, and shrubbery. Apartment unit windows survey grounds and bordering streets. The walk from street to lobby is direct and short. (Photo by author)

ing liberal, have no constructive objectives to achieve—they are content simply with using the new opportunities to "rip-off" who and what they can.

It is strange, then, to find the enlightened middle class fleeing to the ghettoes of suburbia, fleeing from the liberalized atmosphere they have worked at creating in the cities; stranger still to observe their flight and apparent content with leaving behind an immobile population far more vulnerable to the ravages of criminals, addicts, and abusive agents of authority. For the middle class, criminal assault is a survivable nuisance;

for the poor and working class, it may mean a total wipe-out: a life's work gone, a psychological disaster. For our low-income population, security in their residential environment—security from the natural elements, from criminals, and from authority—is the first essential step to liberation.

The problem is that the opening up and change in our cities may have occurred too quickly for beneficiary and recipient alike. Too much has been created to cope with too soon. The decision to opt out is an easy one—the pastures of suburbia alluring and becoming—but for those who remember the rich advantages of city life, and who have experienced the "poverty" of suburbia, the city is not so easily relinquished, nor are the motivations behind the work put into the opening up of society. However, to be able to retain the purpose and carry out the goal beyond the heady moment of liberation may now require a restructuring of our cities. Defensible space may be the last stand of the urban man committed to an open society.

It is probably premature to come to this conclusion, but it is possible that an inadvertent result of a socially mobile and open society is its required segregation into physically separate, subclusters which are inviolable and uniform, both socially and economically. The residential portion

FIG. 170. Vest-pocket housing in London set among traditional 3½-story English row housing. (Photo by author)

of the urban environment, devoted to family life and the raising of children, may have to take place within small exclusive homogeneous clusters. The interaction necessary to business, education, and the pursuit of recreation, on the other hand, will involve intermingling of economic groups, but within a framework in which roles and behavior norms are very defined.

If this is to be the required format for future cities, the quesion is, at what level is such segregation to occur? Is it to be a core city isolated from the suburb, or is it to take place at the scale where collections of defensible residential enclaves share a city, and where mutual association is of mutual benefit?

Within the present atmosphere of pervasive crime and ineffectual authority, the only effective measure for assuring a safe living environment is community control. We are advocating a program for the restructuring of residential developments in our cities to facilitate their control by the people who inhabit them. We see this as the only long-term measure of consequence in the battle for the maintenance of a sane urban society. Short-term measures involving flights to suburbia or additional police manpower and equipment are only palliatives.

The essential ingredient of our proposal is territorial definition coupled with improvements to the capacity of the territorial occupants to survey their newly defined realm. Territorial definition may appear to be the antithesis of the open society, and surveillance a further restriction on its freedom. Territory and surveillance have after all traditionally been understood as the devices of the propertied classes and their agents or police authority. We, however, are advocating territorial definition and the creation of surveillance opportunities to allow the *citizen* of the open society to achieve control of his environment for the activities he wishes to pursue within it—to make him instrumental in curtailing others from destroying his habitat, whether the others are criminals or a reactionary authority.

The functioning of authority in crime prevention has been greatly curtailed by the new format of our evolving residential areas. The policeman's fear of entering projects minimizes his effectiveness—perhaps entirely nullifying it. If police are to be a final resort in dealing with (apprehending) criminals, then community self-assurance is an essential ingredient to intelligent demand and use of police. The difficulty lies in the fact that unlike a middle-class community, low-income neighborhoods hold various attitudes towards police. Where some may view them positively, others react with negative or hostile feelings. It becomes essential, therefore, for residents and police to create a situation in which the residents will assume responsibility for a summoned policeman's safety, just as they will, in turn, be able to require that the policeman perform in accord with a defined set of rules.

If territorial redefinition, as advocated in the "defensible space" program, proves to reinforce certain groups in taking over and controlling previous public space adjacent to their dwelling units, are we not, through these actions, removing much territory in the form of parks and open space from the public domain? Are we not by this exclusion placing further restriction on the already narrowing and limited resources of our cities? Some of our findings suggest that just the opposite may be true. Studies of the use of grounds of housing projects in many different cities —New York, Cleveland, San Francisco—indicate that the grounds of projects which were intentionally left open for public use (as a contribution to the open-space needs of the surrounding city) end up unused and neglected, by housing residents as well as members of the surrounding community. Each group, by experience, had found their activities easily disrupted by other groups and found that their claim to the use of the space for recreation difficult to enforce. By contrast, recreation space located within the interior of a housing project, clearly defined by surrounding dwellings, was found to be used more frequently by both groups. Project residents had clearly laid claim to these play spaces and set up an unwritten, but understood, set of rules for their use. These rules were enforced by parents and other children. Project residents had first claim to this use, followed by surrounding neighborhood children, who came both spontaneously and by invitation. Disputes almost always resulted in the expulsion of the visitors. Since visiting children really had nowhere else to go or to retreat to, the proprietary rights of project children soon became understood and accepted, and further conflict was avoided by mutual desire, whenever possible.

In the course of our work, we have received expressions of concern from members of communities adjacent to the projects we have been working in. Their concern is that our endeavors would only succeed in displacing crime from one area to another. There is some evidence to support their hypothesis. Captain Arnold Berkman, of the New York City Housing Authority Police, keeps careful tabulations of variations in crime rates in all areas of his jurisdiction and has found that as a vigorous police effort is concentrated in one project, criminals respond by moving into adjacent projects. Displacement, however, is seldom a full 100 percent.

The nature of criminal acts is sometimes distinguished by the intent and motivation of the criminal. Much crime is crime of opportunity rather than premeditated. Since a sizable percentage of crimes in housing projects is estimated to be crime of opportunity, the reduction of opportunity may, therefore, result in less crime rather than in displacement.

If, for the sake of argument, one accepts as a proposition that the total amount of crime cannot be diminished, only displaced, this then offers a new question: is a pattern of uniformly distributed crime preferable to one in which crime is concentrated in particular areas? It is our contention that the second situation is more desirable. The home and its environs must be felt secure or the very fabric of society comes under threat. From our interviewing, we have been led to believe that people accept the fact that certain areas of a city are unsafe and, therefore, take steps to avoid, or minimize, the risk of using them. But they all find this an intolerable condition for their own residential environment. People can limit the use of dangerous areas to necessary occasions and, if too frightened, will find ways of collectively using these areas so as to add to their safety. (This often happens when women meet together to go shopping or to use the project laundry room.) In the home and its environs, no one wishes to feel so restricted. The family spends most of its time there. It is where future generations are raised, and where the most susceptible members of society live. It is also the shelter to which we all return from our forays. For these reasons, it must be made secure, even at the expense, if necessary, of making other nonresidential areas more dangerous. In many ways it would be a significant accomplishment to achieve this end alone: allowing displacement of crime to shopping, institutional, and business areas. The argument can be made that these other areas are inheritantly more easily served by formal police protection.

In spite of these justifications, there are serious moral implications to the question of displacement, and they are not as easily dismissed as might be suggested. In the ensuing years of our study we will be examining the changing patterns of crime in the areas surrounding the projects we have altered, just as we observe the changes in the projects themselves. The full extent of the displacement problem is yet to be understood and a means for coping with it developed.

Fundamental to this study is the proposition that through the manipulation of building and spatial configurations, one can create areas for which people will adopt concern. This may suggest that if our data and design methods were sufficiently sensitive it would be possible to predict and control a wide range of behavior and social relationships through provision of particular architectural settings. While this may or may not be true, it is not the focus of our research. Ours is a much smaller thesis: that it is possible, through the provision of facilities in certain juxtapositions, to release potential behavioral attitudes and positive social relationships. As an example: the provision of a play facility for infants at each floor level of an apartment building may bring families out to use it and may further result in the development of limited friendships and the cognizance of neighbors. This, in turn, may lead to a commonly shared effort at maintaining the facility so as to make it secure for the children, an act which also entails a screening of all intruders to these areas.

These relationships should be understood as those of mutual assistance to support a commonly desired situation. They may, in some instances, lead to further friendships, and the sharing of responsibilities in the care of children, but this is a peripheral outcome, and one which is not central to our immediate thesis. The recorded instances of a few welfare-supported mothers cooperatively sharing child rearing responsibilities is not, we feel, a by-product of a shared architectural setting, but of a social and possibly cultural need. No group of buildings or architectural setting is likely to give birth to a particular utopian society. Isomorphism remains a happy delusion of very few architects and physical planners.

We are concerned that some might read into our work the implication that architectural design can have a direct causal effect on social interactions. Architecture operates more in the area of "influence" than control. It can create a setting conducive to realizing the *potential* of mutual concern. It does not and cannot manipulate people toward these feelings, but rather allows mutually benefiting attitudes to surface. Some might conclude that, if it were found desirable, it might be possible to apply our findings in reverse. That is, for a malignant authority to intentionally set about developing environments which isolate people and elicit their antagonisms, fears, and paranoia. It might be argued that a system developed for one end, if valid, may be employed to achieve another. Our research indicates that even the most disadvantaged will not tolerate for very long extreme negativism in their living environment. Pruitt-Igoe and other public housing monstrosities, while created accidentally, did for a while succeed in creating a subculture victimized by criminals and the deranged preying on each other. But, in a short time, most residents rebelled and simply moved out; the remaining few got together to insist on administrative and physical changes. With a 65 percent vacancy rate, in a city where housing for welfare recipients is in very short supply, there appears to be little future in negative planning to achieve negative results.[2]

The past few years have witnessed efforts by the Federal Government, in partnership with large corporations, to apply large-scale technological and financial methods to the mass production of housing (as in Project Breakthrough). One danger is all too clear: in our concern for coming to grips with the problem of providing mass housing, we may be moving into a period where technological and economic acumen in the provision and construction of buildings have become ends in themselves. A parallel empirical and theoretical breakthrough is necessary in defining the social and psychological constraints with which these new forms will have to reckon. It is our hope that this initial study will serve as the first of many steps in this direction.

NOTES

1. New York City Housing Authority insurance liability reports show a total of twenty-one deaths of children as a result of elevator accidents between 1969 and 1971.

2. St. Louis Housing Authority, "Annual Statistical Report," 1970.

APPENDIX A

Methodology

I. Introduction

II. Available Data
   A. Police Crime Reports
      1. New York City Housing Authority Police
      2. New York City Police Crime Reports
   B. Physical Variables
   C. Tenant Characteristics
   D. Interview Methodology

III. Approaches
   A. Stepwise Multiple Regression Analysis
   B. Trend Analysis
   C. Analysis of Variance

Tables
   A1. Police Crime Data Existing on Tape
   A2. Preliminary List of Physical Variables
   A3. Physical Characteristics
   A4. Tenant Data Existing on Tape
   A5. Record Format of Tenant Data Statistics Tape
   A6. Correlation Coefficients of Physical and Social Variables with Robberies
   A7. Regression Analysis of Physical and Social Variables with Indoor Robberies

Illustrations
   Fig. A1. New York City Housing Authority—Police Department incident report
   Fig. A2. New York City Housing Authority—Police Department transcript of incident report
   Fig. A3. List of coded crimes included in New York City Housing Police data
   Fig. A4. New York City Housing Authority transcript of tenant data

I. INTRODUCTION

The purpose of this statistical study was to analyze the relationship between physical design elements and criminal activity. Analysis of past experience may demonstrate that particular physical configurations, in terms of site planning, building design, and interior layout, have demonstrably affected crime patterns. The basic task was to discern the statistical technique that could significantly demonstrate this effect, within the constraints of available data.

There are two fundamental problems in attempting to accurately define the relationship between crime and physical elements. First, crime is caused by a multiplicity of factors—economic, social, and governmental as well as physical—and it is extraordinarily difficult to isolate one sort of characteristic and discern its particular influence. In order to deal solely with physical variables, it was necessary to comprehend and account for the role of non-physical characteristics. Secondly, to a considerable extent we were attempting to measure something that does *not* happen—crime is least in evidence when certain design elements are most effective.

In attempting to find the proper solution to these problems, we began by considering available data, and then proceeded to develop a series of approaches intended to illuminate specific areas of information.

II. AVAILABLE DATA

A. Police Crime Reports

I. NEW YORK CITY HOUSING AUTHORITY POLICE

The New York City Housing Authority Police record complete and accurate information concerning virtually every incident in which a Housing Authority Police Officer is involved. Table A1 is a detailed breakdown of this data. Also included are copies of the actual forms and computer format used to record this data (figs. A1, A2, and A3). Of particular note is the fact that locational breakdowns, such as apartment, hallway, lobby, and grounds are recorded. Also important is the fact that data is kept on a project, but not an individual building basis.

TABLE A1

Police Crime Data Existing on Tape

Columns	*Data*
1	*Nature of Report*
	1 = initial
	2 = subsequent
	3 = additional
2–6	Incident number
7–9	Housing Authority *Police* number (range 200–699)
10–11	*Place of occurrence*
	10 = apartment
	12 = basement
	13 = community or child center
	14 = commercial establishment
	15 = elevator
	16 = lobby
	18 = hallway
	19 = parking lot
	21 = project area
	23 = roof and landing
	25 = stairway
	26 = public sidewalk, contiguous
	27 = unclassified, inside
	28 = unclassified, outside
	11 = off project park
	17 = off project street
	20 = off project, unclassified
12–17	*Date of occurrence*
	month columns = 12–13
	day columns = 14–15
	year columns = 16–17
18–19	*Day and tour of occurrence*

Time	Sun.	Mon.	Tue.	Wed.	Thurs.	Fri.	Sat.
12–4	1–1	2–1	3–1	4–1	5–1	6–1	7–1
4–8	1–2	2–2	3–2	4–2	5–2	6–2	7–2
8–12	1–3	2–3	3–3	4–3	5–3	6–3	7–3
12–4	1–4	2–4	3–4	4–4	5–4	6–4	7–4
4–8	1–5	2–5	3–5	4–5	5–5	6–5	7–5
8–12	1–6	2–6	3–6	4–6	5–6	6–6	7–6
Unknown	1–0	2–0	3–0	4–0	5–0	6–0	7–0

Unknown date and time = 0–0

Columns	*Data*
20	*Intrahousehold incident*
	1 = yes
	2 = no
21–23	*Type of incident*
	001–027 = felonies
	100–137 = misdemeanors
	200–212 = violations/offenses
	300–314 = investigations/aided
	400–417 = breach of rules

TABLE A 1—Continued

Columns	Data
24–25	
	01 = inside
	02 = outside
26	*Complainant*
	1 = Housing Authority patrolman
	2 = employee, tenant
	3 = tenant
	4 = nontenant
	5 = cross complaint
	6 = not applicable
	0 = Housing Authority patrolman
27–28	Age of complainant or aided
	00 = unknown or not applicable; Housing Authority Patrolman
29	*Race of complainant*
	1 = white
	2 = Negro
	3 = Puerto Rican
	4 = other
	5 = not applicable
	0 = Housing Authority Patrolman
30	*Sex of aided or complainant*
	1 = male
	2 = female
	3 = not applicable
	0 = Housing Authority Patrolman
31	*Reporting officer's assignment*
	1 = project
	2 = UF 61—report from New York City Police
	3 = detective squad
	4 = site and buildings squad
	5 = special patrol
	6 = other
32–36	Reporting officer's shield number
NOTE: From 37–70 Arrest/Apprehensions/Dispositions only	
37–39	*Type of incident*
	001–027 = felony
	100–137 = misdemeanors
	200–212 = violations/offenses
	300–317 = investigations
	401–417 = breach of rules
	500–502 = breach of rules
40–45	Date of arrest or apprehension
46	*Place of arrest*
	1 = off project
	2 = on project
	3 = not applicable

TABLE A 1—Continued

Columns	Data
47	Arresting officer's assignment (see column 31)
48–52	Arresting or apprehending officers shield number
53	*Status of first apprehended individual*
	1 = tenant
	2 = nontenant
	3 = not applicable
54–55	Age of first apprehended individual
56	Race of first apprehended individual (see column 29)
57	Sex of first apprehended individual (see column 30)
58	*Disposition*
	1 = arrested
	2 = apprehended
	3 = youthful offender
	4 = summons issued
	5 = referred to court
	6 = refusal to press charges
	7 = arrested by other authority
	8 = unfounded
Cols. 59–64 repeat 53–58 for second apprehended individual	
59	Status
60–61	Age
62	Race
63	Sex
64	Disposition
Cols. 65–70 repeat 53–58 for third apprehended individual	
65	Status
66–67	Age
68	Race
69	Sex
70	Disposition

NYCHA 080.003&R (RE[illegible]64)

INCIDENT REPORT

NEW YORK CITY HOUSING AUTHORITY • POLICE DEPARTMENT

1. REPORT ☐ INIT. ☐ SUBS. ☐ ADDIT.	2. INCIDENT #	3. PROJECT *(name)*	IBM #	5. INCIDENT: ☐ FELONY ☐ MISDEM. ☐ OFFENSE ☐ H.A.R.R. ☐ AIDED		DAY	DATE	TIME	9. INTRA-HOUSEHOLD ☐ YES ☐ NO
		4. PLACE OF OCCURRENCE *(Bldg., apt., walk, etc.)*		6. BLDG. ☐ IN ☐ OUT PROJ. ☐ ON ☐ OFF	7. OCCURRED				MGR. REPORT NO.
					8. REPORTED				

10. **SECTION Ⓐ : COMPLAINANT(S) / WITNESS(ES) / AIDED**

	NAME *(last, first, middle)*	ADDRESS *(no., st., apt., borough)*	PHONE NO.	AGE	RACE *(color)*	SEX M	SEX F	TENANT YES	TENANT NO	C'PLT	WIT.	AIDED
1												
2												
3												

AIDED DELIVERED TO: ☐ HOSPITAL *(name of hospital)* ☐ HOME ☐ MORGUE ☐ CLAIMED ☐ S.P.C.C.
(name, licence no., relationship)

DRIVEN BY:

11. SPECIFY — CRIME, OFFENSE, VIOL. H.A.R.R., AID — CODE #

12. **SECTION Ⓑ : VIOLATOR(S) / ARRESTED / WANTED**

	NAME *(last, first, middle, aliases)*	ADDRESS *(no., st., apt., borough)*	OCCUPATION/ SCHOOL	TENANT YES	TENANT NO	AGE	RACE *(color)*	SEX M	SEX F	YD'ED. YES	YD'ED. NO	HT.	WT.
①													
②													
③													

REPORTING OFFICER'S NAME, RANK | ASSIGNMENT | SHIELD NO.

SECTION Ⓒ DETAILS

(Give pertinent circumstances and conditions, property or objects involved and their values, seriousness of injury or illness, by whom aided person is claimed, action taken, etc.)

13. ARRESTS/ APPREHENSIONS		Ⓑ ①	Ⓑ ②	Ⓑ ③
SPECIFY CRIME OFFENSE OR VIOL.H.A.R.R. ▶		CODE #	CODE #	CODE #
PRECINCT NUMBERS	UF 61			
	ARREST			
	AIDED			
GANG NAME				

P.D. PCT. # ☐ PICK-UP ☐ COMPLAINT

ARREST/APPREH. DATE | TIME ☐ AM ☐ PM | ARREST/APPREH. OFF. PROJ. ☐ ON PROJ. ☐

ARREST/APPREH. OFFICER'S
NAME, RANK
ASSIGNMENT | SHIELD #

D/O ONLY: RPT. REC'D. DATE | TIME ☐ AM ☐ PM | INIT. | CODERS ONLY DATE | INI[T.]

STATUS OF INCIDENT REPORT			FINAL DISPOSITION		
CLOSED WITH RESULTS BY:	DATE	COURT	FINAL CHARGE	ACTION OF COURT	JUDGE
ARRESTS(S) _____ AR(S)_____ OTHER_____	B1)				
YD-1 (S)________ JR(S)_____ CLOSED NO RESULTS	B2)				
UNFOUNDED	B3)				

FOLLOW UP INFORMATION

DATE	REMARKS	INITIAL

FIG. A1. New York City Housing Authority—Police Department incident report

NYCHA 080.005 (REV. 10/67)

TRANSCRIPT OF INCIDENT REPORT — NEW YORK CITY HOUSING AUTHORITY • POLICE DEPARTMENT

NOTE: USE GREEN TRANSCRIPTS TO CODE SUBSEQUENT OR ADDITIONAL INCIDENT REPORTS.

A. REPORT OF INCIDENT	CODE
1. Nature of Report *(Circle one)*	*(Col 1)*
a. Initial	1
b. Subsequent	2
c. Additional	3
2. Incident Number	*(Cols 2-6)*
3. Project Number — ADDIT. OR SUBS. PROCEED TO ITEM #16	*(Cols 7-9)*
4. Place of Occurrence	*(Cols 10-11)*
Unknown	oo
5. Date of Occurrence	*(Cols 12-17)*
6. Day and Tour of Occurrence	*(Cols 18-19)*
Unknown	oo
7. Intra-Household Incident *(Circle one)*	*(Col 20)*
a. Yes	1
b. Not Applicable	2
8. Type of Incident	*(Col 21-23)*
9. *(Circle one)*	*(Cols 24-25)*
Inside	01
Outside	02
10. Complainant or Aided *(Circle one)*	*(Col 26)*
a. Housing Patrolman	1
b. Employe Tenant	2
c. Tenant	3
d. Non-Tenant	4
e. Cross Complainant	5
f. Not Applicable	6
11. Age of Complainant or Aided	*(Cols 27-28)*
a. Tenant or Non-Tenant	
b. Unknown or Not Applicable-a, b, e, f, of Item 10	oo
12. Race of Complainant or Aided *(Circle one)*	*(Col 29)*
a. White	1
b. Negro	2
c. Puerto Rican	3
d. Other	4
e. Not Applicable-a, b, e, f, of Item 10	o
13. Sex of Complainant or Aided *(Circle one)*	*(Col 30)*
a. Male	1
b. Female	2
c. Not Applicable-a, b, e, f, of Item 10	o
14. Reporting Officer's Assig. *(Circle one)*	*(Col 31)*
a. Project Assignment	1
b. U.F.61	2
c. Detective Squad	3
d. Site & Buildings Squad	4
e. Special Patrol	5
f. Other *(Supervisor/Recruit)*	6
15. Reporting Officer's Shield Number	*(Cols 32-36)*

B. ARREST/APPREHENSION/DISPOSITION	CODE
16. Type of Incident	*(Col 37-39)*
17. Date of Arrest or Apprehension	*(Cols 40-45)*
Not Applicable	oooooo
18. Place of Arrest/Appreh. *(Circle one)*	*(Col 46)*
a. Off Project Grounds	1
b. On Project Grounds	2
c. Not Applicable	3
19. Arrest/Appreh. Officer's Assig. *(Circle one)*	*(Col 47)*
a. Project Assignment	1
b. U.F.61	2
c. Detective Squad	3
d. Site & Buildings Squad	4
e. Special Patrol	5
f. Other *(Supervisor/Recruit)*	6
g. Not Applicable *(e.g. P.D.)*	7
20. Arresting or Apprehending Officer's Shield Number	*(Cols 48-52)*
Not Applicable	ooooo

	Ⓑ ①	Ⓑ ②	Ⓑ ③
21. Tenant Status *(Circle one)*	*(Col 53)*	*(Col 59)*	*(Col 65)*
a. Tenant	1	1	1
b. Non-Tenant	2	2	2
c. Not Appl.	3	3	3
22. Age	*(Col 54-55)*	*(Col 60-61)*	*(Col 66-67)*
Not Appl.	oo	oo	oo
23. Race (Color) *(Circle one)*	*(Col 56)*	*(Col 62)*	*(Col 68)*
a. White	1	1	1
b. Negro	2	2	2
c. Puerto Rican	3	3	3
d. Other	4	4	4
e. Not Appl.	5	5	5
24. Sex *(Circle one)*	*(Col 57)*	*(Col 63)*	*(Col 69)*
a. Male	1	1	1
b. Female	2	2	2
c. Not Appl.	3	3	3
25. Arrest/Appreh. *(Circle one)*	*(Col 58)*	*(Col 64)*	*(Col 70)*
a. Arrested	1	1	1
b. Appreh.	2	2	2
c. Y D I	3	3	3
d. Sumns. Iss.	4	4	4
e. Referred to Court	5	5	5
f. Refused to Press Chgs.	6	6	6
g. Arrest by other Auth.	7	7	7
h. Unfounded	8	8	8

FIG. A2. New York City Housing Authority—Police Department transcript of incident report

CODE INTERPRETATION
SECURITY DEPARTMENT

PLACE OF OCCURRENCE

Code	
10	Apartment
11	Building: Outside or Inside Entrance Of
12	Basement
13	Community Center, Nursery, etc.
14	Commercial Establishment (Laundry, Milk Station, Store)
15	Elevator Inside
16	Lobby
17	Lawn & Shrub Area
18	Public Hallway
19	Parking Area
20	Project Walk or Bench
21	Project Playground
22	Rear Exit - Vicinity
23	Roof
24	Roof Landing
25	Stairway
26	Sidewalk Contiguous to Project
27	Other Places on Project
28	Off Project

FELONIES

001	Assault, Felonious (Except Officer)
002	Assault, Felonious (On Officer)
003	Arson
004	Burglary
005	Burglar's Instruments
006	Criminally Receiving (Stolen Goods)
007	Carnal Abuse
008	Drugs: Narcotic Drugs, Sale, Possession
009	Drugs: Amphetamines & Barbiturates, Sale, Possession
010	Dangerous Weapons
011	Grand Larceny (Pocketbook Snatch)
012	Grand Larceny (Mail Theft from Tenant Mail Box)
013	Grand Larceny (Motor Vehicle)
014	Grand Larceny (Other)
015	Incest
016	Murder & Non-Negligent Manslaughter (Criminal Homicide)
017	Murder & Non-Negligent Manslaughter (Foetus of 5 months or more)
018	Manslaughter, other (Negligence)
019	Malicious Mischief (Mail & Mailbox)
020	Malicious Mischief, Other
021	Rape (Forcible)
022	Rape Attempted (Force)
023	Robbery, Any Weapon
024	Robbery, No Weapon
025	Sodomy
026	Seduction
027	Other Felonies

MISDEMEANORS

Code	
100	Assault
101	Criminally Receiving (Stolen Goods)
102	Carnal Abuse
103	Drugs: Narcotic Drugs (Possession)
104	Drugs: Amphetamines & Barbiturates
105	Drugs: Narcotic Instruments - Hypodermic Syringe/Needle (Sale or Possession)
106	Dangerous Weapons
107	Endangering Health & Morals (Children)
108	Fireworks (Sale or ssession)
109	Indecent Exposure
110	Indecent Prints, Possession
111	Indecent Performan
112	Liquor Laws
113	Motor Laws (Including Intoxicated Driving)
114	Malicious Mischief (H.A. Trees, Shrubs, Lawns)
115	Malicious Mischief (H.A. Benches)
116	Malicious Mischief (Windows in Public Areas)
117	Malicious Mischief (Light Bulbs)
118	Malicious Mischief (Fire Hoses)
119	Malicious Mischief, other Authority Property including Apartment Windows
120	Malicious Mischief, Non-Authority Property
121	Malicious Mischief (Elevators)
122	Possession of Burglar's Instruments (Tools)
123	Petit Larceny (Authority Property)
124	Petit Larceny (Mail Theft from Tenant's Box)
125	Petit Larceny, other (Except Vehicle Theft)
126	Petit Larceny, Less than $5
127	Petit Larceny, $5 to $49
128	Petit Larceny, $50 to $100
129	Policy, Gambling & Lottery, Bookmaking
130	Prostitution and Commercialized Vice
131	Resisting or Interfering with Arrest
132	Rape
133	Sodomy
134	Unlawful Entry
135	Unlawful Assembly
136	Unlawful Intrusion
137	Other Misdemeanors

OFFENSES

Code	
200	Disorderly Conduct, Jostling
201	Disorderly Conduct, Sex Offenses (Degenerates)
202	Disorderly Conduct, Gambling (Dice and Cards)
203	Disorderly Conduct, Other
204	Vagrancy (Prostitution, Soliciting)
205	Vagrancy, Other
206	Other Offenses

AIDED/INVESTIGATIONS/WARRANTS

300	Dead Human Body (Non-Suicide)
301	Drugs: Found - Narcotics or Paraphernalia, Unverified Report of Narcotic Use or Sale
302	Fires (Including Unknown Origin)
303	Foetus Found on H.A. Property
304	Lockouts
305	Missing Person (Lost, Runaway, Stranded, Destitute, Neglected Child)
306	Report of Lost Property or Property Recovered
308	Suicides, Attempted or Accomplished
309	Sick, Injured (Mentally Ill, Accidents)
310	Weapons: Found or Surrendered
311	Warrants, Arrests
312	Other: Aided/Investigations, Warrants, Summonses
313	Truancy

VIOLATION HOUSING AUTHORITY RULES AND REGULATIONS/DAMAGE

400	Bicycle Riding Prohibited Areas
401	Damaged Interior or Exterior Walls
402	Damage to Trees, Shrubs, Lawn and Greenery
403	Damage to Benches
404	Damage to Doors
405	Damage to Windows
406	Damage to Elevators or Equipment
407	Damage to and Missing Bulbs
408	Damage to Fire Hoses, Nozzles, Connections
409	Damage to Mail Boxes
410	Damages, Other
411	Exploding Fireworks
412	Loitering
413	Playing, Walking Prohibited Area
414	Tenant and/or Family Dispute
415	Unauthorized Parking
416	Other Violations

DAY AND TOUR CODE

TIME	SUNDAY	MONDAY	TUESDAY	WEDNESDAY	THURSDAY	FRIDAY	SATURDAY
12 Mid.- 4 A.M.	1-1	2-1	3-1	4-1	5-1	6-1	7-1
4 A.M.- 8 A.M.	1-2	2-2	3-2	4-2	5-2	6-2	7-2
8 A.M.-12 P.M.	1-3	2-3	3-3	4-3	5-3	6-3	7-3
12 P.M.- 4 P.M.	1-4	2-4	3-4	4-4	5-4	6-4	7-4
4 P.M.- 8 P.M.	1-5	2-5	3-5	4-5	5-5	6-5	7-5
8 P.M.-12 Mid.	1-6	2-6	3-6	4-6	5-6	6-6	7-6
UNKNOWN							
Day & Tour	0-0	0-0	0-0	0-0	0-0	0-0	0-0
Tour	1-0	2-0	3-0	4-0	5-0	6-0	7-0

FIG. A3. List of coded crimes included in New York City Housing Authority Police data

2. NEW YORK CITY POLICE DEPARTMENT CRIME REPORTS

In order to compare project crime with crime in surrounding communities, we have collected New York City Police data on a precinct basis, for the same time period. These reports include FBI Index crimes—murder, rape, robbery, assault, burglary, and larceny (auto theft was excluded)—which correspond to selected felonies in the Housing Authority Police reporting system.

B. Physical Variables

In attempting to ascertain the relationship between physical elements and crime, it is crucial to define precisely and measure accurately those physical attributes involved.

We began with a complete listing of all the standard physical measures; such as height, acreage, coverage, density, and floor area ratios, as shown in table A2, Preliminary List of Physical Variables. However, as hypotheses developed, it became clear that most of these did not deal with those precise qualities that we hypothesized were related to crime. Rather, these standard measures were intended to serve for quite different purposes.

In order to resolve this problem, and deal directly with the physical features we believed to be crucial, we developed our own measures (categories 9 and 14 in table A2 are indicative). While based upon objective criteria, these measures concern the specific physical elements hypothesized to be crucial. These measures were applied largely by the analysis of site and building plans by staff architects, and by visits to the site (see table A3).

TABLE A2

Preliminary List of Physical Variables

PROJECT AS UNIT OF ANALYSIS

Columns	*F-Code*	*Physical Variables as on Punch Card Forms*
1–3	3.1	1. Coverage, percent of area covered by buildings
4–7	4.0	2. Number of apartments
8–10	3.2	3. Floor area ratio (FAR): total area of all building floors, divided by land area of project
11–13	3.2	4. Average number of rental rooms per apartment
14–17	4.0	5. Total population
18–20	3.0	6. Density, in persons per acre
21–22	2.0	7. Number of site units, ranges from 1 to 10 This is: number of separate areas of spaces into which project is divided. Divisions are usually made by through streets

TABLE A 2—Continued

Columns	*F-Code*	*Physical Variables as on Punch Card Forms*
23–26	4.1	8. Total area in acres
27–29	3.1	9. Average length is shortest span, in hundreds of feet. This is: shortest length across spaces, averaged if there is more than one site unit or if space is irregularly shaped
30–32	3.0	10. Number of stories, total for all buildings
33–35	3.0	11. Number of buildings
36–38	3.0	12. Number of street addresses
39	1.0	13. *Code for ranges of rent, 1–5* 1 = \$14.99 or under 2 = \$15.00 to \$17.99 3 = \$18.00 to \$20.99 4 = \$21.00 to \$23.99 5 = \$24.00 or over
40–42	3.0	14. Percent of building walls facing and within fifty feet of the street; total distance of wall parallel to street (and prorated for angles to street): 0–50 feet away = 100 percent 50–75 feet away = 50 percent 75–100 feet away = 25 percent
43	1.0	15. *Building type, four types* 1 = row or rehabilitation 2 = type A, Williamsburg or Breukelen prototype 3 = cruciform 4 = slab
44–46	3.1	16. Precinct felony rate per 1,000
47–48	2.0	17. Year project completed
49	1.0	18. *Height, category: rank in order from I to VII* I = 2 II = 3 and 7 III = 7 IV = 6,7 + 13,14 V = 13,14 VI = 15–19 or 15 + 21 VII = 20+
50–51	2.0	19. Weighted height, i.e., number of stories
78–80	3.0	20. Project number as per NYCHA Police

$$\text{Weighted Height} = \frac{\overbrace{(\text{No. units} \times \text{No. stories})}^{\textit{Height 1}} + \overbrace{(\text{No. units} \times \text{No. stories})}^{\textit{Height 2}}}{\text{Total No. of units}}$$

TABLE A3
Physical Characteristics

Column	*F-Code*	*Description*
	1.0	1. *Building type* 1– row house (no elevator; long rows) 2– walk-up (no elevator; free-standing) 3– low elevator (up to 6 floors) 4– single-loaded corridors 5– point block (7 floors+; short corridors) 6– double-loaded corridors (7 floors+; long corridors) 9– rehabilitation (usually walk-up)
2	1.0	2. *Special building characteristics* 1– 5-pointed "star" plan; enclosed circular corridor around core 2– garage for residents' cars 3– upper-floor lobbies glazed and/or have balcony 4– building fronts directly on sidewalk; virtually no "grounds" 5– elevators and stairs located in different "blocks" which are connected at each floor by a gallery 6– two elevator cores joined by a long corridor on each floor (i.e., choice of 2 cores for egress) 7– elevator blocks flanked by attached walk-up wings with separate entries 8– 3-pointed "star" plan; central core connected to wings by halls 9– covered "pass-through" under center of building provides access to an elevator lobby at each end
3–4	2.0	3. *Number of floors per building* (basements excluded)
5–6	2.0	4. *Number of buildings of this type*
7	1.0	5. *Number of lobbies per building* (i.e., separate entries to elevator or stair cores)
8	1.0	6. *Number of elevators per lobby*
9–11	3.0	7. *Number of apartments per lobby* (averaged for building type)
2–14	3.2	8. Proportion of apartments whose primary entrances face and are within 120 feet of a through public street (0.50 = ½ the apartments).
15	1.0	9. *Degree to which entry is defined by shape of building*
16	1.0	10. *Stair type* 1– scissors stair 2– two conventional stairs (function like scissors) 3– three stairways (usually one scissors, one conventional) required in very large buildings

TABLE A 3—Continued

Column	*F-Code*	*Description*
		7– conventional stair: (2-run) stair landings separated from hallway 8– conventional stair: (2-run) hallway serves as one landing 9– conventional stair: (straight-run) staircase exposed in hallway

7

8

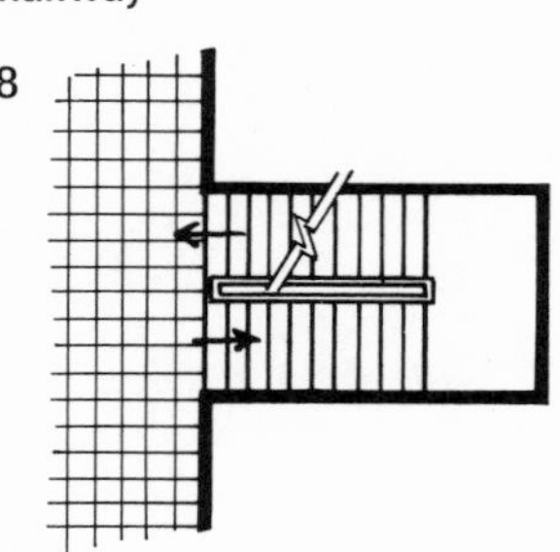

9

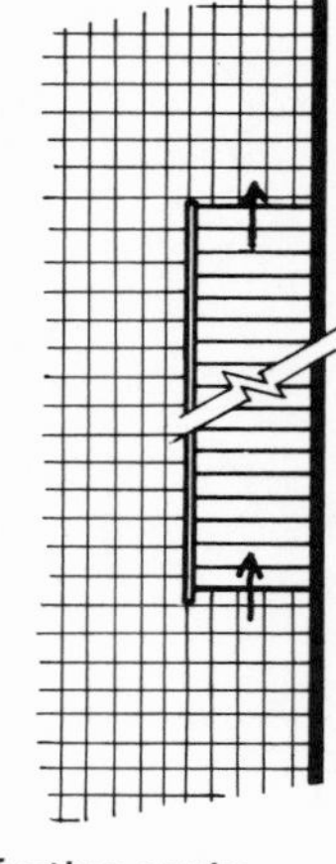

Column	*F-Code*	*Description*
17	1.0	11. *Location of exit doors of stairways* (most furtive route—usually second scissors) 1– into short exit hall, or down to basement or cellar or directly outside 2– into public hall (hidden from lobby) 3– into public hall (visible from lobby) 4– directly into lobby 6– cannot tell from drawings
18	1.0	12. *Egress to outside from second scissors or stair (furtive)* 1– via basement/cellar—not connected to lobby 2– via basement/cellar—connected to lobby 3– out opposite side of building—not connected to lobby 4– out opposite side of building—connected to lobby 5– out near primary entry door: visible from entry—not connected to lobby 6– out near primary entry door—connected to lobby 7– forced into lobby and through primary entry doors 8– cannot tell from drawings
19	1.0	13. *Visibility of elevator from outside primary entry door* 0– no elevator 1– not visible 2– barely visible (obstructed view, bad angle, etc.) 3– visible 4– fully visible, including insides of elevators 5– mixed: some lobbies good; some very bad 6– cannot tell from drawings
20	1.0	14. *Visibility of lobby from outside primary entry door* 0– no lobby 1– generally not visible (0–25 percent)

TABLE A 3—Continued

Column	F-Code	Description
		2– partly visible (25–50 percent)
		3– visible, but corridors not visible (50–75 percent)
		4– fully visible, including corridors (75–100 percent)
		5– mixed: some lobbies good; some bad
		6– cannot tell from drawings
21–40	none	15. *Project name spelled out*
41–46		16. *Total number of apartments for project* (computed: product of No. 4 × No. 5 × No. 7)
61–63	3.0	*Card number* (sequentially numbered)
68	1.0	*Additions to project*
		0– no additions
		1– one addition (ie., two Housing Authority project numbers)
		2– two additions (three numbers)
69–70	2.0	*Date of full occupancy:* 19___
71	1.0	*Fudge Factors*
		0– no manipulation of data
		1– building heights lumped to most common height (maximum shift of one floor)
		2– building sizes "standardized" (ie., lobbies-per-building number averaged)
		3– six- or seven-floor buildings grouped into one designation, because project is primarily one or the other
		4– one private-entry apartment grouped to lobby
		5– date of occupancy estimated from drawing dates
		6– type-5 or type-6 buildings switched to other type
		7– six-floor blocks flanked by three-floor wings
		8– building heights modified by more than two floors (high-rise only)
72	1.0	*Number of building types*
73	1.0	*Number of cards for this Housing Authority Police*
74–76	3.0	*Housing Authority project number*
77	1.0	*Card number:* 5
78–80	3.0	*Housing Authority Police project number*

Neighborhood Indices

I. Comparison of project site plan to neighborhood texture
- 1 = project indiscernible from neighborhood
- 4 = project immediately distinguishable from neighborhood

II. Comparison of project height to height of buildings in surrounding neighborhood
- 1 = project same height as neighborhood
- 2 = project low, elevator; neighborhood walk-up
- 3 = project high-rise; neighborhood low, elevator
- 4 = project high-rise; neighborhood walk-up

III. Projects in vicinity
- 1 = two or more projects in immediate vicinity
- 2 = one other project nearby
- 3 = no other projects in vicinity

Precinct Felony Rate

C. Tenant Characteristics

While we are primarily concerned with the relationship of physical and crime variables, tenant characteristics inevitably enter the picture. Essentially, the issue is to have enough knowledge of tenant characteristics to assume that any difference in crime patterns attributed to physical differences, is not, in fact, due to variations in tenant characteristics.

The New York City Housing Authority maintains detailed data on all families residing within Authority projects, as listed in table A4, Tenant Data Existing on Tape (see table A5 for record format of tape data), and indicated on original application and annual follow-up forms (fig. A4).

It is also true that the New York City Housing Authority applies uniform tenant admittance criteria, and thus there is some consistency throughout all projects. However, it is clear from even a cursory glance at tenant data, that differences in tenant characteristics do exist and must be accounted for in any causal description of crime.

TABLE A4

Tenant Data Existing on Tape

Column	Description
25	*Total assets at admission*
	0 = none or unknown
	Y = less than $1,000
	1 = $1,000 to $1,999
	2 = $2,000 to $2,999
	3 = $3,000 to $3,999
	4 = $4,000 to $4,999
	5 = $5,000 to $5,999
	6 = $6,000 to $6,999
	7 = $7,000 to $7,999
	8 = $8,000 to $8,999
	9 = $9,000 to $9,999
	10 = $10,000 or more
26–27	*Source of income at admission*
	01 private employment
	02 government employment
	03 own business
	04 Department of Welfare
	05 V.A. Service connected
	06 Social Security
	07 Military Allotment
	08 other public funds
	09 other nonpublic funds
	Additional and combination codes available. These include numbers up to 99 and number-letter combinations, such as 4X or 9Y

TABLE A 4—Continued

Column	*Description*	
28–30	*Occupation of principal wage earner at admission*	
	000–099–Professional	
	100–199–Managerial	
	200–299–Clerical	
	300–399–Skilled	
	400–499–Semiskilled	
	500–599–Unskilled	
	600–699–Servant	
31–33	Net annual income for rent (packed decimal format)	
34	*Occupancy of previous housing*	
		*Transcience score**
	1 = own apartment	4
	2 = apartment shared with strangers	2
	3 = apartment shared with relatives	3
	4 = rooming house	1
	5 = furnished room	1
	6 = janitor	2
	7 = owner	5
	8 = hotel	1
	9 = split family	0
	X = unknown	0
35	Apartment size	
	number of full rooms previously occupied by family	
36–38	Gross monthly rent of previous housing in dollars	
39	Percent of income for rent in previous housing	
	(Note: problem—only one column for percent?)	
40	*Length of residence at previous address*	
	0 = less than six months	
	1 = six to eleven months	
	2 = one year, less than two	
	3 = two years, less than three	
	4 = three years, less than four	
	5 = four years, less than five	
	6 = five years, less than ten	
	7 = ten years, less than fifteen	
	8 = fifteen years, less than twenty	
	9 = twenty years or more	
	X = unknown	
	Y = split family	
41–44	Date of current data, month and year	
45	*Basis for report*	
	1 = admitted	
	2 = not admitted	
46	Apartment size, number of full rooms family needs in project	
47–49	Gross income (annually in dollars), packed decimal format	

* Applied later

NYCHA 047.001&R (REV. 9/71)
TRANSCRIPT OF TENANT DATA

NEW YORK CITY HOUSING AUTHORITY

REPORT ON ADMISSION OF NEW TENANT

PROJECT NAME	Cols. 1-3 PROJECT #	Cols. 4-8 ACCT. NO.
Cols. 9-10 TENANT'S NAME *(Please Print)* LAST FIRST	Col. 11 TRANSCRIPT CODE 4	APT. SIZE *(No. of full Rms.)*

ITEM	CODE
DATE ADMITTED Month - Year	Cols.12-15 /
RACE OR ETHNIC GROUP	Col.16
White	1
Black *(Negro)*	2
Puerto Rican	3
Other Spanish American	4
American Indian	5
Oriental	6
Other Minorities *(specify)* ______	7
BASIS FOR SELECTION	Cols.17-18
Former Site Occupant	01
Displaced from N.Y.C.H.A. Site *(Code X)* *Specify* ______	02
Displaced from URA, other Redevelopment Area or Public Improvement Site *(Code Y)* *Specify* ______	03
Displaced by Building Vacate Order *(Code O)*	04
Court Order Eviction *(Code 1)*	10
Health Emergency *(Code 1)*	11
Homeless Family *(Code 1)*	12
Vietnam Veteran or Serviceman	13
Extremely Substandard Housing *(Code 2)*	14
Extreme Hardship *(Code 3)*	15
Grossly Overcrowded Family *(Code 4)*	16
Health Hardship *(Code 5)*	17
Substandard Housing *(Code 6)*	18
Overcrowded Family *(Code 7)*	19
Doubled-up Family *(Code 7)*	20
Split Family *(Code 7)*	21
Rent Hardship *(Code 8)*	22
Other Substandard and/or Hardship Conditions *(Code 7)*	23
Former Tenant Readmitted	24
Resident Employee	25
TENANT ADMITTED ABOVE NORMAL ADMISSION LIMIT	Col.19
Yes - Vietnam Veteran	1
Yes - Other *(specify)* ______	2
No	3
ASSETS	Col.20
None or Unknown	0
Less than $1,000	Y
$1,000 - 1,999	1
2,000 - 2,999	2
3,000 - 3,999	3
4,000 - 4,999	4
5,000 - 5,999	5
6,000 - 6,999	6
7,000 - 7,999	7
8,000 - 8,999	8
9,000 - 9,999	9
10,000 or more *(specify)* $______	X

ITEM	CODE
PREVIOUS HOUSING	
BOROUGH	Col.21
Manhattan	1
Brooklyn	2
Bronx	3
Queens	4
Staten Island	5
Out of Town	6
OCCUPANCY	Col.22
Own Apartment	1
Apartment Shared	2
Rooming House or Furnished Room	3
Hotel	4
Janitor or Superintendent	5
Owner	6
Unknown	7
SIZE OF APARTMENT Number of Full Rooms	Col.23
GROSS MONTHLY RENT FOR APT. Amount *(Dollars only)*	Cols.24-26 $
RESIDENCE AT LAST ADDRESS	Col.27
Less than 6 Mos.	0
6-11 Mos.	1
1 Year, less than 2	2
2 Years, less than 3	3
3 Years, less than 4	4
4 Years, less than 5	5
5 Years, less than 10	6
10 Years, less than 15	7
15 Years, less than 20	8
20 Years, or more	9
Unknown	X

(over)

FIG. A4. New York City Housing Authority transcript of tenant data

ITEM	CODE	ITEM	CODE
CURRENT DATA			
GROSS ANTICIPATED INCOME Amount *(Dollars only)*	Cols.28-32 $	AGE OF HEAD OF HOUSEHOLD Years *(as of last birthday)*	Cols.59-60
NET INCOME FOR RENT Amount *(Dollars only)*	Cols.33-37 $	SEX OF HEAD OF HOUSEHOLD	Col. 61
		Male	1
NET INCOME FOR ELIGIBILITY Amount *(Dollars only)*	Cols.38-42 $	Female	2
		AGE OF SPOUSE Years *(as of last birthday)*	Cols.62-63
MONTHLY GROSS RENT Amount *(Dollars & Cents)*	Cols.43-47 $	DISABLED OR HANDICAPPED *(Circle first code which is applicable)*	Col. 64
CLASSIFICATION OF NEW RENT	Col. 48	Head of Household Disabled	1
Basic Rent	1	Spouse Disabled	2
Surcharge Rent	2	Head of Household Handicapped	3
Maximum Rent	3	Spouse Handicapped	4
Public Assistance Rent	4	Neither Disabled nor Handicapped	5
Brooke Rent	5	SOURCES OF CURRENT INCOME *(Mult.)*	Cols.65-69
Resident Employee Rent	6	Employment	1
SIZE OF FAMILY Number of Persons	Cols.49-50	Own Business	2
FAMILY COMPOSITION	Col. 51	Dept. of Social Services:	
Single Person	0	Family on Public Assistance	3
Husband, Wife, no Children	1	Individual *(Other than head of household or spouse)* on Public Assistance	4
Mother, Father, and Children	2		
Mother and One or More Children	3	Social Security:	
Father and One or More Children	4	Old Age or Disability Ins.	5
Sisters, or Brothers and Sisters	5	Survivors Insurance	6
Other *(specify)* ________	6	Military Allotment & Serviceman's Pay	7
Doubled-up Family	7	V.A. Benefits	8
PERSONS CURRENTLY EMPLOYED Number	Col. 52	Other Benefits from Public Funds *(specify)* ________	9
HEAD OF HOUSEHOLD EMPLOYED *(Male or Female)*	Col. 53	Other *(Non-public)* *(specify)* ________	0
No	0		
Yes	1	NUMBER OF PERSONS IN SPECIFIED AGE GROUPS	Cols.70-79
SPOUSE EMPLOYED	Col. 54	Under 2 years (Col.70	
No or Not Applicable	0	2 - 3 years (Col.71	
Yes	1	4 - 5 years (Col.72	
MINORS CURRENTLY EMPLOYED Number	Col. 55	6 - 9 years (Col.73	
		10-13 years (Col.74	
OTHER ADULTS CURRENTLY EMPLOYED Number	Col. 56	14-17 years (Col.75	
		18-20 years (Col.76	
MINORS OUT OF SCHOOL WORKING PART TIME Number	Col. 57	21-49 years (Col.77	
		50-61 years (Col.78	
MINORS OUT OF SCHOOL NOT WORKING Number	Col. 58	62 years and over (Col.79	
		Prepared by ________ *Date* ________	

TABLE A 4—Continued

50–52 Net income for rent (annually in dollars), packed decimal format
53–54 Monthly gross rent (dollars and cents), packed decimal format
55–56 Percent of income for rent (currently in project)
57 Rent adjustment made inapplicable; new tenant = 9
58 *Classification of new rent*
  1 = basic rent
  2 = surcharge rent
  3 = maximum rent
  5 = welfare rent
59 Eligibility for continued occupancy
  1 = eligible
60–61 Family size (current number of persons)
62 *Family composition*
  0 = single person
  1 = husband and wife, no children
  2 = mother, father, and children
  3 = mother and one or more children
  4 = father and one or more children
  5 = sisters, or brothers and sisters
  6 = other
  7 = doubled-up family
63–64 Number of children under 21
65 Number of persons currently employed

TABLE A 4—Continued

Column	*Description*
66	*Employment of wife or mother* 0 = inapplicable, not with family 1 = not employed and did not work in past year 2 = not employed but worked during past year 3 = employed as principal wage earner 4 = employed as secondary wage earner
67	Number of minors currently employed
68–69	*Sources of current income* (Same additional codes as columns 26–27) 01 = private employment 02 = government employment 03 = own business 04 = Department of Welfare 05 = Veterans Administration 06 = Social Security 07 = military allotment 08 = other public funds 09 = other nonpublic funds
70–71	Age of head of household in years
72	*Sex of head of household* 1 = male 2 = female
73–74	Age of spouse
75	*Military service* 1 = disabled veteran 2 = deceased veterans or servicemen 3 = other veterans or servicemen X = Korean veteran 4 = no veterans or servicemen
76–78	Net income for eligibility, packed decimal format
80	Previous subsidy___
81	Combined apartment___
82	Program___

TABLE A5

Record Format of Tenant Data Statistics Tape

DUPLICATE TENANT STATISTICS TAPE

Fixed-length records
Blocked 20
Standard RCA labels
Record size = 82 bytes

Record Format

1–3	Project number
4–8	Account number
9–10	Tenant's name
11	Borough of previous residence
12–15	Month and year of admission
16–18	Project number at admission
19–20	Family size at admission
21	Race or color
22–23	Birthplace of head of family
24	Basis for selection
25	Total assets at admission
26–27	Sources of income at admission
28–30	Occupation of principal wage earner at admission
31–33	Net income for rent at admission (packed)
34	Occupancy of previous housing
35	Apartment size
36–38	Gross monthly rent of previous housing
39	Percent of income for rent (previous)
40	Length of residence at previous address
41–44	Date of current data (month & year)
45	Basis for report
46	Apartment size
47–49	Gross income (packed)
50–52	Net income for rent (packed)
53–54	Monthly gross rent (packed)
55–56	Percent of income for rent
57	Rent adjustment made
58	Classification of new rent
59	Eligibility for continued occupancy
60–61	Family size
62	Family composition
63–64	Number of children under 21
65	Number of persons currently employed
66	Employment of wife or mother
67	Number of minors currently employed
68–69	Sources of current income
70–71	Age of head of household
72	Sex of head of household
73–74	Age of spouse
75	Military service record
76–78	Net income for eligibility
79	Current subsidy code
80	Previous subsidy code
81	Combined apartment code
82	Program code

D. Interview Methodology

The following is an outline of the purposes and procedures involved in the interviewing of the residents of four New York City public housing projects.

CLASON POINT AND BRONXDALE

It was our intention to interview the residents of Clason Point and Bronxdale before any architectural plans were carried out. This would allow us to create an in-depth profile of each project, one which would give a base line for such indexes as neighboring, responsibility, fear location, parental supervision, space usage, and the nature and extent of criminality. Basic psychological tendencies or social propensities were recognized as not likely to change in response to redefinition of physical form. However, a psychological and social baseline would enable us to determine the background on which more superficial changes might be wrought. Once defensible space modifications are completed in these two projects, it is our plan to repeat the interviewing process. The resultant data will allow us to measure the exact nature and degree of change that the modifications have had on the variables and will enable us to create a theory regarding the impact of defensible space design on behavior and attitudes. In addition, this data will allow for a generalization of principles on a more universal level.

In the case of Clason Point, indices were developed that measured the general, relevant psychological characteristics and a specific index was derived from the concrete details of living in Clason Point Gardens. It is the specific index that is expected to change as a result of modifications to the project. The areas of measurement examined in relationship to both these indices were (1) alienation, (2) isolation, (3) personal space (sense of privacy and ownership), (4) social space (concept of neighborhood and neighborhood visiting networks), (5) crime and victimization, and (6) moral judgment and governance. In the post-test, certain additional questions have been added to supply needed information unobtained by the original. Naturally, these additions will not have pretest equivalency.

At Bronxdale, extensive piloting of preliminary interviews was possible. Based on tabulations and test results, only those questions that proved most promising (i.e., elicited statistically significant data) were included in the final questionnaire used in interviewing the residents of those buildings chosen to be tested. This questionnaire assumed two forms: one for young tenants with children under twelve, and one for elderly tenants. We specifically wished to investigate where mothers permitted their children to play and with what degree and type of supervision. With the elderly, we wanted to know if they sat outside, where they sat, and the reasons involved in their choice. These activities, it was felt, would be the ones most likely to be measurably affected by any physical and electronic modifications at Bronxdale. As a result of our careful selection of the buildings whose tenants were to be interviewed, it will be possible, once post-modifications interview data are accumulated, to measure the effect on attitudes and behavior of (1) lobby modifications, independent of video and audio installation; (2) video equipment, independent of audio installations; (3) audio equipment, independent of video equipment; (4) video and audio equipment, in combination.

A precautionary measure to eliminate the effects of initial measurement, maturation, and contemporaneous events on the attitude and behavior of Bronxdale residents was taken by choosing certain buildings as controls; these buildings were planned to have no video or audio alterations.

In both Clason Point and Bronxdale, detailed comparisons were done between tenants interviewed and not interviewed in those buildings selected for study, as well as between those interviewed and the project population as a whole. Characteristics investigated for comparison were race, source of income, average number of years in the project, family age, etc. No marked differences appeared between those interviewed and those who were not.

BROWNSVILLE AND VAN DYKE

The methods developed in the preliminary interviewing in Bronxdale were adapted for use in the study of Brownsville and Van Dyke projects. Here, the main purpose in interviewing was to determine what differences, if any, existed between the two physically different projects, and which design (high- or low-rise) was more conducive to a safe environment. To achieve this, a building-by-building analysis was conducted to separate the distinct architectural types within the two projects, and a building type comparison of the results was done. Three basic questions relating to crime were asked, in addition to neighboring and responsibility questions. No modifications were planned for these two projects, and hence no post-tesing is necessary.

A more detailed description of our interviewing methodology and results will be included in a forthcoming publication revealing the results of the defensible space experiment in Clason Point and Bronxdale.

III. APPROACHES

A. Stepwise Multiple Regression Analysis

The first effort began by developing a conceptual model consisting of a listing of all the various factors that were believed to affect crime (see the following outline). From a list of several hundred factors, we selected a more limited list of those variables we believed to be crucial, and for which data were available.

Conceptual Model Outline
Selected Factors Affecting Location and Frequency of Crimes in 133 New York City Housing Authority Projects

I. Physical Variables
   - A. Number and Groupings of Buildings: project size, coverage, floor area ratio (FAR), height variation, subdivisions in site plan, location and use of open space, relation of buildings to streets, organization of path system in relation to buildings, project building density, and height in relation to surrounding area
   - B. Building Characteristics: apartments per entrance, apartments per corridor, height, tenants per elevator, semipublic vestibules, and average apartment size
   - C. Surveillance: positioning of entrances in relation to street, relation of apartments to corridors, number of windows facing entrance and grounds, visibility of elevator from street, case of visual access by police, motorists, or pedestrians

II. Tenant Variables
   - A. Family and Individual Characteristics
     1. Population: age, sex, race, ethnicity
     2. Education: grade completed
     3. Occupation and Income: socio-economic level, percent receiving welfare assistance
     4. Family Constellation: percent of female heads of household, percent divorced, number of children
   - B. Social and Community Characteristics
     1. Transience of Population: turnover rates for apartments, average years in project, and previous housing (i.e., owner-occupied versus rooming house or hotel)
     2. Community Facilities: recreational and commercial facilities, precinct crime rate, closeness to central city, and density
     3. Transportation and Journey to Work: closeness of buses, trains, distance from central city, and auto ownership

III. Crime Variables
   - A. Type of Crime: *general categories*—felonies, misdemeanors, violations, warrants and investigations, breach of rules. *Specific crimes*—robbery, burglary, mischief, loitering, and lingering
   - B. Location of Crime: *public areas*—sidewalk, path, parking lot. *Semipublic areas*—commercial zones, community center, roof, and landing. *Semiprivate areas*—elevator, lobby, and stairwell. *Shared private areas*—hallway and apartment vestibule
   - C. Time of Day; Year: seasonal variation, time of day, and day of week
   - D. Age and Race of Complainant or Aided
   - E. Comparison of Complaints, Investigations, and Arrests

As is often the case in new fields, multiple regression was the statistical technique originally selected. Essentially, this approach does not assume or directly deal with any hypothesis. Each independent variable offered is correlated with all dependent variables. By utilizing a stepwise technique, it is possible to analyze partial and individual correlations.

Certain basic problems, common to multiple regression, afflicted this original effort. There was strong multicolinearity within each of the three categories of variables (as well an among all variables) that was difficult to resolve within the limits of existing data. Also, as was stated, it is inherent in the nature of this study that physical variables account for only a proportion of crime: social and economic inputs also have a strong role. Thus, the anticipated coefficient of correlation between crime and physical variables might be low. This, coupled with the other difficulties, would tend to make initial proof of any hypothesis concerning physical environment and crime rather difficult, utilizing this statistical approach.

All of the regressions conducted utilized crime as the dependent variable. Robbery was selected as a particularly indicative crime, as it is subject to variation and capable of occurring in any location. The actual number of crimes, the rate of crime, and the percentage of crime in various locations were all utilized.

The first set of regressions used ten physical features as independent variables. The results of these regressions pinpointed which physical variables influences crime patterns. In general, the direct influence of physical variables alone upon crime seemed more directed at location than at total rate. Physical variables did achieve a .05 level of significance and an r^2 of .17 in terms of rate. However, in terms of locational percentages, the r^2 was .38 and the level of significance .04. A similar sequence with fifteen social variables indicated an across-the-board general influence of social variables upon crime, with r^2 often over .40.

The combination of physical and social variables used only twelve selected independent variables, half social and half physical. The results indicated that while social variables play a key role in accounting for overall variations in crime, physical variables had a compounding influence and a relatively strong influence upon crimes in particular locations.

In specific instances, physical characteristics were particularly crucial in accounting for variations in crime. For example, building height had a correlation coefficient of .45 with elevator crime. In general, the combination of five key physical and social variables alone approached an r^2 of .50. This influence included both the actual rate of crime and the percentage of crime in each location (see tables A6 and A7).

B. Trend Analysis

In order to expeditiously discover if the specific hypotheses developed were reasonable, a relatively quick system of trend analysis was developed.

At this point the computer materials included detailed information for each project. We proceeded to group projects according to specific variable(s) and compare rates for particular crimes in particular locations between groups. By repeating this process, we were immediately able to ascertain if the trend was in the direction hypothesized.

These trend analyses were done only between physical and crime variables. It was discovered that due to homogeneity of tenants within the New York projects, plus the lack of any correlation between building types or tenant characteristics and project location, randomly selected groups of more than ten projects reasonably assured a representative sample, in terms of tenant characteristics and project location.

This trend analysis enabled us to more accurately select those relationships for which statistical testing would be useful. In addition, these results often led to efforts to further define and specify the precise relationships involved. "T" tests were conducted to demonstrate potentially significant differences and to isolate these differences and the cut-off points that appeared crucial.

C. Analysis of Variance

In order to compare the effects of two or more experimental treatments with no experimental treatment, or for testing hypotheses about the joint contribution of two or more independent variables in influencing a dependent variable, an analysis of variance is necessary. A design which permits an analysis of variance makes possible a study of complex interrelationships. In addition, such a design permits more hypotheses with fewer cases than does a design which tests hypotheses in separate studies.

The relationship between selected physical variables and criminal activity in certain housing projects was examined, using a variety of descriptive and analytic techniques. In each instance, the dependent variable was assigned a value which was a transformation of the measure (number of incidents) of criminal activity.

1. Number of incidents

Data from the criminal activity source tape was reduced by grouping individual incidents into twenty basic categories. This reduced data matrix was then tallied, and control reports on each crime incident were produced, cataloguing crime by total, by project, and by specific location in the project. The information generated from the data tape was checked against published reports to verify its content. Once these control reports were validated, they were then analyzed for patterns of occurrence of criminal activity.

Two problems then had to be dealt with. Firstly, how could projects of differing crime levels be described and/or categorized in terms of physical and other variables? Secondly, could this range or pattern of variation be related to the fluctuations of activities in indoor/outdoor spaces?

The wide range of variation in the number of incidents reported within projects indicated that the random variable, "number of incidents," severely limited the range of applicable statistical techniques for "within project" experiments. For instance, in those projects with a low crime incident level per month, statistical significance could be demonstrated only if the project maintained a zero level (no crimes) for a period of six months.

In addition, the wide variation in the size of project populations, along with the demonstrated relationship between population size and total numbers of incidents, precluded the use of "number of incidents" as the dependent variable in between-project comparative analysis.

2. Annual rate of incidents

The solution was to arrive at a standard measure for the dependent variable which would allow for interproject comparisons. Thus the annual rate of incidents (annual number of incidents per unit of population) was devised to overcome our initial difficulty. It was felt that since a project population tends to maintain its size throughout a selected time slice, we could examine (using established statistical techniques) the ways in which selected physical variables influenced the *rate* of incidents within a specified category of crime, for a particular location classification.

However, as in any data analysis, extreme care had to be taken in interpreting the results. For example, when testing the hypothesis that an increase in the number of apartments/lobby (the physical variable) would increase the rate of mailbox crime (the dependent variable), we found the results, although statistically significant, counter-intuitive and contrary to most other trends. The general trend had been that those projects containing over 1000 apartments demonstrated a high, statistically significant incident rate. How could we explain these contrary results?

In order to assess the possible explanations, we first had to examine some related assumptions and validate or reject them by an independent analysis of the project data file. These assumptions were:

1. Buildings which contain a large number of apartments produce lobbies with large numbers of mailboxes.

2. There are only specific days of the month, and time periods within those days, in which the bulk of mailbox robberies occur (i.e., Welfare and Social Security check day immediately following mail delivery).

3. A large group of criminals do not simultaneously descend upon a project for the purpose of mailbox robbery. (This has been demonstrated by examining the number of incidents within time periods.)

The trend indicated by the counter-intuitive finding was that an increase in the number of apartments per lobby, tends to decrease the rate of mailbox crime. This finding reflects the change in rate generated by an increase in population size, if the *number of incidents* remains relatively the same for any project. Therefore, because successful mailbox crimes must be committed quickly, in a specific time period, there is a safety in numbers.

The statistical technique which was employed in an examination of this question was a partitioned analysis. After partitioning the sample by population size, we were able to examine the hypothesized role of the physical variable, within each group, as well as across groups.

However, the rate transformation alone still did not supply us with a complete description of the relation between any physical variable and crime. It is only in combination with social variables that we are able to deal with the proposition that with the same value for the physical variable there still appears to be a variation in rate of crime.

3. Percent of crime categories by location

In response to this difficulty, we introduced the notion of "opportune" areas for criminal activity. That is, regardless of social factors, given a variable range of incidents and specific class of projects, there are certain areas which the criminal sees as "areas of greatest opportunity." The hypothesis to be tested was that specific physical components generate specific areas of opportunity for the criminal. An operational test of this hypothesis would demonstrate that the percent of a particular crime occurring in the same location tends to be higher in those projects which are lower on the scale (running from worst to best) for a specified physical characteristic.

It was especially important not to ignore variation in reporting significance for percentages. That is, those items which we reported as demonstrating a trend were those in which there was a low level of variation. It is these items which provide one of the most conclusive demonstrations of the role of the physical variable.

The overall result of the analyses of variance coupled with the trend analysis and the regressions, is that relationships between physical design features and crime patterns have been established. For example, six-story elevator buildings were shown to have significantly less elevator crime (F test score of 5.485, significance level of under .001) than buildings over fourteen stories, supporting and providing additional information concerning the high correlation between height and elevator crime.

In similar fashion, it is evident that height affects overall indoor crime, and that a high building in a low-rise neighborhood has even greater problems. Lobby and elevator visibility (in terms of the tenant or policeman approaching the building) clearly influences lobby crime. The size of the project (number of units) apparently affects crime generally, with 1,000 units being one possible cutoff point.

The regression results indicated the interrelationship of physical features, social variables, and crime. At this point, however, we have not conducted additional statistical tests to establish more precisely the nature of this complex interrelationship. Rather, we have been concerned primarily with the influence of physical design features.

TABLE A6

Correlation Coefficients of Physical and Social Variables with Robberies

A value of 99.00000 is printed
if a coefficient cannot be computed.
Significance ± .2701

	Rtindoor	Rtlobby	Rtelevtr	Rtstair	Rthalway	Pcindoor	Pclobby	Pcelevtr	Pcstair	Pchalway	Over 60	Famsize
RTINDOOR	1.00000	0.59491	0.88893	0.73311	0.82073	0.87521	0.56619	0.68866	0.55095	0.74165	−0.05270	0.07234
RTLOBBY	0.59491	1.00000	0.31268	0.38252	0.32922	0.68045	0.89884	0.27762	0.44593	0.35184	0.30116	−0.31462
RTELEVTR	0.88893	0.31268	1.00000	0.61051	0.60767	0.69195	0.32245	0.80332	0.37115	0.48509	−0.15054	0.17565
RTSTAIR	0.73311	0.38252	0.61051	1.00000	0.52340	0.67735	0.40799	0.44469	0.82871	0.58534	−0.15942	0.20153
RTHALWAY	0.82073	0.32922	0.60767	0.52340	1.00000	0.70708	0.30048	0.41400	0.36981	0.91146	−0.10034	0.11330
PCINDOOR	0.87521	0.68045	0.69195	0.67735	0.70708	1.00000	0.77717	0.67449	0.66363	0.75402	0.09950	−0.07384
PCLOBBY	0.56619	0.89884	0.32245	0.40799	0.30048	0.77717	1.00000	0.32276	0.43966	0.35148	0.38633	−0.35015
PCELEVTR	0.68866	0.27762	0.80332	0.44469	0.41400	0.67449	0.32276	1.00000	0.42534	0.41781	−0.16384	0.21643
PCSTAIR	0.55095	0.44593	0.37115	0.82871	0.36981	0.66363	0.43966	0.42534	1.00000	0.53933	−0.12869	0.14940
PCHALWAY	0.74165	0.35184	0.48509	0.58534	0.91146	0.75402	0.35148	0.41781	0.53933	1.00000	−0.10134	0.11294
OVER 60	−0.05270	0.30116	−0.15054	−0.15942	−0.10034	0.09950	0.38633	−0.16384	−0.12869	−0.10134	1.00000	−0.82369
FAMSIZE	0.07234	−0.31462	0.17565	0.20153	0.11330	−0.07384	−0.35015	0.21643	0.14940	0.11294	−0.82369	1.00000
FEMLHEAD	0.41307	0.45336	0.25879	0.26590	0.35102	0.36775	0.39975	0.12124	0.15107	0.30876	0.42370	−0.26029
PCWELFRE	0.46045	0.22318	0.37864	0.42911	0.42476	0.36221	0.17732	0.28825	0.34899	0.40415	−0.05328	0.36672
INCOME	−0.39153	−0.36715	−0.26250	−0.25544	−0.35387	−0.38122	−0.36986	−0.19052	−0.15502	−0.34561	−0.49436	0.21120
INDEX 2	0.13507	0.04012	0.16146	0.27546	0.01353	0.22535	0.16059	0.26340	0.28487	0.12650	−0.00511	0.10774
INDEX 3	−0.25720	−0.10416	−0.24419	−0.33103	−0.17099	−0.31500	−0.19583	−0.35662	−0.31325	−0.24221	0.15432	−0.19634
FELNRATE	0.31219	0.22737	0.31738	0.25615	0.15630	0.33577	0.34249	0.20117	0.14258	0.07638	0.11511	0.00214
HEIGHT	0.35477	−0.04438	0.45012	0.22583	0.30447	0.36156	0.12056	0.47069	0.12123	0.26532	0.00195	0.11683
FACINGST	0.19502	0.03094	0.24120	−0.08117	0.21296	0.21747	0.16130	0.23381	−0.20520	0.15885	0.00802	−0.02652
ELEVISIB	0.01179	−0.27108	0.11571	−0.07456	0.10143	0.03828	−0.12959	0.21322	−0.15166	0.10759	0.01102	0.08706
LOBBYVIS	0.08684	0.21546	0.04029	−0.13047	0.07423	0.27367	0.37273	0.10544	−0.15897	0.05256	0.34346	−0.24254
UNITS	0.25958	0.22667	0.13463	0.31130	0.25012	0.19730	0.09102	0.06954	0.35120	0.35711	−0.22381	0.11665

TABLE A 6—Continued

	Femlhead	Pcwelfre	Income	Index 2	Index 3	Felnrate	Height	Facingst	Elevisib	Lobbyvis	Units
RTINDOOR	0.41307	0.46045	−0.39153	0.13507	−0.25720	0.31219	0.35477	0.19502	0.01179	0.08684	0.25958
RTLOBBY	0.45336	0.22318	−0.36715	0.04012	−0.10416	0.22737	−0.04438	0.03094	0.27108	0.21546	0.22667
RTELEVTR	0.25879	0.37864	−0.26250	0.16146	−0.24419	0.31738	0.45012	0.24120	0.11571	0.04029	0.13463
RTSTAIR	0.26590	0.42911	−0.25544	0.27546	−0.33103	0.25615	0.22583	−0.08117	−0.07456	−0.13047	0.31130
RTHALWAY	0.35102	0.42476	−0.35387	0.01353	−0.17099	0.15630	0.30447	0.21296	0.10143	0.07423	0.25012
PCINDOOR	0.36775	0.36221	−0.38122	0.22535	−0.31500	0.33577	0.36156	0.21747	0.03828	0.27367	0.19730
PCLOBBY	0.39975	0.17732	−0.36986	0.16059	−0.19583	0.34249	0.12056	0.16130	−0.12959	0.37273	0.09102
PCELEVTR	0.12124	0.28825	−0.19052	0.26340	−0.35662	0.20117	0.47069	0.23381	0.21322	0.10544	0.06954
PCSTAIR	0.15107	0.34899	−0.15502	0.28487	−0.31325	0.14258	0.12123	−0.20520	−0.15166	−0.15897	0.35120
PCHALWAY	0.30876	0.40415	−0.34561	0.12650	−0.24221	0.07638	0.26532	0.15885	0.10759	0.05256	0.35711
OVER 60	0.42370	−0.05328	−0.49436	−0.00511	0.15432	0.11511	0.00195	0.00802	0.01102	0.34346	−0.22381
FAMSIZE	−0.26029	0.36672	0.21120	0.10774	−0.19634	0.00214	0.11683	−0.02652	0.08706	−0.24254	0.11665
FEMLHEAD	1.00000	0.72464	−0.89391	−0.21891	0.12149	0.21545	−0.10044	0.10366	−0.27408	0.07913	0.00315
PCWELFRE	0.72464	1.00000	−0.72678	−0.06016	−0.15468	0.32638	0.08752	0.06561	−0.10475	−0.02911	0.09144
INCOME	−0.89391	−0.72678	1.00000	0.08510	0.02562	−0.27675	−0.05041	−0.20875	0.10924	−0.13775	0.09405
INDEX 2	−0.21891	−0.06016	0.08510	1.00000	−0.18828	0.29698	0.69257	0.07401	0.43910	0.14048	0.12248
INDEX 3	0.12149	−0.15468	0.02562	−0.18828	1.00000	−0.25746	−0.31941	−0.24219	−0.25093	−0.15736	−0.01443
FELNRATE	0.21545	0.32638	−0.27675	0.29698	−0.25746	1.00000	0.54394	0.37618	0.20673	0.34079	−0.13426
HEIGHT	−0.10044	0.08752	−0.05041	0.69257	−0.31941	0.54394	1.00000	0.40254	0.49145	0.33186	−0.04579
FACINGST	0.10366	0.06561	−0.20875	0.07401	−0.24219	0.37618	0.40254	1.00000	0.19212	0.33117	−0.21567
ELEVISIB	−0.27408	−0.10475	0.10924	0.43910	−0.25093	0.20673	0.49145	0.19212	1.00000	0.53619	0.05193
LOBBYVIS	0.07913	−0.02911	−0.13775	0.14048	−0.15736	0.34079	0.33186	0.33117	0.53619	1.00000	−0.06508
UNITS	0.00315	0.09144	0.09405	0.12248	−0.01443	−0.13426	−0.04579	−0.21567	0.05193	−0.06508	1.00000

RT = Rate
PC = Percent
OVER 60 = Percent of population over 60 years of age
ELEVISIB = Elevator visibility
INDEX 2 – Height relationship with surrounding neighborhood
INDEX 3 – Number of contiguous projects

TABLE A7

Regression Analysis of Physical and Social Variables with Indoor Robberies

DEPENDENT VARIABLE: RATE OF INDOOR ROBBERIES

SUMMARY TABLE

VARIABLE	*Multiple R*	*R Square*	*RSQ Change*	*Simple R*	*B*	*Beta*
PCWELFRE	0.46045	0.21202	0.21202	0.46045	0.00428	0.00827
HEIGHT	0.55828	0.31167	0.09966	0.35477	0.37649	0.51079
UNITS	0.60606	0.36730	0.05563	0.25958	0.00167	0.22843
FEMLHEAD	0.64581	0.41707	0.04976	0.41307	0.16378	0.38149
OVER 60	0.67105	0.45031	0.03325	—0.05270	—0.16704	—0.47040
INDEX 3	0.69332	0.48069	0.03037	—0.25720	—0.98747	—0.16704
FAMSIZE	0.69941	0.48917	0.00848	0.07234	—2.14467	—0.26910
INDEX 2	0.70251	0.49352	0.00434	0.13507	—0.46024	—0.10868
ELEVISIB	0.70514	0.49723	0.00371	0.01179	—0.30849	—0.09317
INCOME	0.70674	0.49948	0.00225	—0.39153	—0.00076	—0.20279
FACINGST	0.70851	0.50198	0.00250	0.19502	—0.00936	—0.07276
LOBBYVIS	0.70890	0.50254	0.00055	0.08684	0.13884	0.03364
(CONSTANT)					12.26192	

APPENDIX B:

Additional Statistics

This appendix contains additional statistics related to the comparative analysis of coupled projects—Brownsville and Van Dyke—appearing in chapter 2.

TABLE B1

Comparison of Crime Incidents Per Thousand Population
1965–1969

BROWNSVILLE (B) VERSUS VAN DYKE (V)

	1965		*1966*		*1967*		*1968*		*1969*	
	(B)	*(V)*	*(B)*	*(V)*	*(B)*	*(V)*	*(B)*	*(V)*	*(B)*	*(V)*
Total Crimes per Type										
Felonies	13.91	19.31	15.21	17.28	14.48	17.28	14.84	22.89	16.70	23.83
Misdemeanors	27.27	24.61	16.88	21.03	11.68	16.82	25.97	52.80	22.82	35.98
Offenses	19.48	21.50	1.30	4.67	3.05	4.05	14.65	12.74	21.70	17.60
Investigations/Warrants	104.26	96.11	105.19	89.10	115.76	98.60	83.48	81.15	97.59	108.72
Violation Housing Authority Rules	211.87	251.56	126.90	155.45	110.01	147.35	7.61	16.36	8.56	7.32
Sampled Specific Crimes										
Robbery	3.15	6.23	4.63	7.47	4.08	6.07	4.64	9.81	5.01	9.66
Drugs—Possession	2.78	2.80	1.48	5.29	1.48	2.49	2.37	2.95	2.04	8.10
Mischief—Criminal/ Tampering—Criminal	.92	2.34	1.11	2.02	.92	1.40	5.19	19.63	6.50	11.68
Fire	4.82	5.45	4.26	7.01	2.78	5.61	3.90	8.41	4.26	7.17
Lingering	16.51	23.05	8.16	11.21	8.71	16.51	5.38	9.65	4.65	5.60

SOURCE: New York City Housing Authority Police data.

Tenant Statistics 1962–1968

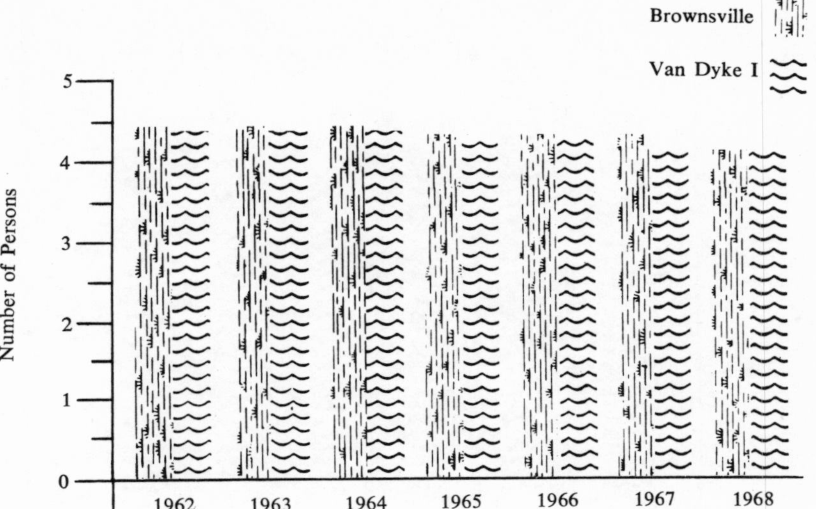

FIG. B1. Average family size

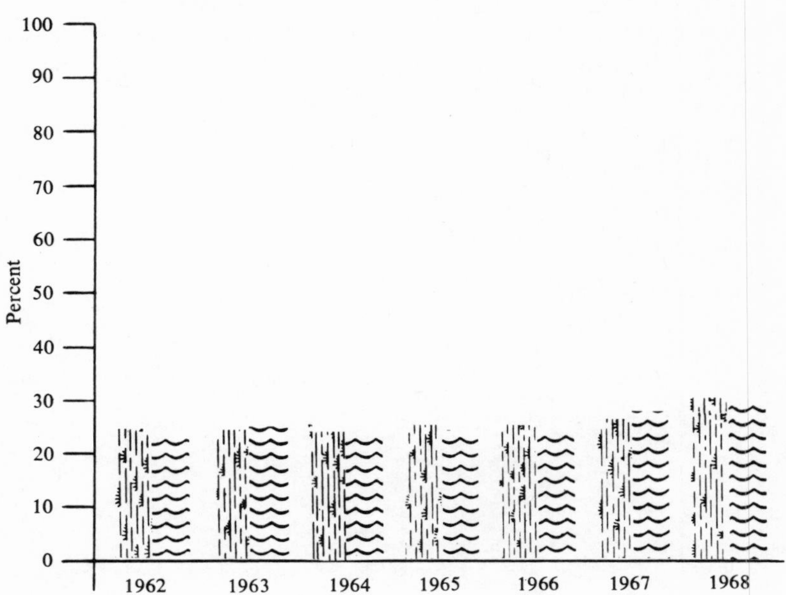

FIG. B2. Percent broken families

Tenant Statistics 1962–1968

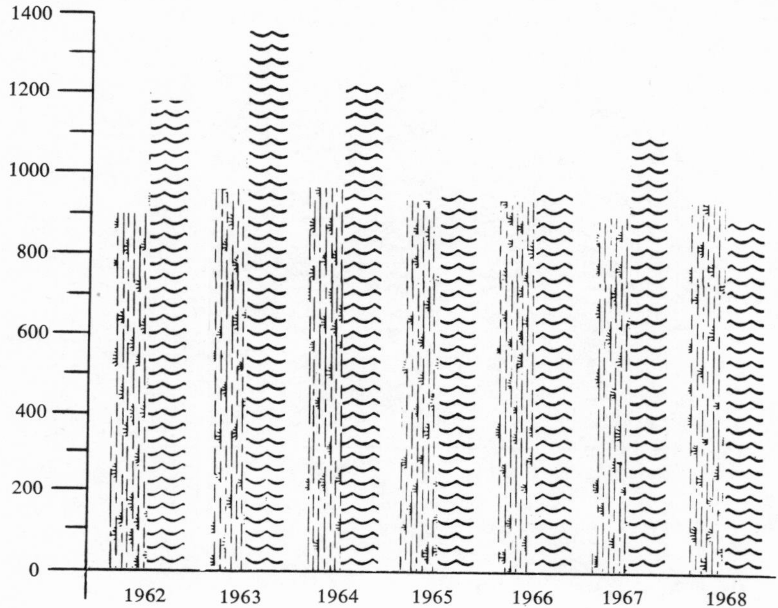

FIG. B3. Number of children in grades 1–6

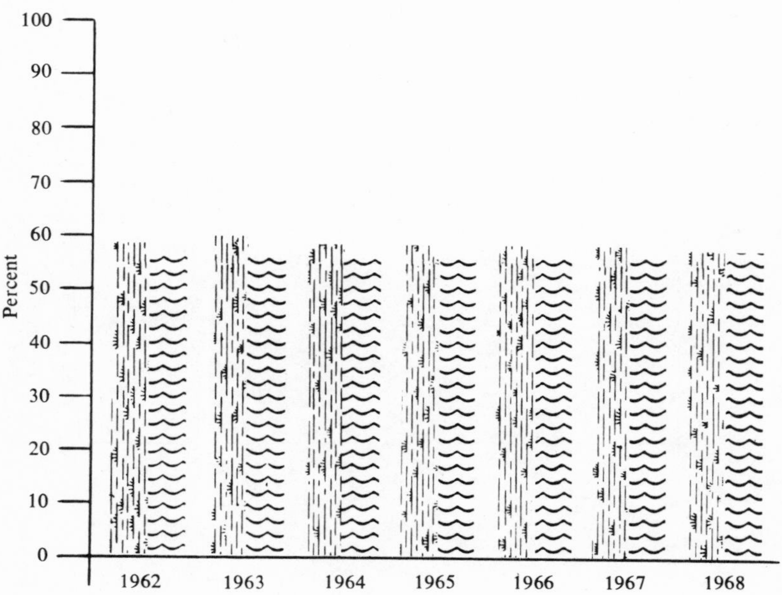

FIG. B4. Percent population minors

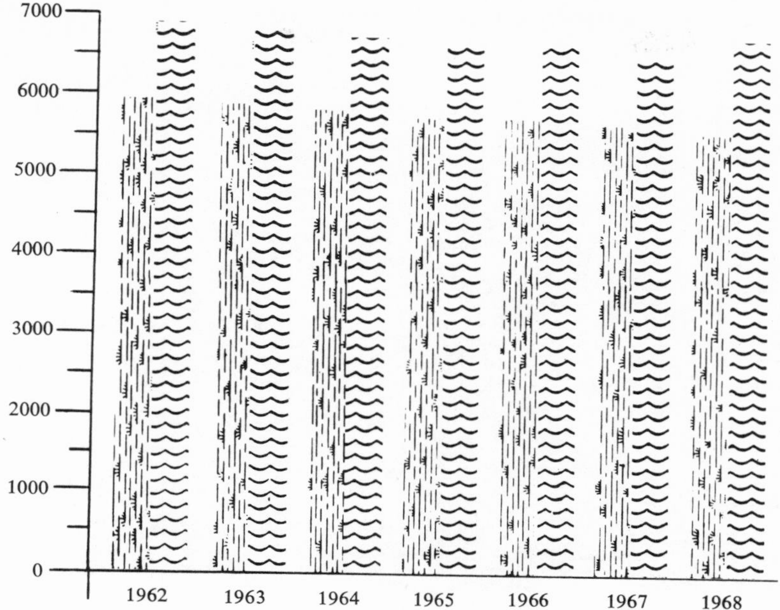

FIG. B5. Total population

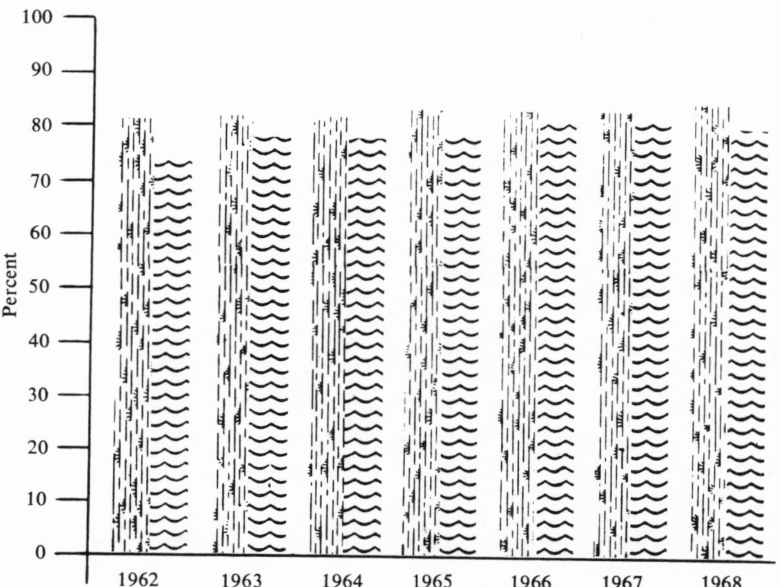

FIG. B6. Percent population black

Tenant Statistics 1962–1968

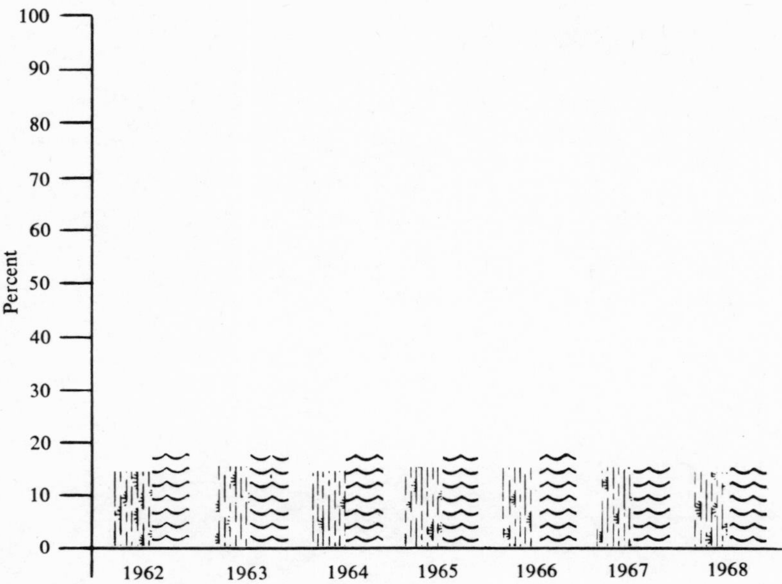

FIG. B7. Percent population Puerto Rican

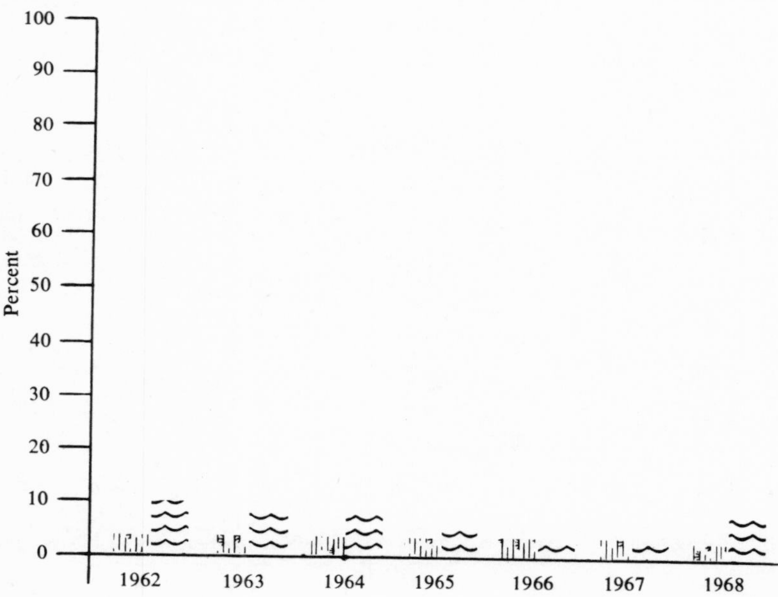

FIG. B8. Percent population white

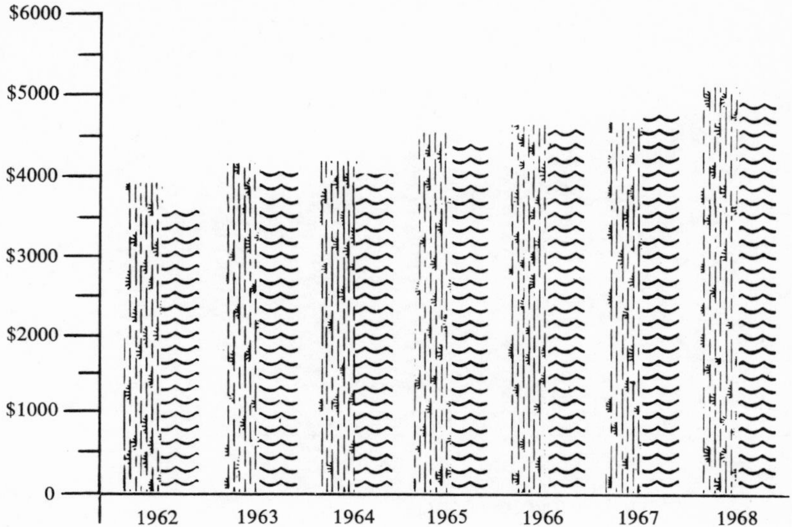

FIG. B9. Average gross income

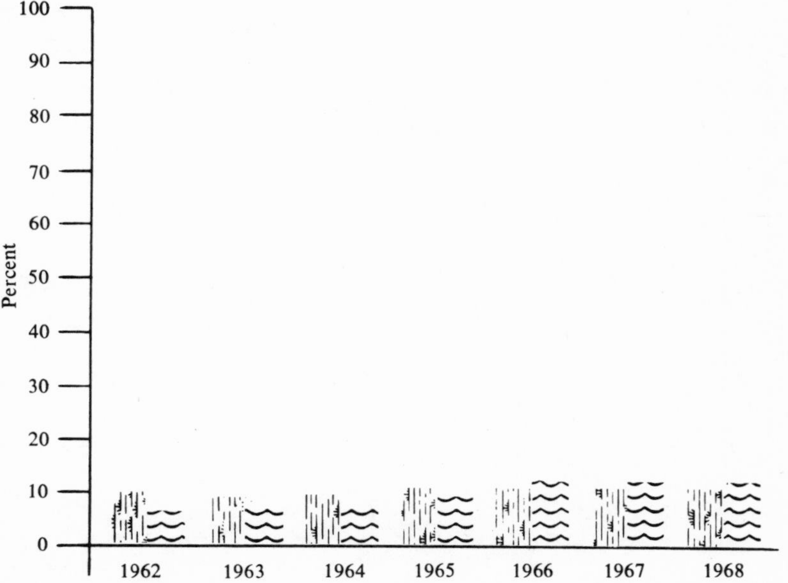

FIG. B10. Percent families with two wage earners

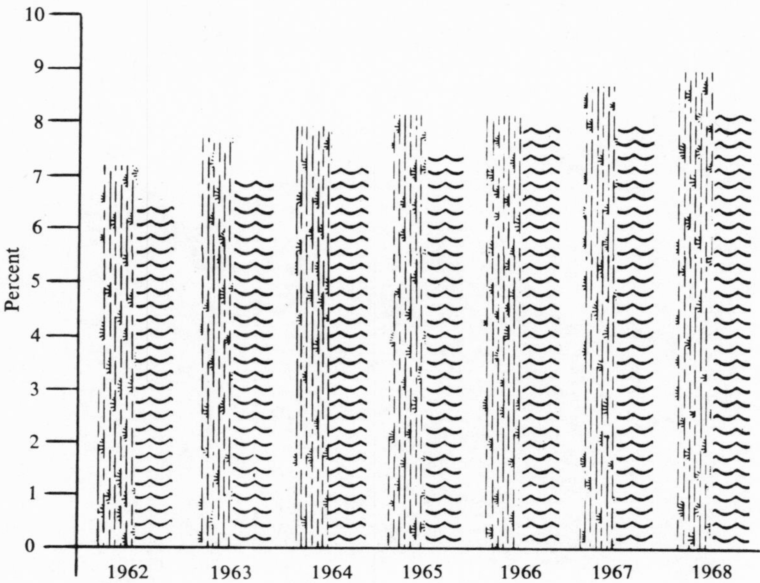

FIG. B11. Average number of years in project

Frequency Distribution of Family Size

BROWNSVILLE (B)

VAN DYKE I (VI)

VAN DYKE II (VII)

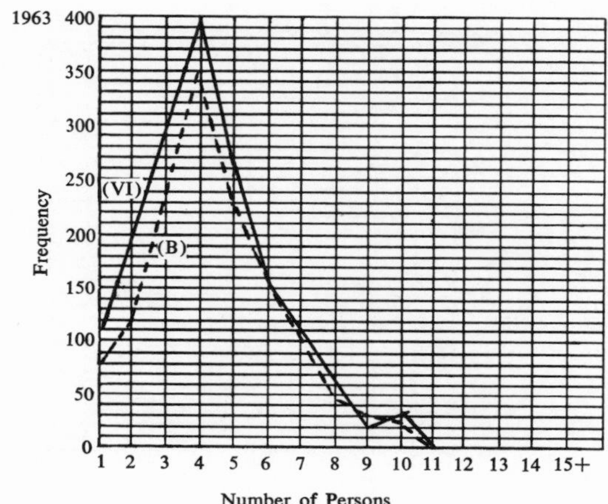

FIG. B12. Distribution for 1963

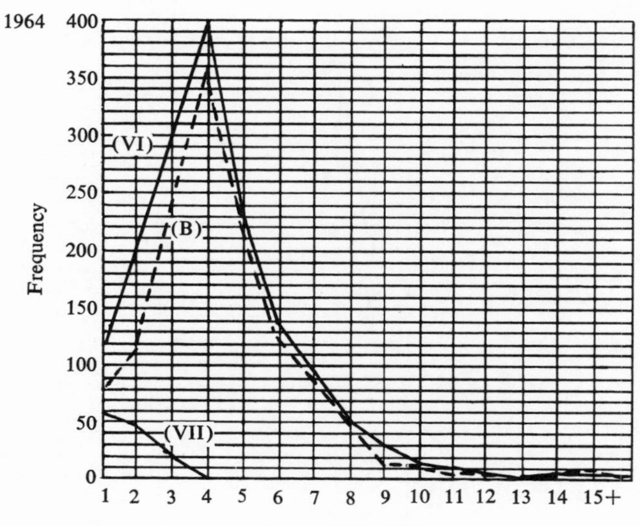

FIG. B13. Distribution for 1964

Frequency Distribution of Family Size

BROWNSVILLE (B)

VAN DYKE I (VI)

VAN DYKE II (VII)

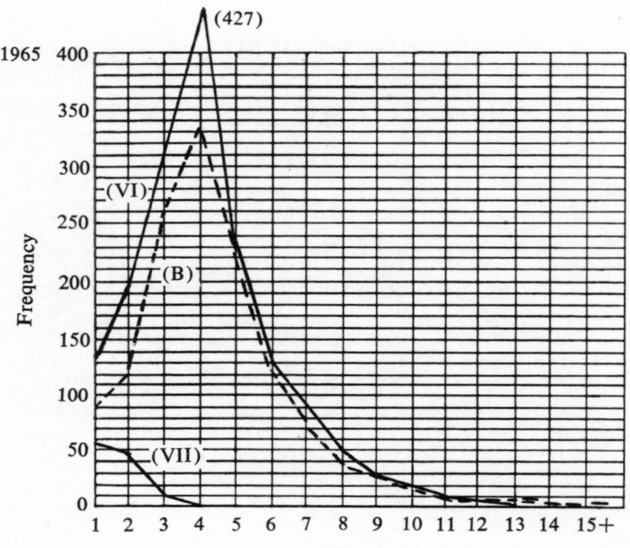

FIG. B14. Distribution for 1965

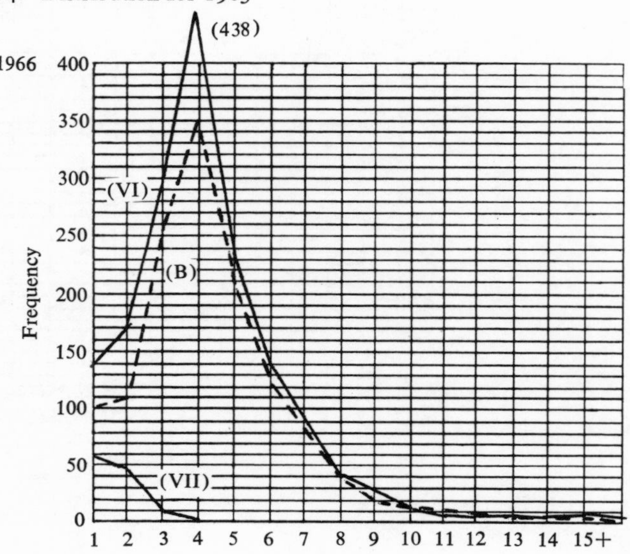

FIG. B15. Distribution for 1966

Frequency Distribution of Family Size

BROWNSVILLE (B)

VAN DYKE I (VI)

VAN DYKE II (VII)

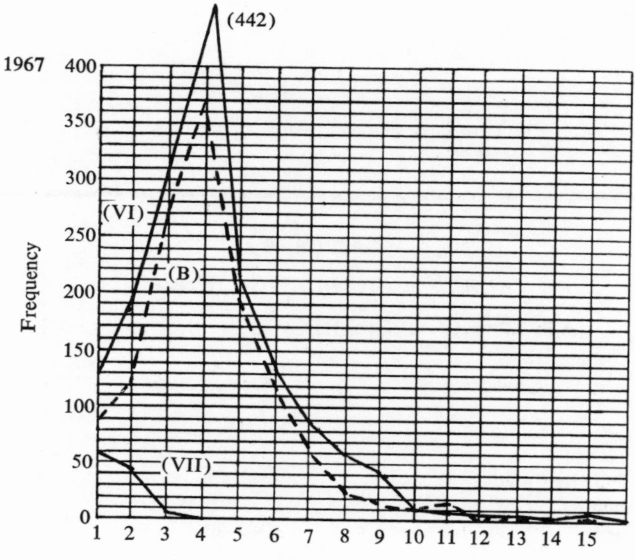

FIG. B16. Distribution for 1967

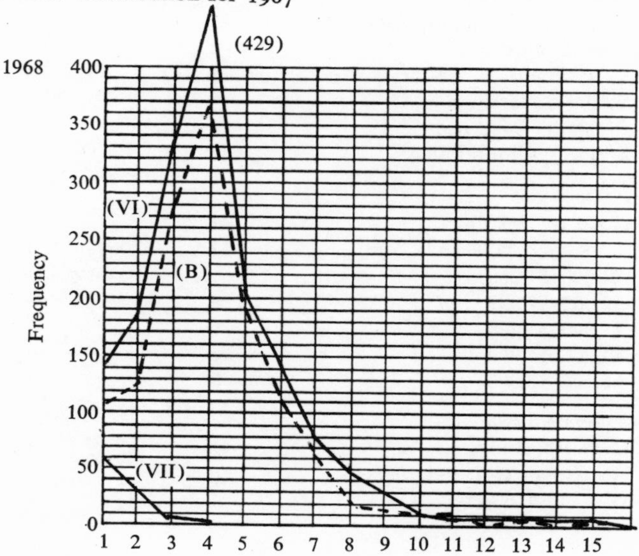

FIG. B17. Distribution for 1968

TABLE B2

Move-Ins: A Three-Year Comparison

Year	*Brownsville*	*Van Dyke*
1967	109	158
1968	118	127
1969	75	93

SOURCE: New York City Housing Authority tenant data.

TABLE B3

Tenant Statistics for Move-Ins

(A SAMPLE OF ONE-FIFTH OF MOVE-INS, 1967–1969)

Characteristic	*Brownsville*	*Van Dyke*
Race		
Negro	51	41
Puerto Rican	7	10
White	0	0
Total	58	51
Source of Income		
Private Employment	34	36
Government Employment	5	1
Own Business	0	1
Department of Welfare	16	9
Social Security	1	1
Disability Insurance	0	1
Military Allotments	2	2
Assets		
None or Unknown	27	51
Less than $1,000	1	0
$1,000–$1,999	3	0
$2,000–$2,999	9	0
$3,000–$3,999	5	0
$4,000–$4,999	8	0
$5,000–$5,999	5	0
Previous Housing		
Own Apartment	46	43
Apartment with Relatives	10	0
Furnished Room	1	7
Hotel	1	1

TABLE B 3—Continued

Characteristic	Brownsville	Van Dyke
Residence at Last Address		
Less than 6 months	7	4
6–11 months	8	7
1 year–less than 2	13	16
2 years–less than 3	8	10
3 years–less than 4	6	6
4 years–less than 5	3	1
5 years–less than 10	6	4
10 years–less than 15	3	2
15 years–less than 20	2	1
20 years or more	2	0
Family Composition		
Single Person	3	1
Married Couple	4	3
Father, Mother, Children	34	33
Father with one or more Children	1	0
Mother with one or more Children	14	14
Other	2	0
Sex of Head of Household		
Male	38	36
Female	20	15
Age of Head of Household		
Less than 20 years	2	2
20–29 years	27	26
30–39 years	11	13
40–49 years	8	3
50–59 years	5	3
60–69 years	3	4
70–79 years	2	0
Number of Children Under 21		
0	10	6
1	17	20
2	23	20
3	4	2
4	2	2
5	2	0
7	0	1

SOURCE: New York City Housing Authority tenant data.

BIBLIOGRAPHY

ENVIRONMENTAL FORM:

Alexander, Christopher. *Notes on the Synthesis of Form.* Cambridge, Mass.: Harvard University Press, 1964.

Alonso, William. "The Mirage of New Towns." *The Public Interest* 19 (Spring 1970): 3–17.

Boulding, Kenneth E. *The Image.* Ann Arbor: The University of Michigan Press, 1956.

Chermayeff, S. and Alexander, C. *Community and Privacy*, Garden City: Anchor Books, 1965.

Jennings, Burgess H., and Murphy, John E. *Interactions of Man and His Environment.* New York: Plenum Press, 1966.

Lynch, Kevin. *The Image of the City.* Cambridge, Mass.: The M.I.T. Press, 1966.

———. "*City Design and City Appearance.*" In *Principles and Practice of Urban Planning.* Washington, D. C.: International City Managers' Association, 1968.

Meier, Richard L. *A Communications Theory of Urban Growth.* Cambridge, Mass.: The M.I.T. Press, 1970.

Parr, A. E. "City and Psyche." *Yale Review* 54 (Autumn 1965): 71–85.

Pawley, Martin. *Architecture versus Housing.* New York: Praeger, 1971.

Stripe, Robert E., ed. *Perception and Environment.* Chapel Hill: The Institute of Government, University of North Carolina, 1966.

Webber, Melvin et al. *Explorations into Urban Structure.* Philadelphia: University of Pennsylvania Press, 1964.

Wingo, Lowdon Jr. *Cities and Space: Future Use of Urban Land.* Baltimore: Johns Hopkins Press, 1963.

SOCIAL POLICY:

Abrams, Charles. "Housing In The Year 2000." In *Environment and Public Policy, The Next Fifty Years*, edited by William R. Ewald, Jr. Bloomington: Indiana University Press, 1968.

Bell, Daniel. *The End of Ideology*. New York: The Macmillan Company, 1960.

Duhl, Leonard, ed. *The Urban Condition*. New York: Simon and Schuster, 1963.

Ewald, William R., Jr., ed. *Environment and Public Policy: The Next Fifty Years*. Bloomington: Indiana University Press, 1968.

Frieden, Bernard J. and Robert Morris, eds. *Urban Planning and Social Policy*. New York: Basic Books, 1968.

Jacobs, Jane. *The Death and Life of Great American Cities*. New York: Vintage Books, 1961.

Mayor's Urban Task Force. *The Threatened City: A Report on the Design of the City of New York*. New York: City of New York, 1967.

Montgomery, Roger. "Improving the Design Process in Urban Renewal." *Journal of the American Institute of Planners* 31 (February 1965): 7–20.

———. "Comment on 'Fear and House-as-Haven in the Lower Class.'" *Journal of the American Institute of Planners* 32 (January 1966): 31–37.

New York City Planning Commission. *Plan for New York*. New York: City of New York, 1969.

Newman, Oscar. *Park-Mall Lawndale*. St. Louis, Urban Renewal Design Center. St. Louis: Washington University, 1968.

———. *New Frontiers in Architecture*. New York: Universe Books, 1961.

Roslansky, John D., ed. *The Control of the Environment*. Amsterdam, North-Holland, 1967.

Starr, Roger. *Urban Choices: The City and Its Critics*. Baltimore: Penguin Books, 1966.

Urban Renewal Administration. *Design Objectives in Urban Renewal*. Technical Guide #16. Washington, D.C.: U.S. Government Printing Office, 1965.

Wilson, James O., ed. *Urban Renewal*, Cambridge, Mass.: The M.I.T. Press, 1966.

HOUSING AND THE SOCIOLOGY OF THE FAMILY

Adams, Bert N. *Kinship in an Urban Setting*. Chicago: Markham Publishers, 1968.

Brolin, Brent C., and Zeisel, John. "Mass Housing: Social Research and Design." *Architectural Forum*, 129 (July/August 1968): 66–71.

Festinger, Schacter, Back. *Social Pressures in Informal Groups (A Study of Human Factors in Housing)*. Stanford: Stanford University Press, 1950.

Firey, Walter. *Land Use in Central Boston*. New York: Greenwood Press, 1968.

Fried, Marc, and Gleicher, Peggy. "Some Sources of Residential Satisfaction in an Urban Slum." *Journal of the American Institute of Planners* 27 (1961): 305–315.

Gans, Herbert J. *The Urban Villagers*. New York: The Macmillan Company, 1962.

———. *People and Plans, Essays On Urban Problems and Solutions*. New York: Basic Books, 1968.

———. "Planning and Social Life." *Journal of the American Institute of Planners* 27 (1961): 134–140.

Gutman, Robert. *A Sociologist Looks at Housing.* Urban Studies Center, New Brunswick, New Jersey: Rutgers University Press, 1967.

Lewis, Oscar. *Five Families.* New York: Mentor, 1959.

———. *La Vida.* New York: Vintage, 1965.

———. *The Children of Sanchez.* New York: Vintage, 1963.

Morris, R. N., and Mogey, John. *The Sociology of Housing.* London: Routledge and Kegan Paul Ltd., 1965.

Rainwater, Lee. "Fear and the House-as-Haven in the Lower Class." *Journal of the American Institute of Planners* 32 (January 1966): 23–37.

———. *Behind Ghetto Walls.* Chicago: Aldine-Atherton Inc., 1970.

———. *Workingman's Wife.* New York: Oceana Publications, 1959.

Schorr, Alvin L. *Slums and Social Insecurity.* Washington, D.C.: U.S. Government Printing Office, 1963.

Thomlinson, Ralph. *Urban Structure, The Social and Spatial Character of Cities.* New York: Random House, 1969.

Van der Ryn, S. *Amenity Attitudes of Residential Location.* San Francisco: A. D. Little, 1965.

Van der Ryn, S., and Silverstein, M. *Dorms at Berkeley: An Environmental Analysis.* Berkeley: University of California, 1967.

Young, Michael, and Willmott, Peter. *Family and Kinship in East London.* Baltimore: Penguin Books, 1957.

Wilner, Walkley et al. *The Housing Environment and Family Life.* Baltimore: Johns Hopkins, 1962.

Wood, Elizabeth. *Housing Design: A Social Theory.* New York: Citizens' Housing and Planning Council of New York, Inc., 1961.

HUMAN TERRITORIALITY:

Ardrey, Robert. *African Genesis.* New York: Dell Publishing Company, 1961.

———. *The Territorial Imperative.* New York: Dell Publishing Company, 1966.

Barker, Roger. *Ecological Psychology.* Stanford: Stanford University Press, 1968.

Barker, Roger, and Gump, Paul. *Big School, Small School: High School Size and Student Behavior.* Stanford: Stanford University Press, 1964.

Goffman, Erving. *Behavior in Public Places.* New York: The Macmillan Company, 1963.

———. *Interaction Ritual.* New York: Doubleday, 1967.

Hall, Edward T. *The Silent Language.* New York: Fawcett, 1959.

Sommer, Robert. *Personal Space: The Behavioral Basis of Design.* Englewood, New Jersey: Prentice-Hall, 1969.

Stea, David. "Space, Territory and Human Movements." *Landscape* 15 (Autumn 1965): 13–16.

Theodorson, George A. *Studies in Human Ecology.* New York: Harper and Row, 1961.

URBAN CRIME:

Angel, Schlomo. *Discouraging Crime Through City Planning.* Berkeley: The University of California, 1968.

Annals, The. "Patterns of Violence," *The Annals of the American Academy of Political and Social Science,* Vol. 364 (March 1966).

———. "Combatting Crime," *The Annals of the American Academy of Political and Social Science,* Vol. 374 (November 1967).

Chicago Housing Authority. *Annual Statistical Report.* Chicago: City of Chicago, 1969.

Federal Bureau of Investigation. *Crime in the United States: Uniform Crime Reports.* Washington, D.C.: U.S. Government Printing Office, 1970.

Hoffman, Richard B. *The Transfer of Space and Computer Technology to Urban Security.* Berkeley: University of California, 1966.

Morris, Norval, and Hawkins, Gordon. *The Honest Politician's Guide to Crime Control.* Chicago: The University of Chicago Press, 1970.

The National Commission on Civil Disorders. *Report of the National Commission on Civil Disorders.* New York: Bantam, 1968.

New York City Housing Authority Police Department. *Annual Report.* New York: City of New York, 1969.

New York City Housing Authority. *Tenant Data.* New York: City of New York, 1969.

President's Commission on Law Enforcement and Administration of Justice. *The Challenge of Crime in a Free Society.* New York: Dutton, 1969.

St. Louis Housing Authority. *Annual Statistical Report.* St. Louis: City of St. Louis, 1969.

Westin, Alan F. *Privacy and Freedom.* New York: Atheneum, 1970.

INDEX

Access paths
at The Californian, 152–53
circuitous, 82, 83
glazing, lighting and positioning of, 80–91
transitional, 92
Alexander, Christopher, 148, 150
Ambiguous behavior, territoriality and, 65–66
Angel, Shlomo, 112
Anselivicus and Montgomery (architectural firm), 158
Antisocial behavior, new dormitories and, 74–76
Anxieties, surveillance calming, 78
Apartment towers, *see* High-rise apartments
Apartments, *see specific building types; for example*: High-rise apartments; Row-housing; Walk-up apartments
Architects, characteristics of, 115–16
Architectural design, environmental influences of, 207; *see also* Physical design
Audio intercoms, 185–86
Audio surveillance, 185
Automobile-free superblocks, 24–25

Baruch Houses (New York City), 82, 83
Berkman, Capt. Arnold, 205
Breukelen Houses (New York City)
fears of path system and, 82
ground-floor plan of, 93
grounds differentiation at, 54–56
kitchen windows at, 91
scissors stairs at, 89
stair and corridor system at, 67–69
as territorially intact project, 59–60
transitional paths, buffer and parking area at, 92
Bronxdale Houses (New York City)
crime location profile for, 88
entry and ground-floor plan of, 86, 87
juxtaposition of commercial area with, 112
modification for defensible space, 163, 176–86
site plan of, 113
Brownsville Houses (New York City)
building codes and building of, 118
density at, 195, 197
doors kept ajar at, 69
fear of access paths at, 82
roof landings at, 91
statistical tables on, 46, 47, 239–51
Van Dyke Houses compared with, 38–49
Building codes, changing, 118
Building height
increase in crime rate and, 27–32
tables, 28, 30–31, 72

Building height (*cont.*)
negative distinctiveness of, 103
prototypal defensible space and, 131
Building location, crime rate and, 83–86; *see also* Location
Building prototypes, available, 11–12
Building shape, entrance lobbies and, 84; *see also* Entrance lobbies
Building tradition, effects of breakdown in, 6–7
Buildings
poorly designed, crime rate in, 7
glazing, lighting and positioning of nonprivate areas and access paths among, 80–91
groupings of, for defensible space, 180; *see also types of groupings; for example*: High-rise apartments; Row-housing; Walk-up apartments
Burglaries
in apartment interiors, 33
building height and, 32

Californian, The (Tustin, Calif.)
as prototypal defensible space, 148–55
St. Francis Square compared with, 140–41
Center for Planning and Development Research, 155, 156
Central area, modification for defensible space, 152
Chermayeff, Serge, 148, 150
Children
building types and play of, 44–45
danger of high-rises to, 189–91
in high-rises, and sense of privacy and territory, 13
physical form of residential environment and shaping perception of, 14
playing in corridors, 44
Circulation confusion, fire stairs and, 97–99
Circulation patterns, interruptions of, 103
Cities
changes in, 201–7
lack of tradition in building 20th century, 6–7
Clason Point Gardens (New York City)
fear map of, 171
modification for defensible space, 163–75
Clothiel Smith and Associates, 142
Columbus Homes (Newark, N.J.)
circuitous paths of, 82, 83
destruction of, 188
fire stairs at, 98, 99
territoriality at, 56
transitional differentiating elements at, 66
Community
St. Marks Place used by, 62
territoriality and sense of, 3
Community action, difficulty in initiating, 1–2
Community control of environment, 11, 204
Community and Privacy (Chermayeff and Alexander), 148, 150
Compositional design, organic design vs., 59–60
Co-op City (New York City), 16–18
vulnerability of, 18
Cooper, Clare C., 155–58
Corrective prevention, 4
Corridors
children playing in, 44
crime rate and size of, 69
double-loaded, 88
crime rate and single-loaded vs., 94
as devoid of surveillance, 91–93
as disastrous, 25
examples of, 67, 122
typical, 22–23
open, 132, 134
single-loaded
European, 130
at Riverbend, 122
surveillance and, 93–95
territorial bickering over, 96
for walk-ups, 71
zone of influence over, 67–69
Crime location profiles, 88
Crime rates
apartment surveillance of exterior and, 91
in Brownsville and Van Dyke Houses, table, 47
building location and, 83–86
comparison of two projects and, 38–49
corridor size and, 69
density and, 195
effect of lobby visibility and entry design on, tables, 85
in fire stairs, 89, 90

in high-rises compared with row-houses, 191
housing projects with, 22–50
mechanism producing high rate, 14
modifying projects for defensible space and, 166–67
percentage of elderly, teen-agers and, 38
physical design and, 44
in poorly designed buildings and projects, 7
precinct felony rate, 199
project size
building height and increase in, 27–32
tables, 28, 30–31, 72
relation of visibility to, 83–86
single- vs. double-loaded corridors and, 94
surveillance of lobbies and, 87
variation in crime index offence rates, 36
Crimes engaged in by the poor, 198–200
Criminal acts, nature of, 205–6

Davis, Brody and Associates, 122, 129
Death and Life of Great American Cities (Jacobs), 25
Defensible space
defined, 3
elements of, *see* Juxtaposition; Surveillance; Symbolization; Territoriality
Defensive space prototypes, 118–62
table, 120
Density as culprit, 195–98
Desire Houses (New Orleans, La.), 100
Detached housing, density of, 196
Doormen, workable habitat and, 23–24
Dormitory colleges, problems facing, 74–76
Double-loaded corridors, 88
crime rate and single-loaded vs., 94
definition of, 22–23
as devoid of surveillance, 91–93
as disastrous, 25
examples of, 67, 122
Douglas Park (Chicago, Ill.), 115

Easter Hill Village (Richmond, Va.)
as prototype, 155–59
Edenwald Houses (New York City), 87
juxtaposition of commercial area with, 110
fire stairs at, 97, 98
Elderly, the, housing for, 194–95
Electronic surveillance
devices for, 177–79
modifying high-rises for defensible space, 182–85
Elevator breakdowns, 48
Elevator waiting area
negative distinctiveness of, 104
Riverbend, 126, 127
vandalized, 106
Elevators
Breukelen Houses, 69
Brownsville Houses, 43
children playing in, 189
crime rate in, 86
in double-loaded corridors, 67
as most vulnerable areas, 33–34
subdivisions and apartments using, 73–74
television monitored, 128–29
Van Dyke Houses, 41–42
Entertainment areas, juxtaposition of residential with, 109–13
Entrance lobby
Breukelen Houses, 69
Bronxdale House, 86, 87
Brownsville Houses, 43, 45
The Californian, 152, 154
crime rate and surveillance of, 87
Easter Hill Village, 157
Hyde Park, 147
LaClede Town, 141, 142
modification, for defensible space, 181–82
Pruitt-Igoe, 57
Riverbend Houses, 126
Rosen Apartment, 192
St. Francis Square, 138–40
shape of building and, 84
surveillance and design of, 87–88
Tower Hill, 159–62
Van Dyke Houses, 45
vest-pocket project, 202
vulnerability of, 34
External areas, natural surveillance of, 80–86

Family unit, territorial zone and, 51
Federal Housing Administration, 13
Felony rate
building height and, 28, 29, 32

Felony rate (*cont.*)
 at Van Dyke and Brownsville Houses, 47–48
Fences, 56–58
 workable habitat and, 23–24
Fire stairs
 circulation confusion in, 97–99
 crime rate and, 89, 90
 Riverbend, 128
 scissors described, 35
  in double-loaded corridors, 67
  natural surveillance of, 89
  problems, 88–91
 surveillance and design of, 88–91
 vulnerability of, 34
First Houses (New York City, 64, 65
Fisher Homes (New Orleans, La.), 100
Forest Hills controversy (New York City), 197–98
Forest Park (Mo.), 159

Garfield Park (Chicago, Ill.), 115
Genovese, Kitty, 79
Glazing of nonprivate areas, 80–91
Grounds differentation, 54–56
Guards, 23–24, 125–26
Guste Homes (New Orleans, La.), 100

Halprin, Lawrence, 157
Hardison, DeMars and Associates, 157
Harry Wiess and Associates, 145
Hierarchy
 of defensible space, 9, 10
 of increasingly private zones, 63–66
Highbridge Gardens (New York City), 87, 88
 entry to, and fire exits at, 98
 fire stairs at, 98
High-income families, guidelines for, 194
High-rise apartments
 aerial photo of, 11
 anonymous public streets and, 155
 children, and sense of privacy and territory, 13
 cooperation with police in, 12–15
 crime rate in row-houses compared, 191
 danger of raising children in, 189–91
 density in, 196
 destruction of, 188
 as disastrous, 25–27
 doormen for, 194
 duplex (piggy-back), 129
 electronic surveillance modifying, 182–85
 greater crime rate in, 29
 identical crime and, 23–24
 land costs and, 188, 196–97
 middle-class families withdrawn in, 14–15
 positive and negative distinctiveness of, 103
 prototype for modifying, for defensible space, 163, 176–86
 security and, 14, 22, 25
 surveillance of external areas of, 80–86
 surveillance of internal areas of, 86–91
 surveillance and random positioning of, 82
 as single unit, and territoriality, 54
 vacancy rates in, 193
 vulnerability of, 11–12, 200
High-rise prototypes, 163, 176–86
 limitations of, 7–8
High schools, juxtaposition of residential areas with, 111
Housing projects
 building codes and, 118
 building height in
  building height and prototypal defensible space, 131
  increase in crime rate and, 27–32
  negative distinctiveness of height, 103
  tables, 28, 30–31, 72
 building location and, 83–86; *see also* Location
 building shape in, 84
 building tradition breakdown and effect on, 6–7
 buildings of
  crime rate in poorly designed, 7
  glazing, lighting and positioning of nonprivate areas and access paths among, 80–91
  grouping for defensible space, 180; *see also types of groupings; for example:* High-rise apartments; Row-housing; Walk-up apartments
 federal program, 36–38
 with high crime rates, 22–50
 institutional image of, 105–7
 modifying, for defensible space, 163–86

negative distinctiveness of size of, 102–4
police and type of, 12–75, 42, 49, 90–91
positioning of, in urban locale, 108–9
public, as housing of last resort, 36–38
significance of number in, 71–77
stigma of, 102–3
surveillance and legibility of, 99–101; *see also* Surveillance
tenant satisfaction and design of, 48–49; *see also* Physical design
See also specific housing projects; for example: Breukelen Houses; Bronxdale Houses; Clason Point Gardens; Van Dyke Houses
Hyde Park (Chicago, Ill.), as prototype, 144–47

Industrial areas, juxtaposition of residential with, 109–13
Institutional areas, juxtaposition of residential with, 109–13
Intercoms
audio, 185–86
for defensible space, 126
Interior finishes and furnishings, negative distinctiveness of, 105–6
Internal areas, natural surveillance of, 86–91
Interview methodology, 228–29

Jacobs, Jane, 25, 112
Junior colleges, juxtaposition of residential areas with, 111
Juxtaposition
of activity areas, 91–96
dimensions of areas in, 114–16
of residential with safe facilities, 109–13

"Keeping the Poor in their Place" (Walinsky), 105
Kingsborough Houses(New York City), 81

Lambert Field (Mo.), 159
LaClede Town (St. Louis, Mo.)
Hyde Park compared with, 147
as prototype, 141–44
Land costs, 188, 196–97
Larceny, building height and, 32
Le Corbusier, 24
Lighting of nonprivate areas, 80–91
Location
apprehension by, table, 32
building height and crime, 33
crime rate and building, 83–86
of low-income projects, 34–36
See also Positioning
Low-income families
architects and, 116
avoiding high-rise apartments, 193
crime and identical high-rise apartments for middle- and, 23–24
crime rate and, 198
defensible space as imperative for, 15–16
difficulty of security design for, 19
effect of criminal assault on, 202–3
high-rise apartments and compensations for, 24
high-rise residential developments and needs of, 7–8
housing prototype and life style desired by, 106
middle-class goals of, 19–20
sense of distinctiveness in, 107–8
victimization of, 12
Low-income projects
background to building of, 36–38
location of, 34–36
modifying, for defensible space, 163–75
prototype for, 131–35, 155–59
Low-middle-income housing projects, prototype for, 121–31, 136–44

Marquis, Stoller and Associates, 137
Mechanical prevention, 4
Methodology, 209–37
Middle-income families
crime and identical high-rise apartments for low-middle-income and, 23–24
crime rate and, 198
effect of criminal assault on, 202
exodus to suburbia, 2, 187, 197, 202–3
insecurity involved, 14, 17–19
goals of low-income families as those of, 19–20
high-rise apartments and compensations for, 24
successful living in high-rise apartments of, 189–91

Middle income families (*cont.*)
visual stigma and buildings of, 105
as withdrawn in high-rise apartments, 14–15
Middle-income housing projects, prototypes for, 144–47, 158–62
Model Cities Program, 37
Modifications for defensible space, 163–86
Mud house, 4
Multi-level dwellings, defensible space in, 10

Natural surveillance, 78–101
juxtaposition of activity areas for, 91–96
physical design providing, 78–80; *see also* Physical design
reduction of ambiguity of public and private areas to provide, 96–101
territoriality and, 78–80; *see also* Territoriality
Neolithic settlement, 4
New York City Housing Authority, 10, 27, 29, 32, 96
New York City projects
effect of building locations on crime in, 83–86
motor scooters in, 80
New York University Project for Security Design in Urban Residential Areas, 2
North Beach Place (San Francisco, Calif.)
as prototype, 131–35

Organic design, compositional design vs., 59–60
Outhwaite House (Cleveland, Ohio), 111, 112

Parking area
Bronxdale Houses, 179
The Californian, 150, 151
Hyde Park, 147
Riverbend Houses, 129
St. Francis Square, 140
Tower Hill, 159–61
Parks, site plans of safe and dangerous, 114–15
Paths, *see* Access paths; Streets
Physical design
crime rate and, 44
improved security by means of, 8–9, 178–79
natural surveillance provided by, 78–80
territoriality in, 8–9
design encouraging territoriality, 53–66
Physical variables of housing projects, 217–21
Pei, I. M., 144, 145, 146, 147
Piggy-back row-houses, as prototypal defensible space, 122–25; *see* also Row housing
Play area
Bronxdale Houses, 179
Hyde Park, 146, 147
Tower Hill, 160, 161
Play court
North Beach Place, 134–35
St. Francis Square, 137, 138, 140
Police, project type and effectiveness of, 12–15, 42, 49, 90–91
Police crime reports, 210–17
Pompeii street, 6
Positioning
of housing in urban locale, 108–9
of nonprivate areas, 80–91
Poverty, criminal–victim correlation and, 13
President's Commission on Law Enforcement and Criminal Justice, 108
Private street system, 60
Project Breakthrough, 207
Project for Security Design of Urban Residential Areas, 2
Projects, *see* Housing projects
Prototypes
available building, 11–12
defensible space, 118–62
table of, 120
Pruitt-Igoe (St. Louis, Mo.)
access paths at, 83
density of, 193–94
elevator and mailbox area at, 106
fire stairs at, 99
floating population in, 77
negative distinctiveness of, 105
North Beach Place compared with, 135
as superblock, 56–59
vacancy rate at, 58, 207
vandalized, 66, 107–8, 188
Public housing projects, *see* Housing projects
Rainwater, Lee, 13, 107–8
Rape, 32, 89
elevators and, 33

Recognition of families sharing building entry, territoriality and, 73
Report of the President's Commission on Law Enforecement and Administration of Justice, 35–36
Riverbend Houses (New York City)
corridors at, 96
density at, 162, 195
North Beach Place compared with, 134
as prototype, 121–31
Robberies
building height and rate of, 29, 32
in elevators, 33
in entrance lobbies, 34
in interior of public areas, 33
at Van Dyke and Brownsville Houses, 47–48
Rosen Houses (Philadelphia, Pa.)
destruction of, 188
entrance to, 192
site plan and front yards of, 190
as superblock, 56
Row-house street, superblock design compared with, 81–83
Row housing
jerry-built, 52
as prototype, 141–47, 155–59

St. Bernard Homes (New Orleans, La.), 100
St. Francis Square (San Francisco, Calif.)
as prototype, 136–41
St. Marks Avenue (New York City), street design and, 60–62
Sarah Lawrence College (Bronxville, N.Y.), 74–77
Schuylkyll Falls Housing Project (Philadelphia, Pa.)
elevator waiting area of, 104
vandalized, 107
Scissors stairs
circulation confusion and, 97–99
described, 35
in double-loaded corridors, 67
natural surveillance of, 89
problems from having adopted, 88–91
Secondary exits, vulnerability of, 34
Security
physical design contributing to, 8–9, 178–79
as function of citizenry, 14–15
as need of low-income families, 13
real vs. symbolic barriers and, 63–66
Self-help tools, 10–11
Semidetached housing, 52
Shared facilities, number of people involved in, 73
Single-family unit, 50–52
Single-loaded corridors
European, 130
at Riverbend Houses, 122
surveillance and, 93–95
Space usage, symbolically restricting, 63, 64
Stairs
fire, *see* Fire stairs
at North Beach Place, 131–34
zone of influence over, 67–69
Stapleton Houses (New York City), 93–96
aerial view of, 94
floor plan and view of, 94–96
Stepwise multiple regression analysis in methodology, 229–31
Stigma
of a project, 102–3
visual, 102–5
Street design, territoriality in, 60–63
Streets
ambiguous behavior and public, 65–66
apartments oriented toward, 135
automobile-free superblocks and; 24–25
bordering Riverbend Houses, 127
at The Californian, 150–54
at Clason Point Gardens, 164
Dutch, and nineteenth-century American city, 7
at Easter Hill Village, 158
high-rise apartments and, 155
at Hyde Park, 145–46
interruption of pattern of, 103
juxtaposition of residential areas with safe public, 113–14
at LeClede Town, 141, 142
Pompeiian, 6
row-house, 81–83
at St. Francis Square, 140
surveillance of, from multi-family buildings, 15
Van Dyke Houses and, 41
Suburbia
exodus to, 2, 187, 197, 202–3
insecurity in, 14, 17–19

Superblocks
automobile-free, 24–25
early 50s, 56–59
legibility of project and, 99–107
row-house street compared with, 81–83
Surveillance
electronic, 182–85
devices, 177–79
natural, 78–101
juxtaposition of activity areas for, 91–96
physical design providing, 78–80, *see also* Physical design
reduction of ambiguity of public and private areas to provide, 96–101
territoriality and, 78–80; *see also* Territoriality
purpose in advocating, 204–5
telephone as a means of, 186
television as a means of, 128–29
Surveillance opportunities,
territorial definition reinforced with, 9
Symbolic barriers, real vs., 63–66
Symbolization, design and life style, 106–9

Telephone, surveillance by, 186
Television, surveillance by, 178
Television monitors in modifying projects for defensible space, 178
Tenant characteristics, 222–27
Tenant satisfaction, project design and, 48–49
Territorial definition,
purpose in advocating, 204–5
reinforced with surveillance opportunities, 9
subdivision of building interiors to achieve, 67–69
Territoriality, 51–77
as crime deterrent, 4–6
hierarchy of increasingly private zones and, 63–66
incorporation of amenities, facilities and, 70–71
natural surveillance and, 78–80; *see also* Surveillance
number of apartments and, 71–77
in physical design of space, 8–9
in zones of influence of buildings, 53–66
Tilden Houses (New York City), 90, 91
Tower Hill (St. Louis County, Mo.)
as prototype, 158–62
St. Francis Square compared with, 140
Trend analysis in methodology, 231–32
Turnkey practices, 105

Upper-income families, high-rise apartments and compensations for, 24
Upper-middle-income families
prototype of housing for, 148–55
successful high-rise apartment living by, 193
Urban locale, positioning of housing in, 108–9
Urban Renewal Program, 36, 37

Van Dyke Houses (New York City)
Brownsville House compared with, 38–49
building codes and building of, 119
density at, 194, 195, 197
statistical tables on, 46, 47, 239–51
as superblock, 56
vandalized, 66
Van Dyke II, 194
Variance, analysis of, in methodology, 232–37
Vest-pocket project (Philadelphia, Pa.), 201, 202
Vest-pocket housing (London), 203
Video surveillance, 185
Ville Radieuse (Le Corbusier), 24
Visibility, relationship of crime to, 83–86

Walinsky, Adam, 105
Walk-up apartments
access arrangements for three-story, 71
aerial view of, 11
cooperation with police in, 12–13
density in, 196
as preferable for low-income families, 193
prototypal defensible space in, 136–44
prototype for modifying, for defensible space, 163–75
vulnerability of, 11–12, 200
Washington Park (Boston, Mass.), 194
Weese, Harry, 144, 146, 147
Wood, Elizabeth, 112
Woodhill Homes (Cleveland, Ohio), 82
juxtaposition at, 110–11
Working class
effect of criminal assault on, 202–3
visual stigma of buildings and, 105